CAPTAIN AMERICA
THE KORVAC SAGA

Writer: **BEN McCOOL**
Artist: **CRAIG ROUSSEAU**
Colorist: **RACHELLE ROSENBERG**
Letterer: **VC'S JOE SABINO**
Cover Artists: **CRAIG ROUSSEAU** & **CHRIS SOTOMAYOR**
Editors: **NATHAN COSBY, MICHAEL HORWITZ**
& **JOHN DENNING**

Captain America created by Joe Simon & Jack Kirby

"Tomorrow Dies Today" from *Avengers #167* (1978)
Writer: **JIM SHOOTER**
Artist: **GEORGE PÉREZ**
Inker: **PABLO MARCOS**
Colorist: **PHIL RACHELSON**
Letterer: **JIM ROSEN**
Editor: **ARCHIE GOODWIN**

Collection Editor & Design:
CORY LEVINE
Editorial Assistants:
JAMES EMMETT & **JOE HOCHSTEIN**
Assistant Editors:
MATT MASDEU, ALEX STARBUCK & **NELSON RIBEIRO**
Editors, Special Projects:
JENNIFER GRÜNWALD & **MARK D. BEAZLEY**
Senior Editor, Special Projects:
JEFF YOUNGQUIST
Senior Vice President of Sales:
DAVID GABRIEL
SVP of Brand Planning & Communications:
MICHAEL PASCIULLO

Editor In Chief:
AXEL ALONSO
Chief Creative Officer:
JOE QUESADA
Publisher:
DAN BUCKLEY
Executive Producer:
ALAN FINE

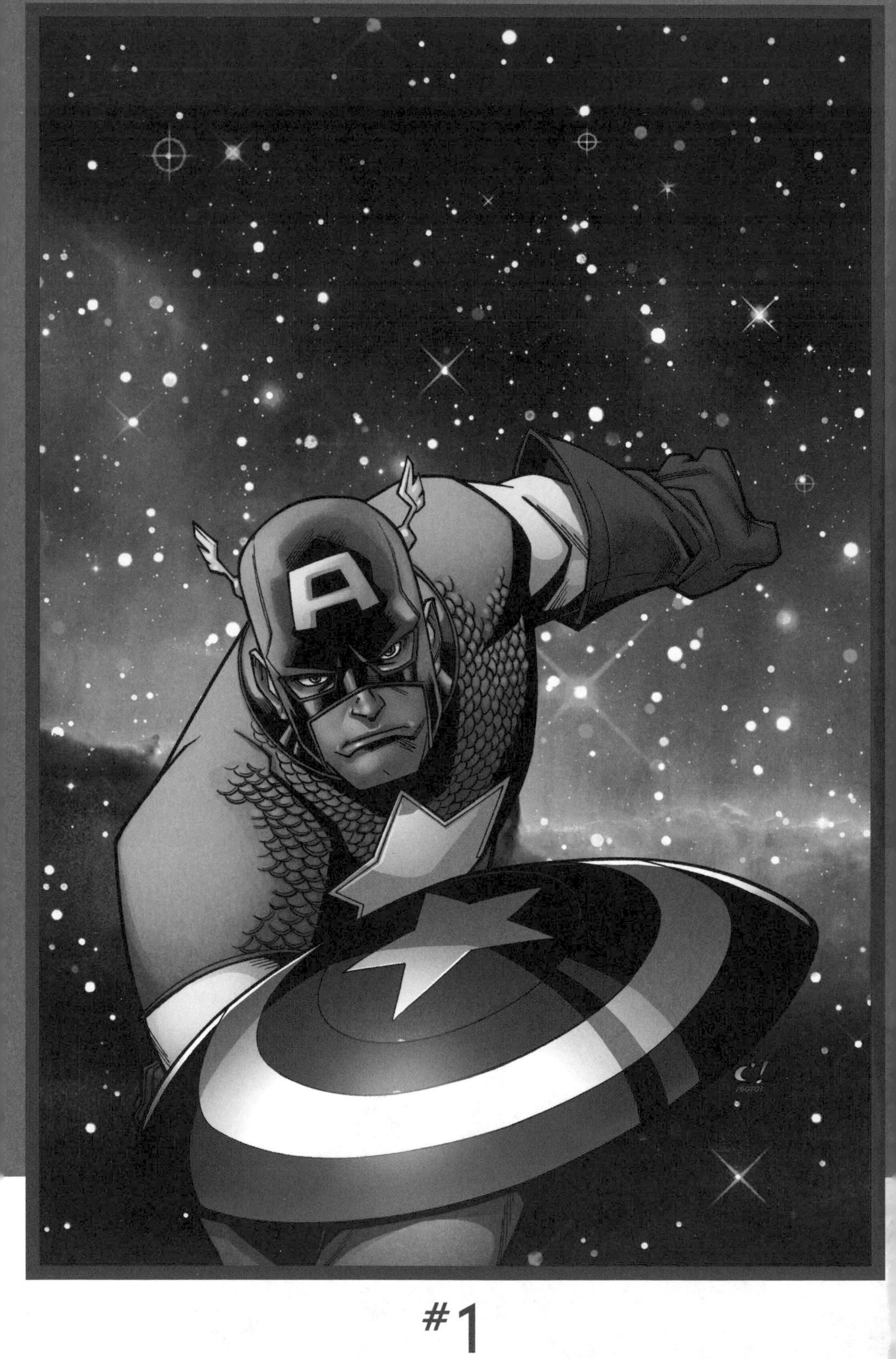

#1

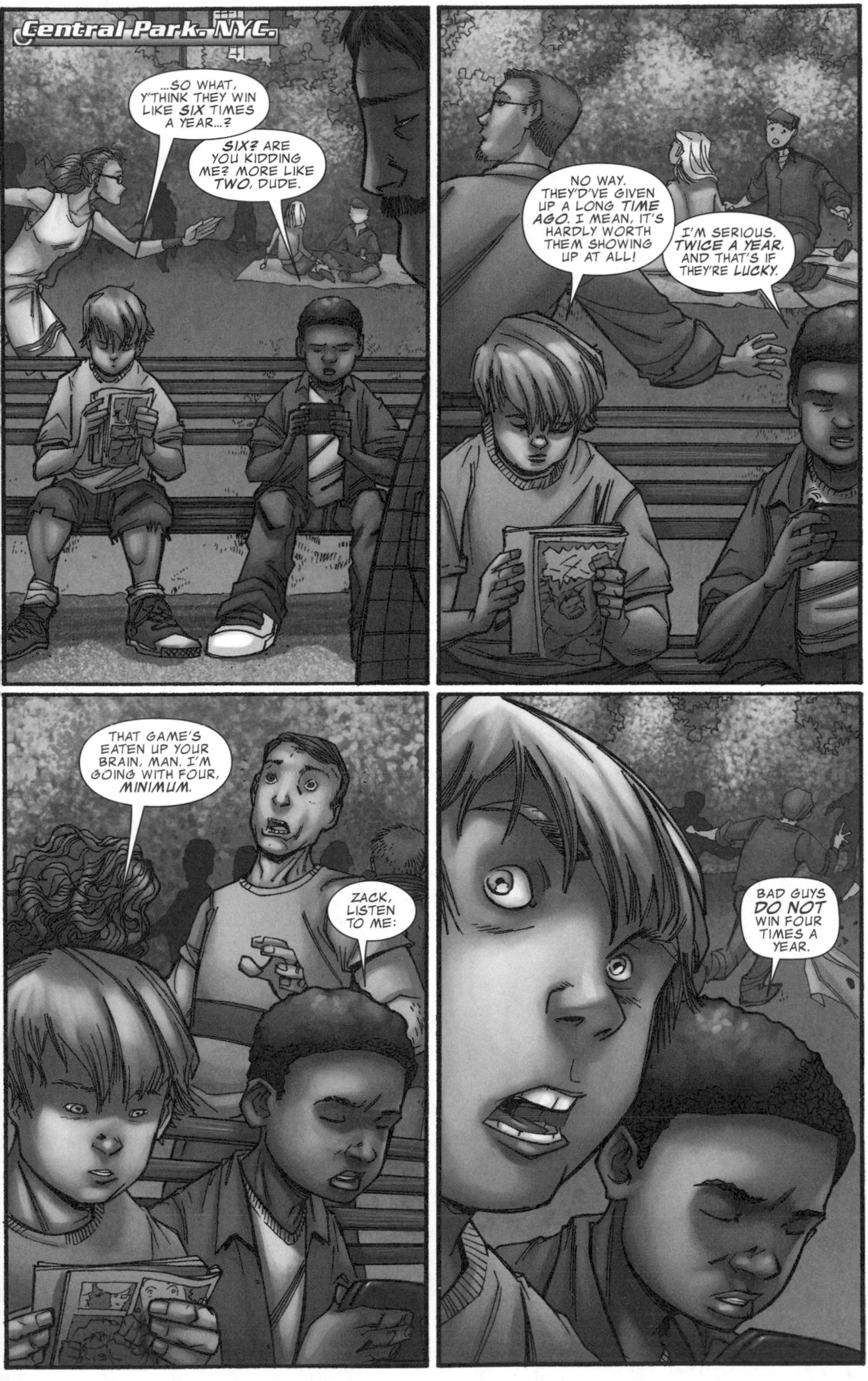
Central Park, NYC.
...SO WHAT, Y'THINK THEY WIN LIKE SIX TIMES A YEAR...?
SIX? ARE YOU KIDDING ME? MORE LIKE TWO, DUDE.
NO WAY. THEY'D'VE GIVEN UP A LONG TIME AGO. I MEAN, IT'S HARDLY WORTH THEM SHOWING UP AT ALL!
I'M SERIOUS. TWICE A YEAR, AND THAT'S IF THEY'RE LUCKY.
THAT GAME'S EATEN UP YOUR BRAIN, MAN. I'M GOING WITH FOUR, MINIMUM.
ZACK, LISTEN TO ME:
BAD GUYS DO NOT WIN FOUR TIMES A YEAR.

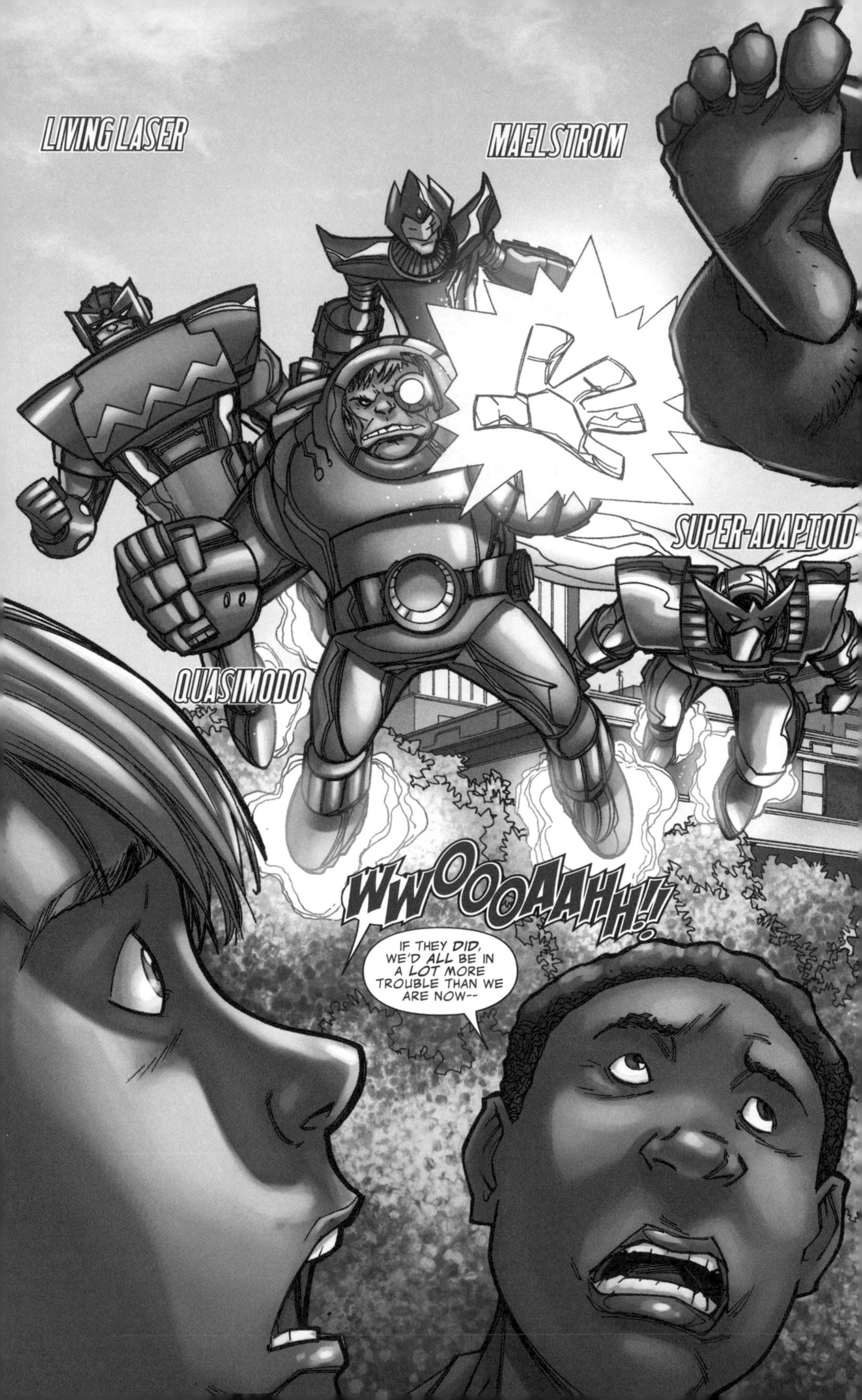
LIVING LASER
MAELSTROM
SUPER-ADAPTOID
QUASIMODO
WWOOOOAAHH!!
IF THEY DID, WE'D ALL BE IN A LOT MORE TROUBLE THAN WE ARE NOW--

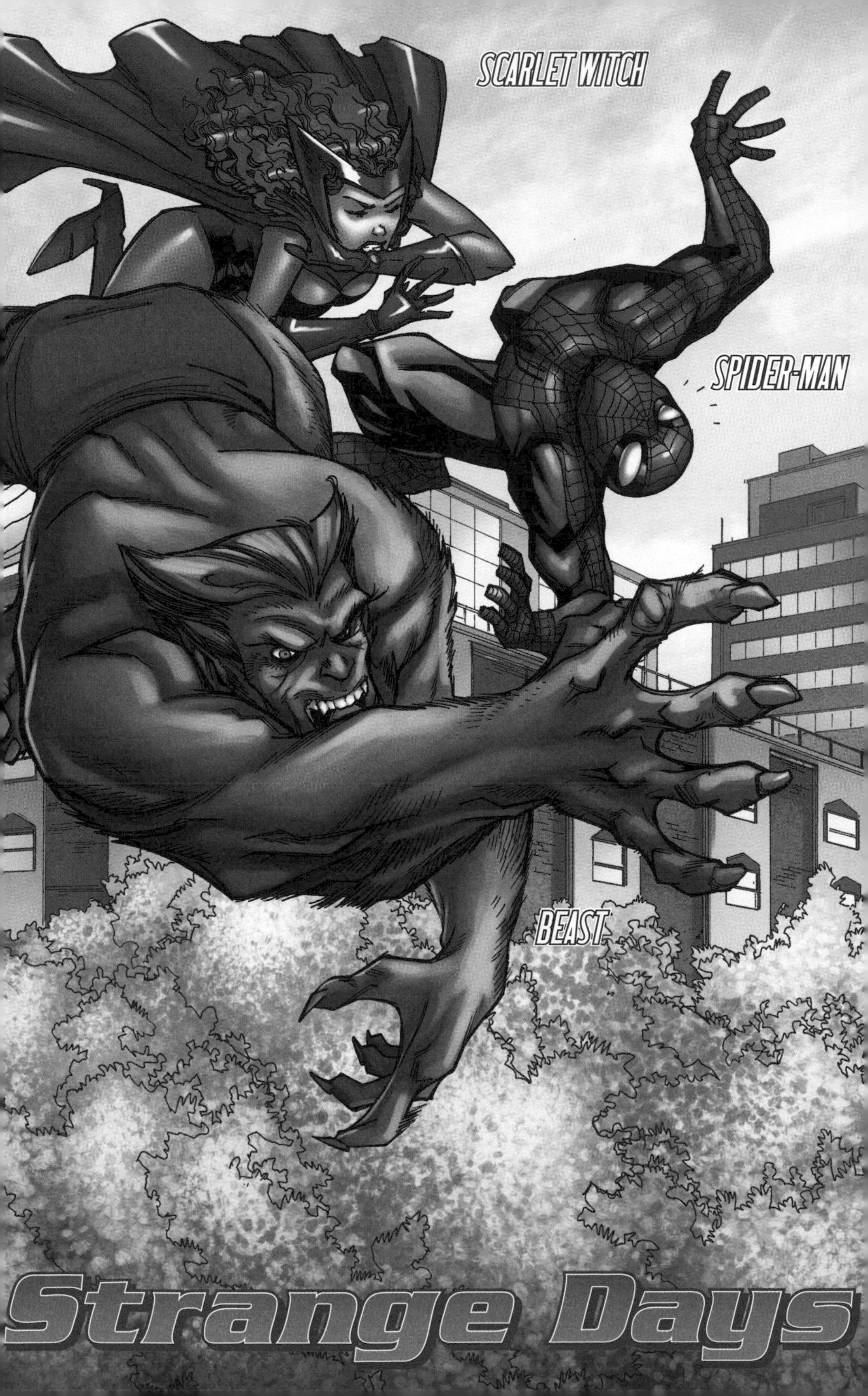
SCARLET WITCH
SPIDER-MAN
BEAST
Strange Days

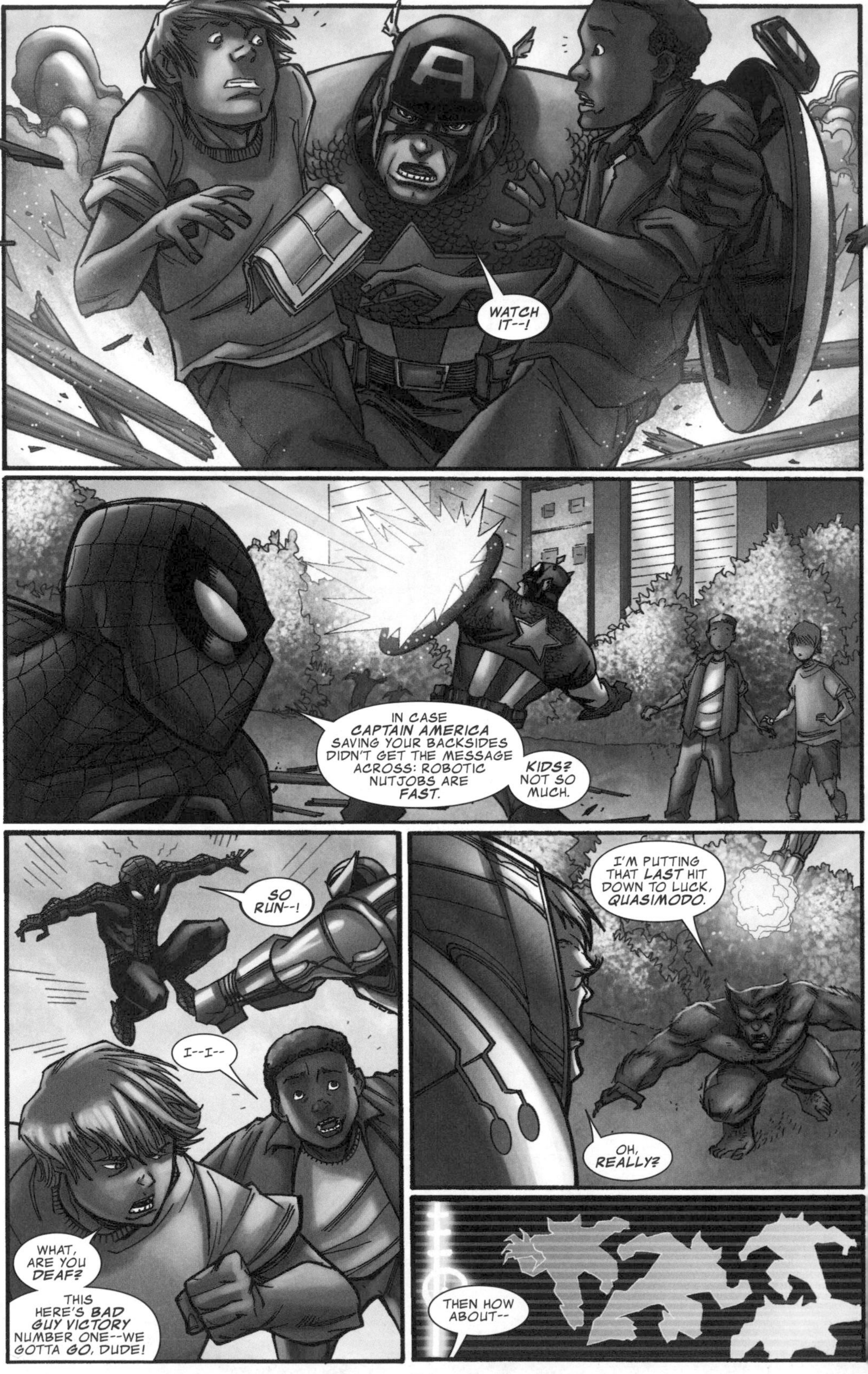
WATCH IT--!
IN CASE CAPTAIN AMERICA SAVING YOUR BACKSIDES DIDN'T GET THE MESSAGE ACROSS: ROBOTIC NUTJOBS ARE FAST.
KIDS? NOT SO MUCH.
SO RUN--!
I--I--
WHAT, ARE YOU DEAF?
THIS HERE'S BAD GUY VICTORY NUMBER ONE--WE GOTTA GO, DUDE!
I'M PUTTING THAT LAST HIT DOWN TO LUCK, QUASIMODO.
OH, REALLY?
THEN HOW ABOUT--

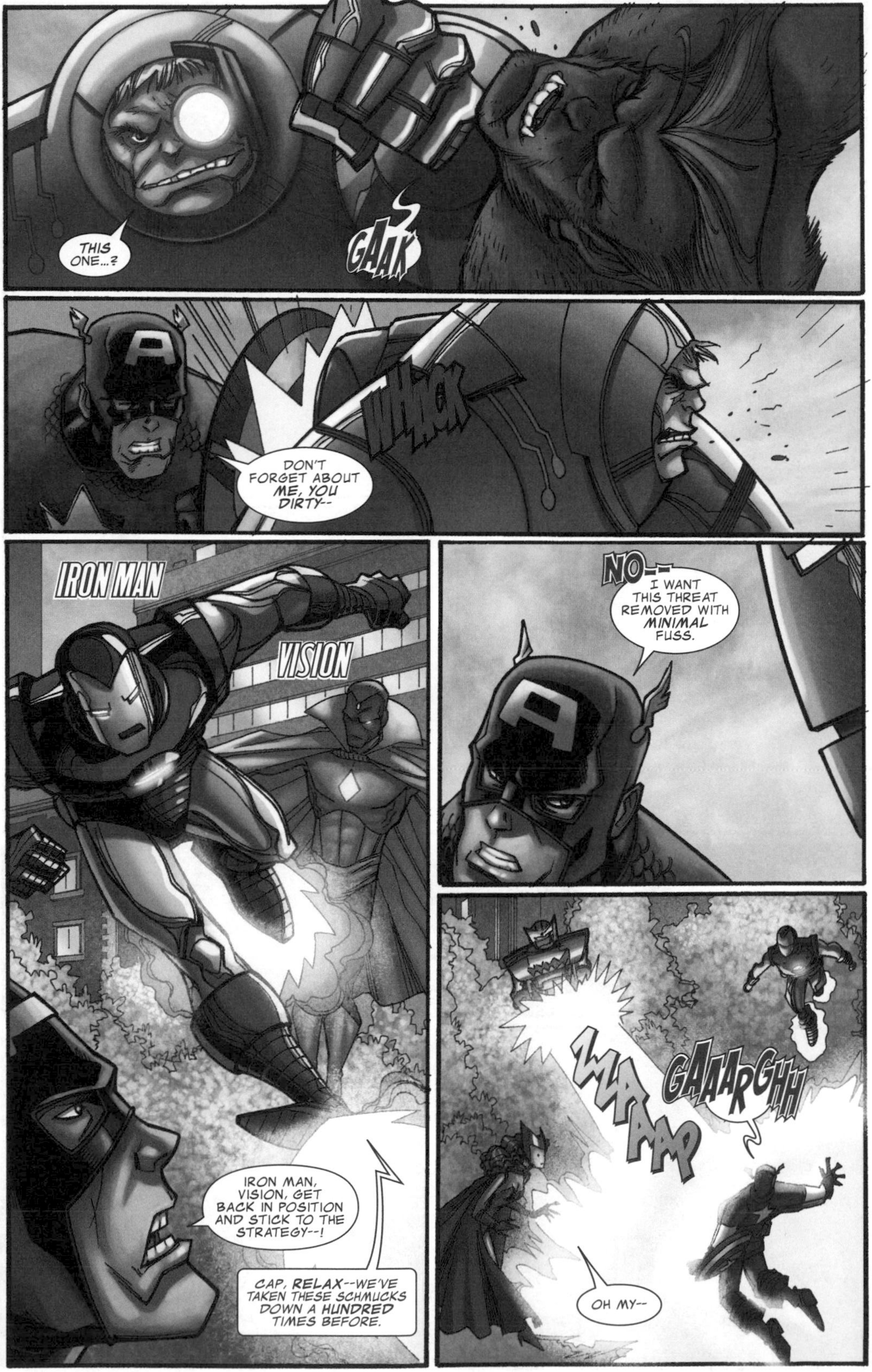
THIS ONE...?
GAAK
WHACK
DON'T FORGET ABOUT ME, YOU DIRTY--
IRON MAN
VISION
IRON MAN, VISION, GET BACK IN POSITION AND STICK TO THE STRATEGY--!
CAP, RELAX--WE'VE TAKEN THESE SCHMUCKS DOWN A HUNDRED TIMES BEFORE.
NO--
I WANT THIS THREAT REMOVED WITH MINIMAL FUSS.
ZZZAPPP
GAAARGHH
OH MY--

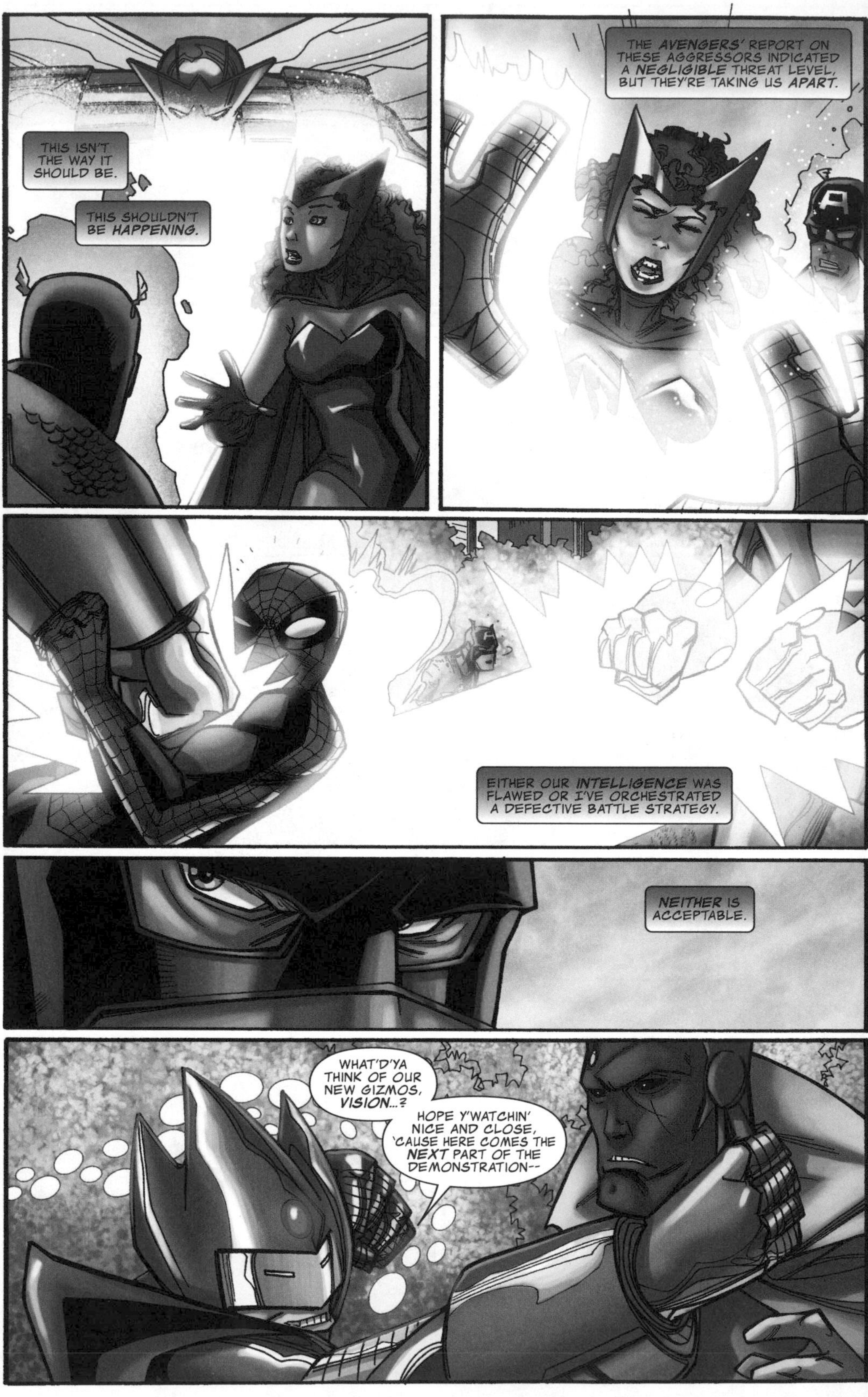
THIS ISN'T THE WAY IT SHOULD BE.
THIS SHOULDN'T BE HAPPENING.
THE AVENGERS' REPORT ON THESE AGGRESSORS INDICATED A NEGLIGIBLE THREAT LEVEL, BUT THEY'RE TAKING US APART.
EITHER OUR INTELLIGENCE WAS FLAWED OR I'VE ORCHESTRATED A DEFECTIVE BATTLE STRATEGY.
NEITHER IS ACCEPTABLE.
WHAT'D'YA THINK OF OUR NEW GIZMOS, VISION...?
HOPE Y'WATCHIN' NICE AND CLOSE, 'CAUSE HERE COMES THE NEXT PART OF THE DEMONSTRATION--

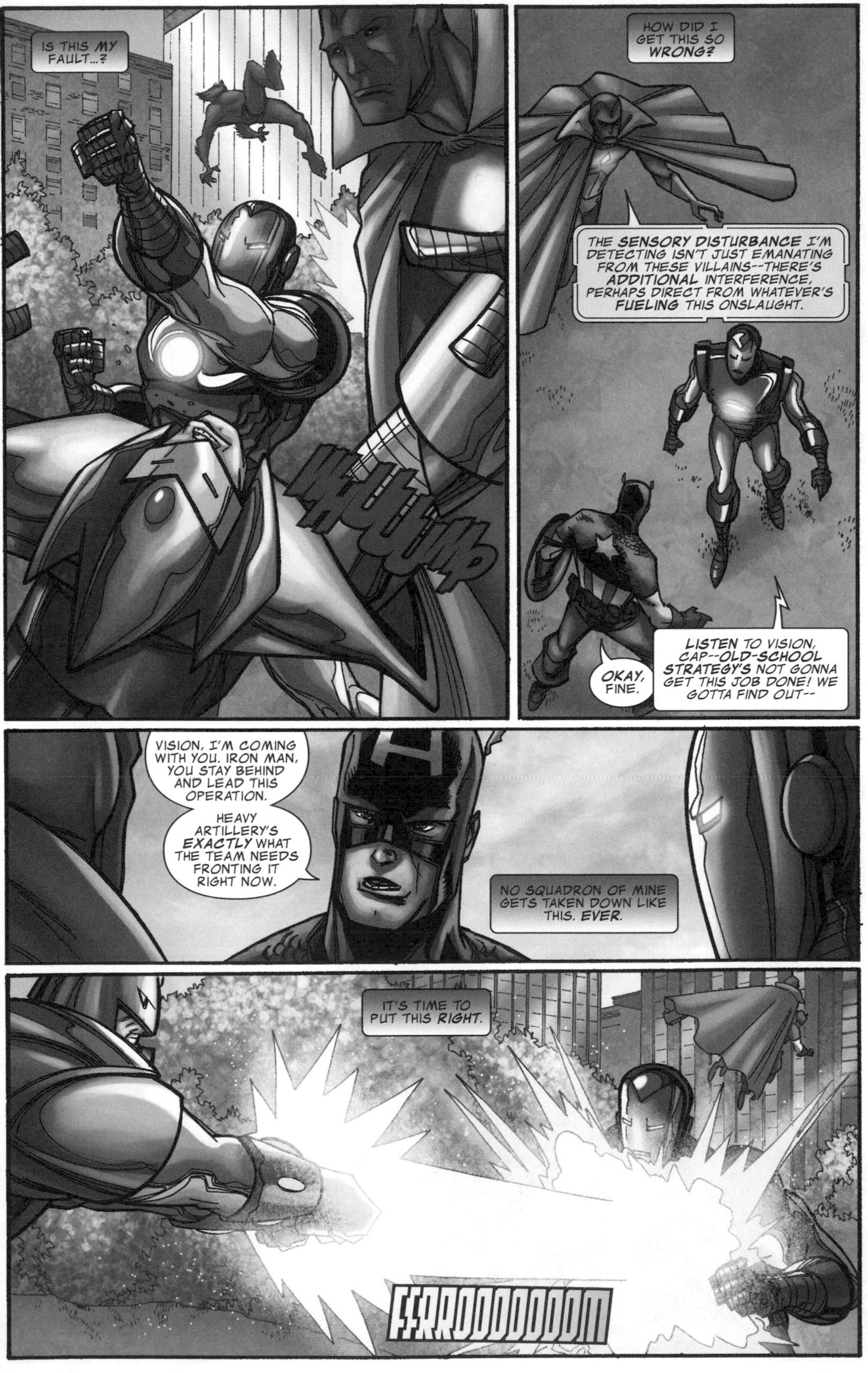
IS THIS *MY* FAULT...?
WHUUUMP
HOW DID I GET THIS SO *WRONG?*
THE **SENSORY DISTURBANCE** I'M DETECTING ISN'T JUST EMANATING FROM THESE VILLAINS--THERE'S **ADDITIONAL** INTERFERENCE, PERHAPS DIRECT FROM WHATEVER'S **FUELING** THIS ONSLAUGHT.
LISTEN TO VISION, CAP--**OLD-SCHOOL STRATEGY'S** NOT GONNA GET THIS JOB DONE! WE GOTTA FIND OUT--
OKAY, FINE.
VISION, I'M COMING WITH YOU. IRON MAN, YOU STAY BEHIND AND LEAD THIS OPERATION.
HEAVY ARTILLERY'S **EXACTLY** WHAT THE TEAM NEEDS FRONTING IT RIGHT NOW.
NO SQUADRON OF MINE GETS TAKEN DOWN LIKE THIS. *EVER.*
IT'S TIME TO PUT THIS *RIGHT.*
FSRROOOOOOOOM

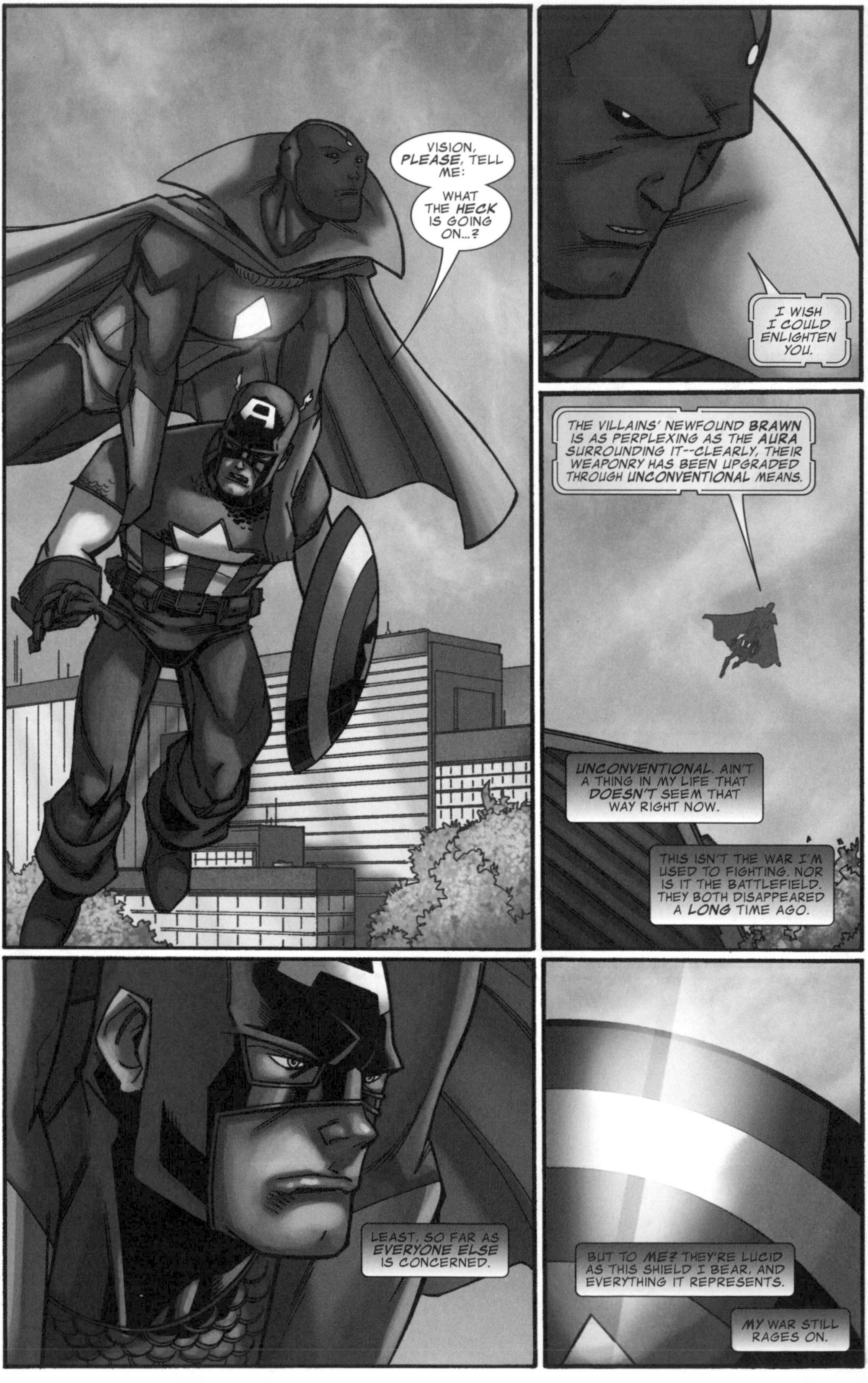
VISION, PLEASE, TELL ME:
WHAT THE HECK IS GOING ON...?
I WISH I COULD ENLIGHTEN YOU.
THE VILLAINS' NEWFOUND BRAWN IS AS PERPLEXING AS THE AURA SURROUNDING IT--CLEARLY, THEIR WEAPONRY HAS BEEN UPGRADED THROUGH UNCONVENTIONAL MEANS.
UNCONVENTIONAL. AIN'T A THING IN MY LIFE THAT DOESN'T SEEM THAT WAY RIGHT NOW.
THIS ISN'T THE WAR I'M USED TO FIGHTING. NOR IS IT THE BATTLEFIELD. THEY BOTH DISAPPEARED A LONG TIME AGO.
LEAST, SO FAR AS EVERYONE ELSE IS CONCERNED.
BUT TO ME? THEY'RE LUCID AS THIS SHIELD I BEAR, AND EVERYTHING IT REPRESENTS.
MY WAR STILL RAGES ON.

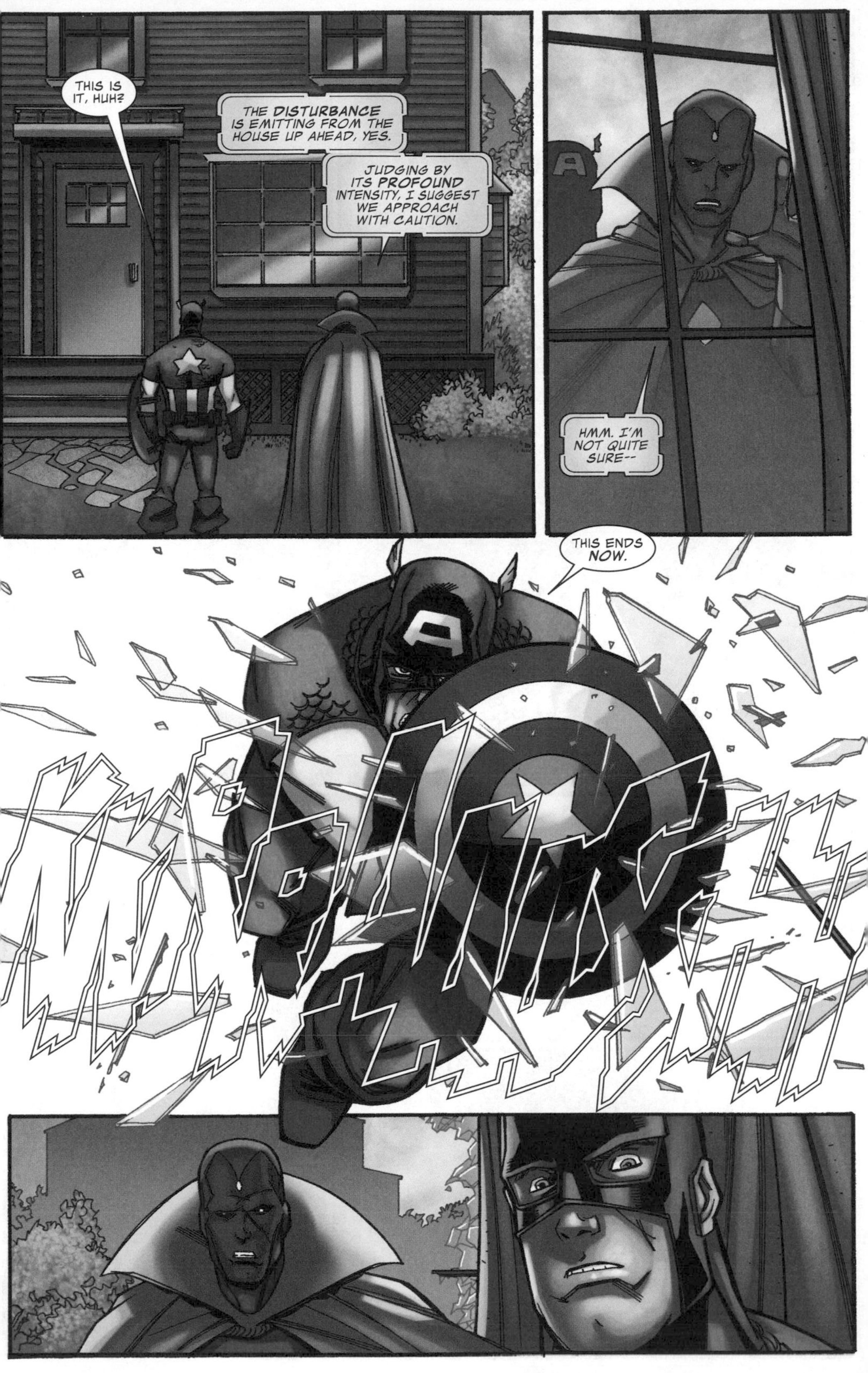
THIS IS IT, HUH?
THE DISTURBANCE IS EMITTING FROM THE HOUSE UP AHEAD, YES.
JUDGING BY ITS PROFOUND INTENSITY, I SUGGEST WE APPROACH WITH CAUTION.
HMM. I'M NOT QUITE SURE--
THIS ENDS NOW.

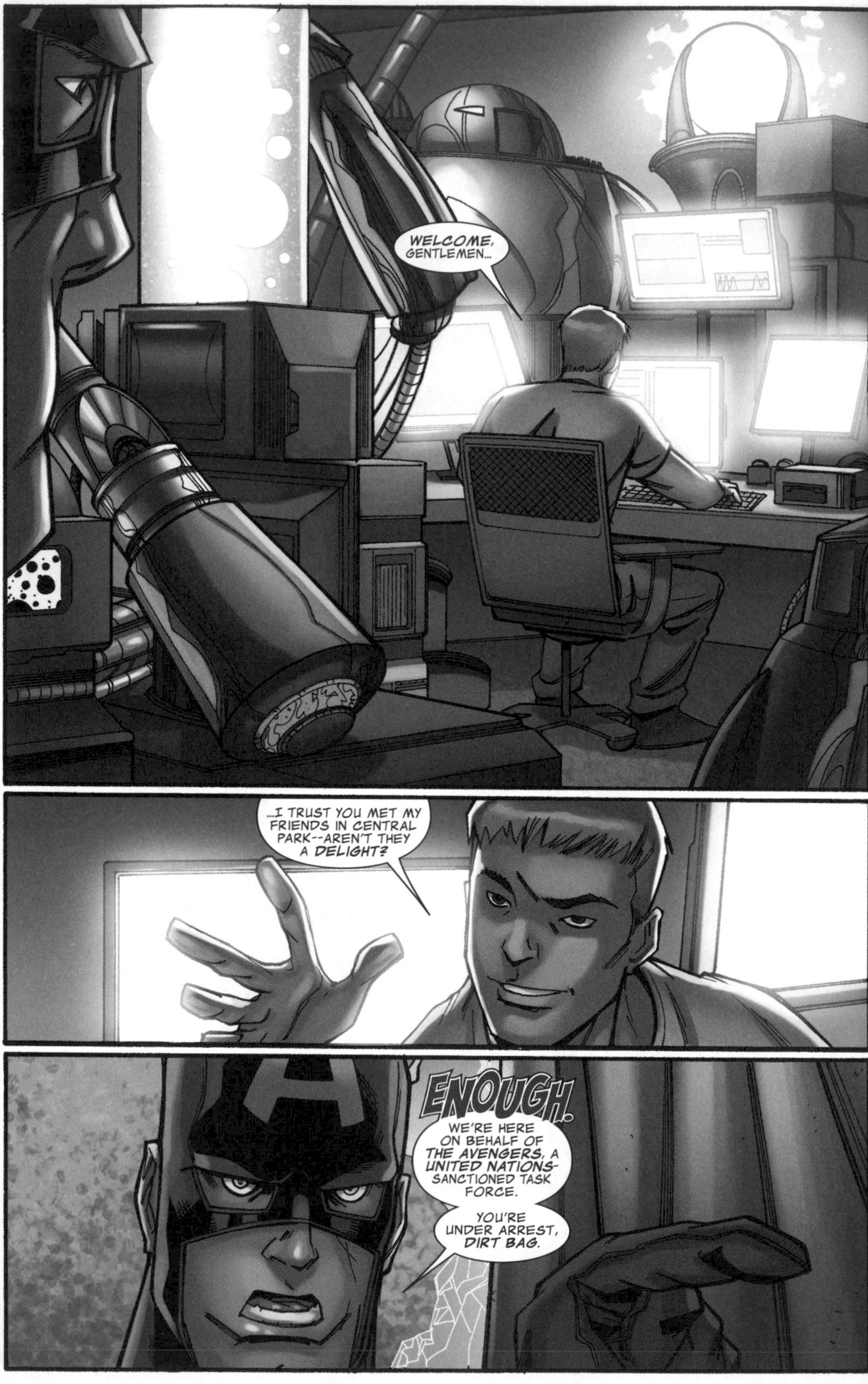
WELCOME, GENTLEMEN...
...I TRUST YOU MET MY FRIENDS IN CENTRAL PARK--AREN'T THEY A DELIGHT?
ENOUGH.
WE'RE HERE ON BEHALF OF THE AVENGERS, A UNITED NATIONS-SANCTIONED TASK FORCE.
YOU'RE UNDER ARREST, DIRT BAG.

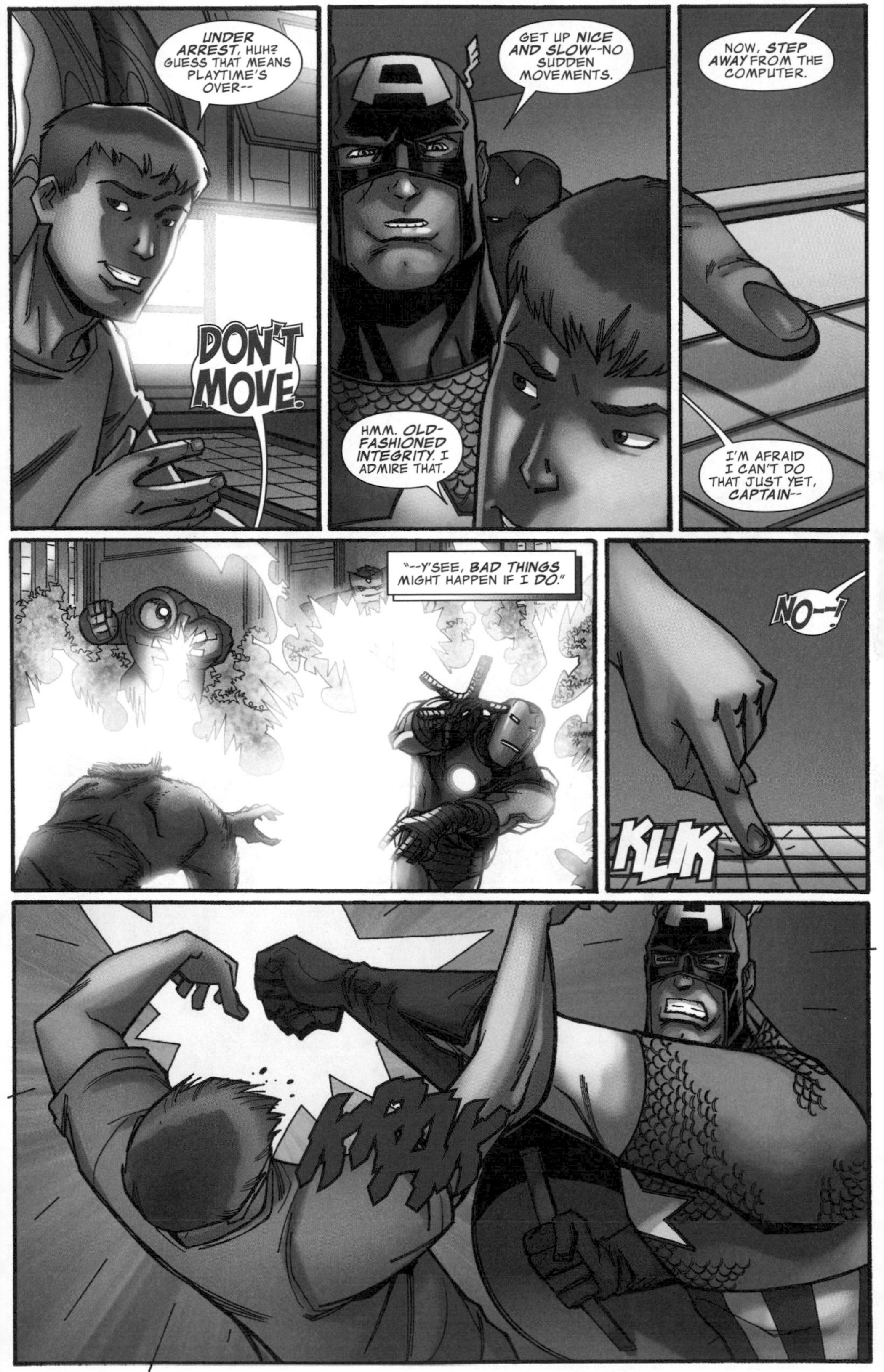

UNDER ARREST, HUH? GUESS THAT MEANS PLAYTIME'S OVER--
DON'T MOVE.
GET UP NICE AND SLOW--NO SUDDEN MOVEMENTS.
HMM. OLD-FASHIONED INTEGRITY. I ADMIRE THAT.
NOW, STEP AWAY FROM THE COMPUTER.
I'M AFRAID I CAN'T DO THAT JUST YET, CAPTAIN--
"--Y'SEE, BAD THINGS MIGHT HAPPEN IF I DO."
NO--!
KLIK
KRAK

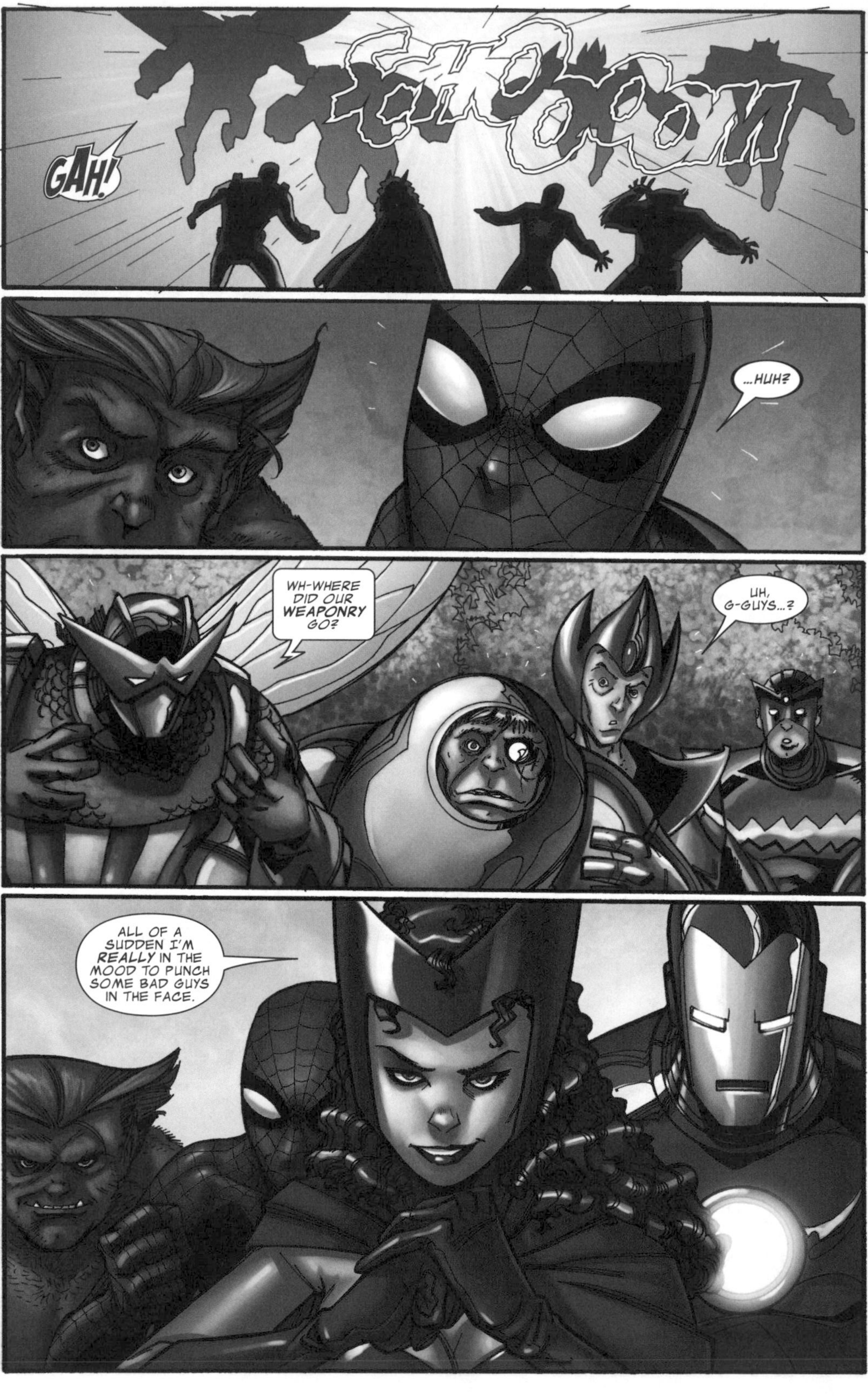
GAH!
...HUH?
WH-WHERE DID OUR WEAPONRY GO?
UH, G-GUYS...?
ALL OF A SUDDEN I'M REALLY IN THE MOOD TO PUNCH SOME BAD GUYS IN THE FACE.

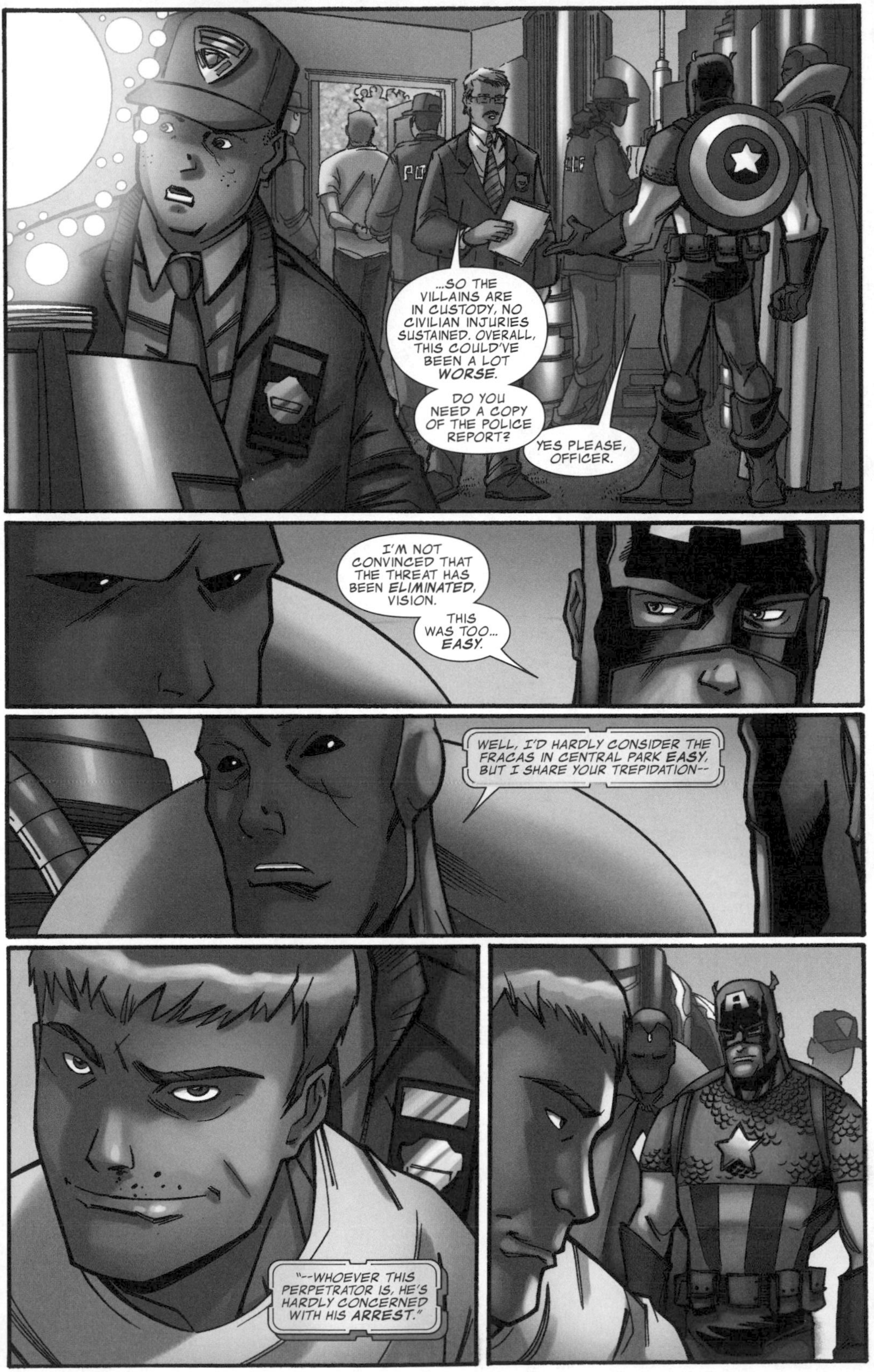
...SO THE VILLAINS ARE IN CUSTODY, NO CIVILIAN INJURIES SUSTAINED. OVERALL, THIS COULD'VE BEEN A LOT WORSE.
DO YOU NEED A COPY OF THE POLICE REPORT?
YES PLEASE, OFFICER.
I'M NOT CONVINCED THAT THE THREAT HAS BEEN ELIMINATED, VISION.
THIS WAS TOO... EASY.
WELL, I'D HARDLY CONSIDER THE FRACAS IN CENTRAL PARK EASY, BUT I SHARE YOUR TREPIDATION--
"--WHOEVER THIS PERPETRATOR IS, HE'S HARDLY CONCERNED WITH HIS ARREST."

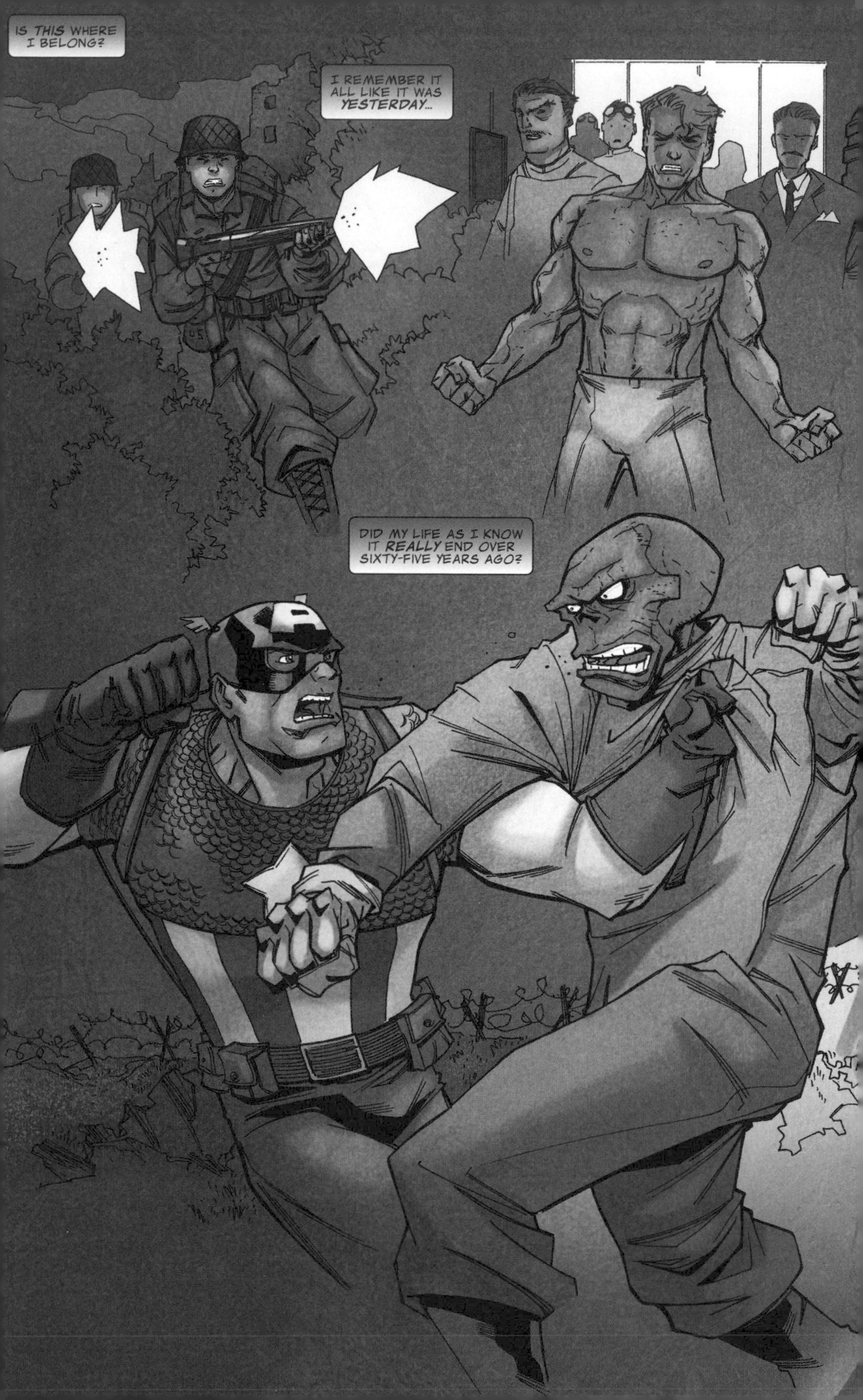
IS THIS WHERE I BELONG?
I REMEMBER IT ALL LIKE IT WAS YESTERDAY...
DID MY LIFE AS I KNOW IT REALLY END OVER SIXTY-FIVE YEARS AGO?

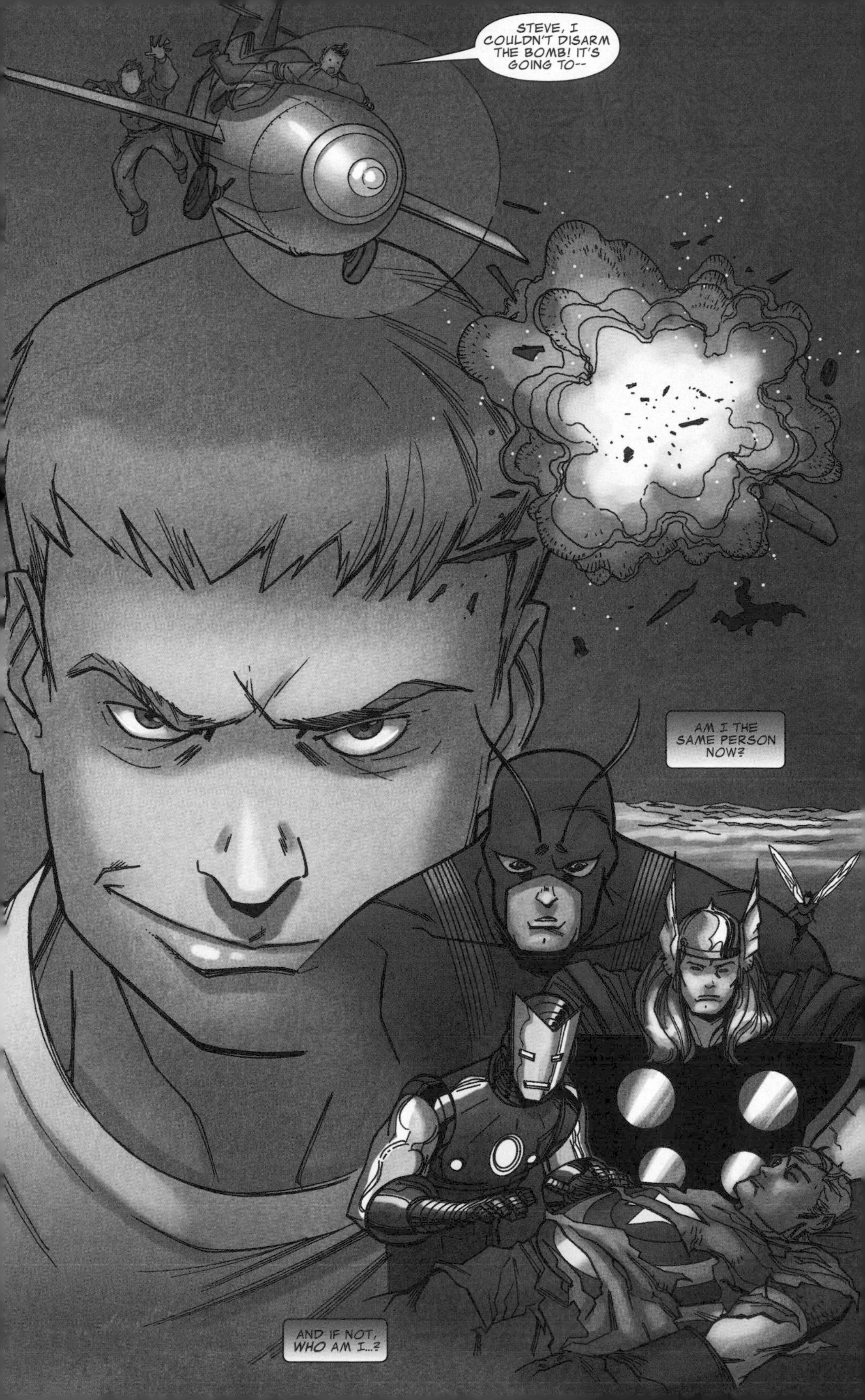
STEVE, I COULDN'T DISARM THE BOMB! IT'S GOING TO--
AM I THE SAME PERSON NOW?
AND IF NOT, WHO AM I...?

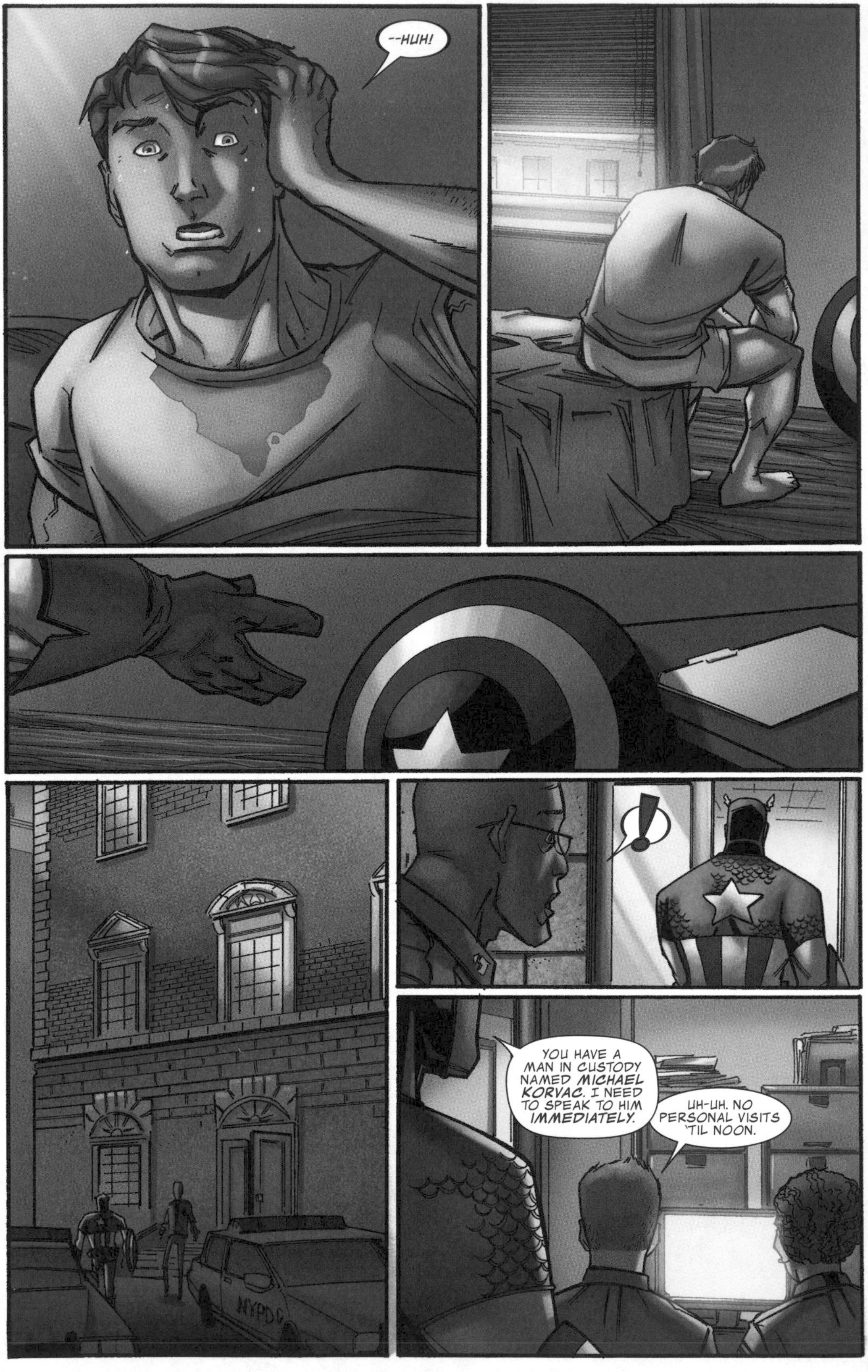
--HUH!
!
YOU HAVE A MAN IN CUSTODY NAMED MICHAEL KORVAC. I NEED TO SPEAK TO HIM IMMEDIATELY.
UH-UH. NO PERSONAL VISITS 'TIL NOON.

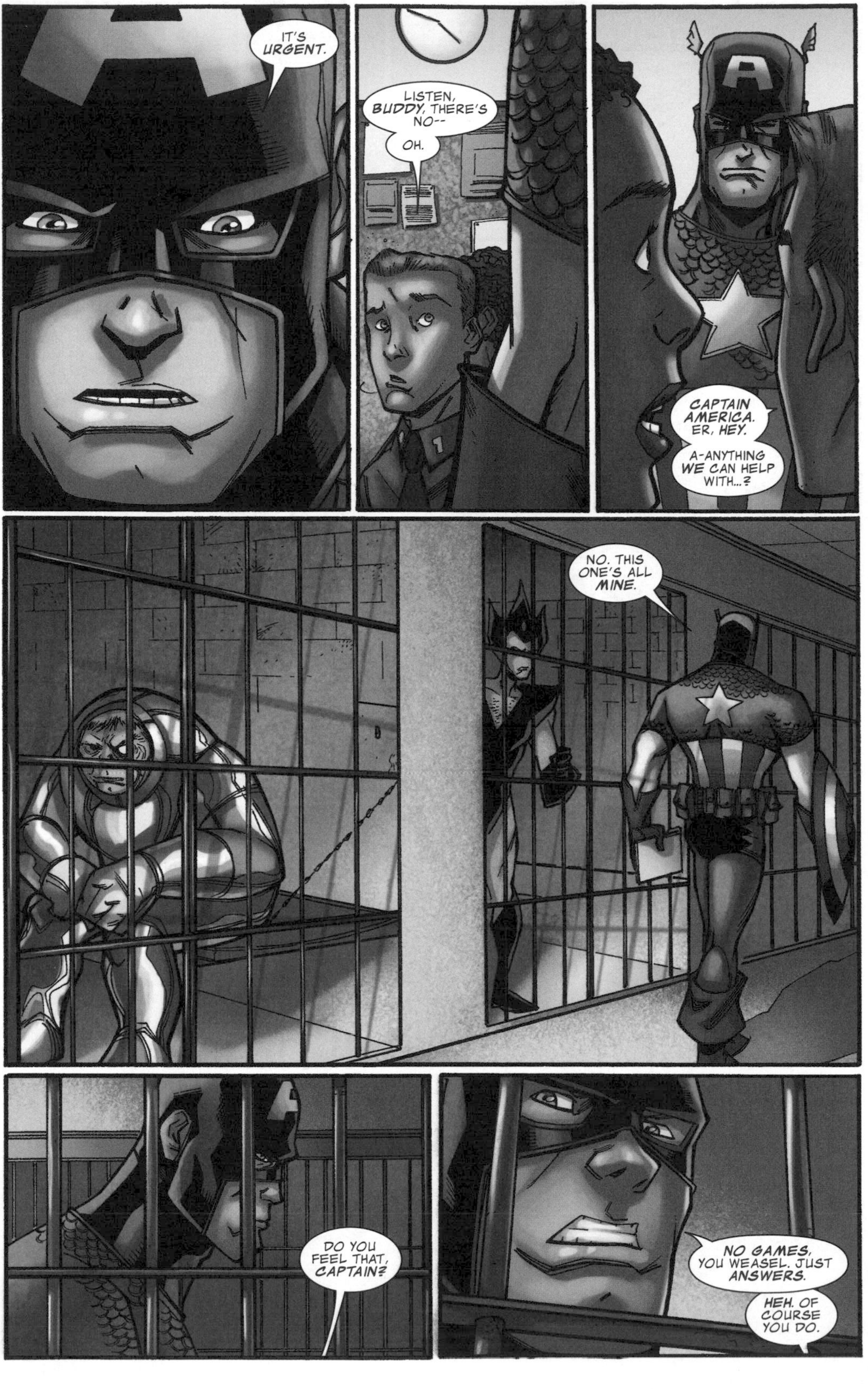
IT'S URGENT.
LISTEN, BUDDY, THERE'S NO--
OH.
CAPTAIN AMERICA. ER, HEY.
A-ANYTHING WE CAN HELP WITH...?
NO. THIS ONE'S ALL MINE.
DO YOU FEEL THAT, CAPTAIN?
NO GAMES, YOU WEASEL. JUST ANSWERS.
HEH. OF COURSE YOU DO.

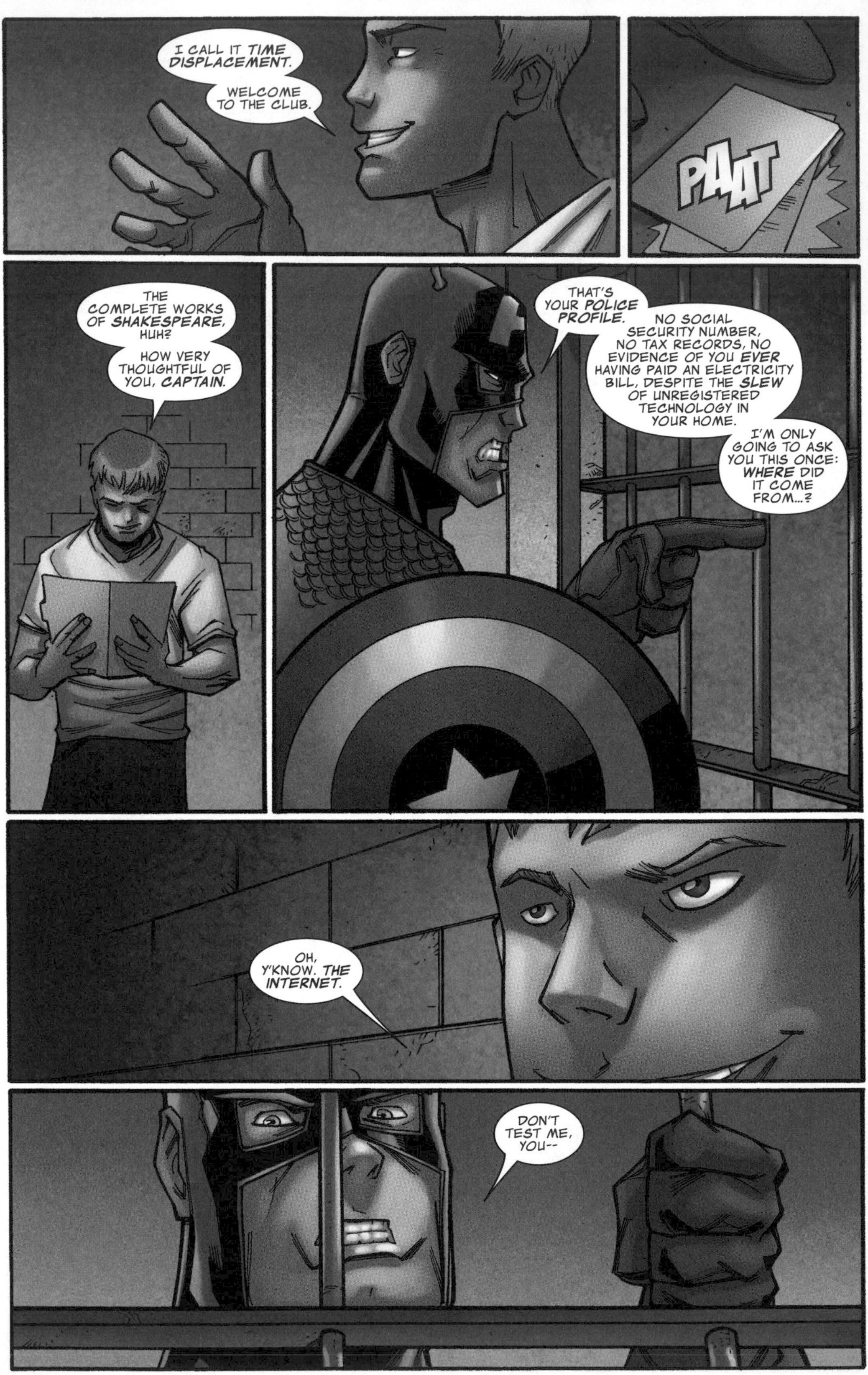
I CALL IT TIME DISPLACEMENT.
WELCOME TO THE CLUB.
PAAT
THE COMPLETE WORKS OF SHAKESPEARE, HUH?
HOW VERY THOUGHTFUL OF YOU, CAPTAIN.
THAT'S YOUR POLICE PROFILE.
NO SOCIAL SECURITY NUMBER, NO TAX RECORDS, NO EVIDENCE OF YOU EVER HAVING PAID AN ELECTRICITY BILL, DESPITE THE SLEW OF UNREGISTERED TECHNOLOGY IN YOUR HOME.
I'M ONLY GOING TO ASK YOU THIS ONCE: WHERE DID IT COME FROM...?
OH, Y'KNOW. THE INTERNET.
DON'T TEST ME, YOU--

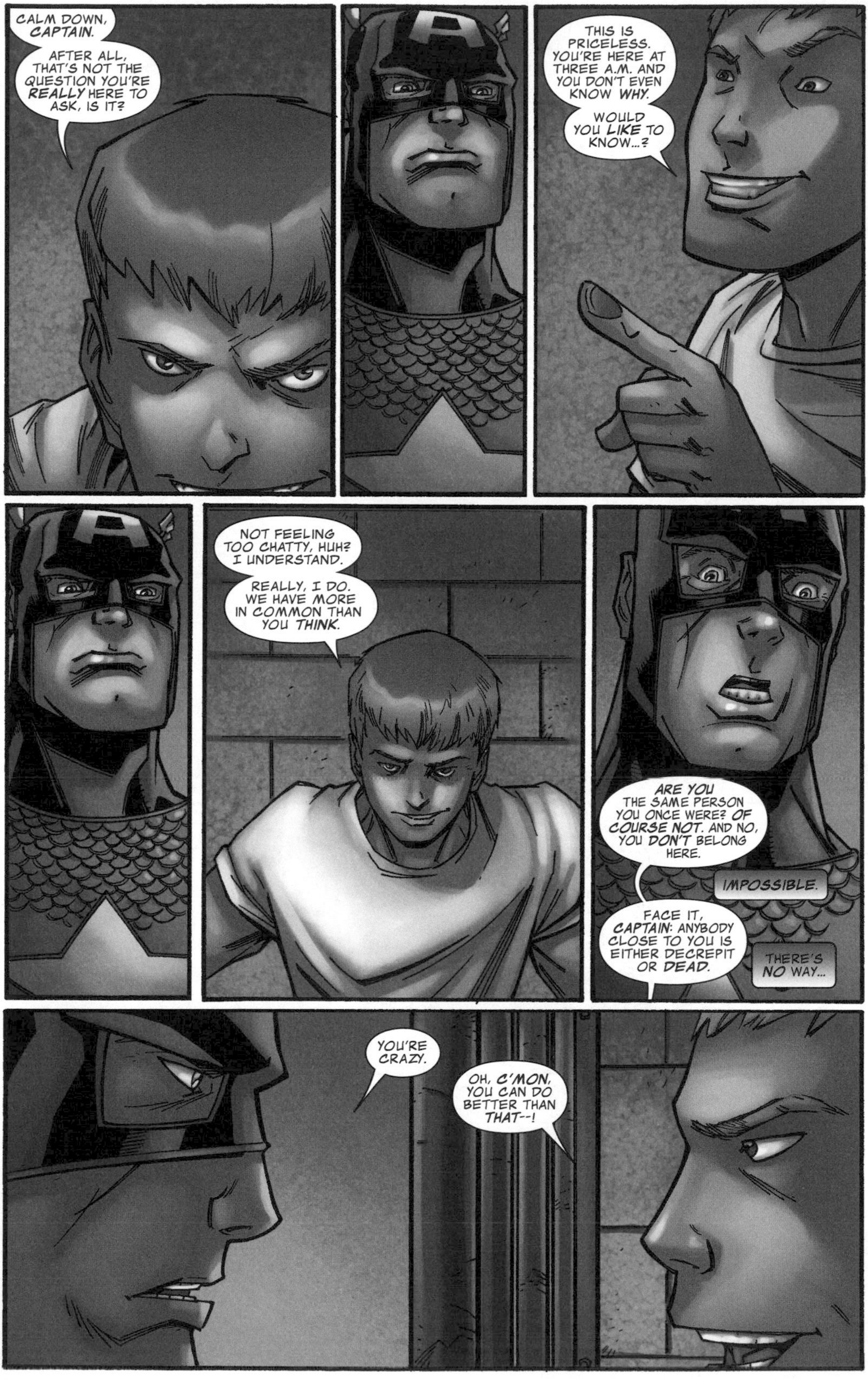
CALM DOWN, CAPTAIN.
AFTER ALL, THAT'S NOT THE QUESTION YOU'RE REALLY HERE TO ASK, IS IT?
THIS IS PRICELESS. YOU'RE HERE AT THREE A.M. AND YOU DON'T EVEN KNOW WHY.
WOULD YOU LIKE TO KNOW...?
NOT FEELING TOO CHATTY, HUH? I UNDERSTAND.
REALLY, I DO. WE HAVE MORE IN COMMON THAN YOU THINK.
ARE YOU THE SAME PERSON YOU ONCE WERE? OF COURSE NOT. AND NO, YOU DON'T BELONG HERE.
IMPOSSIBLE.
FACE IT, CAPTAIN: ANYBODY CLOSE TO YOU IS EITHER DECREPIT OR DEAD.
THERE'S NO WAY...
YOU'RE CRAZY.
OH, C'MON, YOU CAN DO BETTER THAN THAT--!

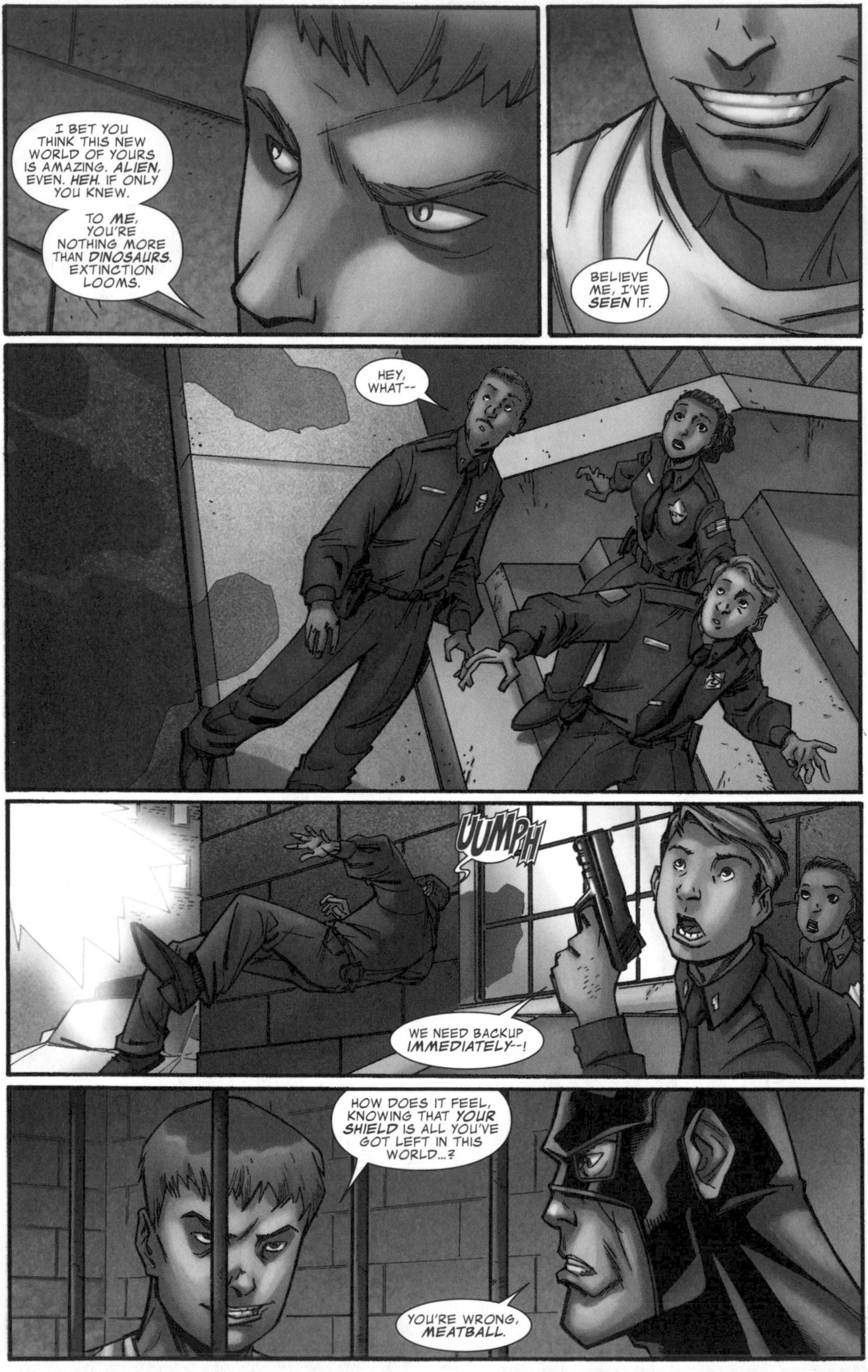
I BET YOU THINK THIS NEW WORLD OF YOURS IS AMAZING. ALIEN, EVEN. HEH. IF ONLY YOU KNEW.
TO ME, YOU'RE NOTHING MORE THAN DINOSAURS. EXTINCTION LOOMS.
BELIEVE ME, I'VE SEEN IT.
HEY, WHAT--
UUMPH
WE NEED BACKUP IMMEDIATELY--!
HOW DOES IT FEEL, KNOWING THAT YOUR SHIELD IS ALL YOU'VE GOT LEFT IN THIS WORLD...?
YOU'RE WRONG, MEATBALL.

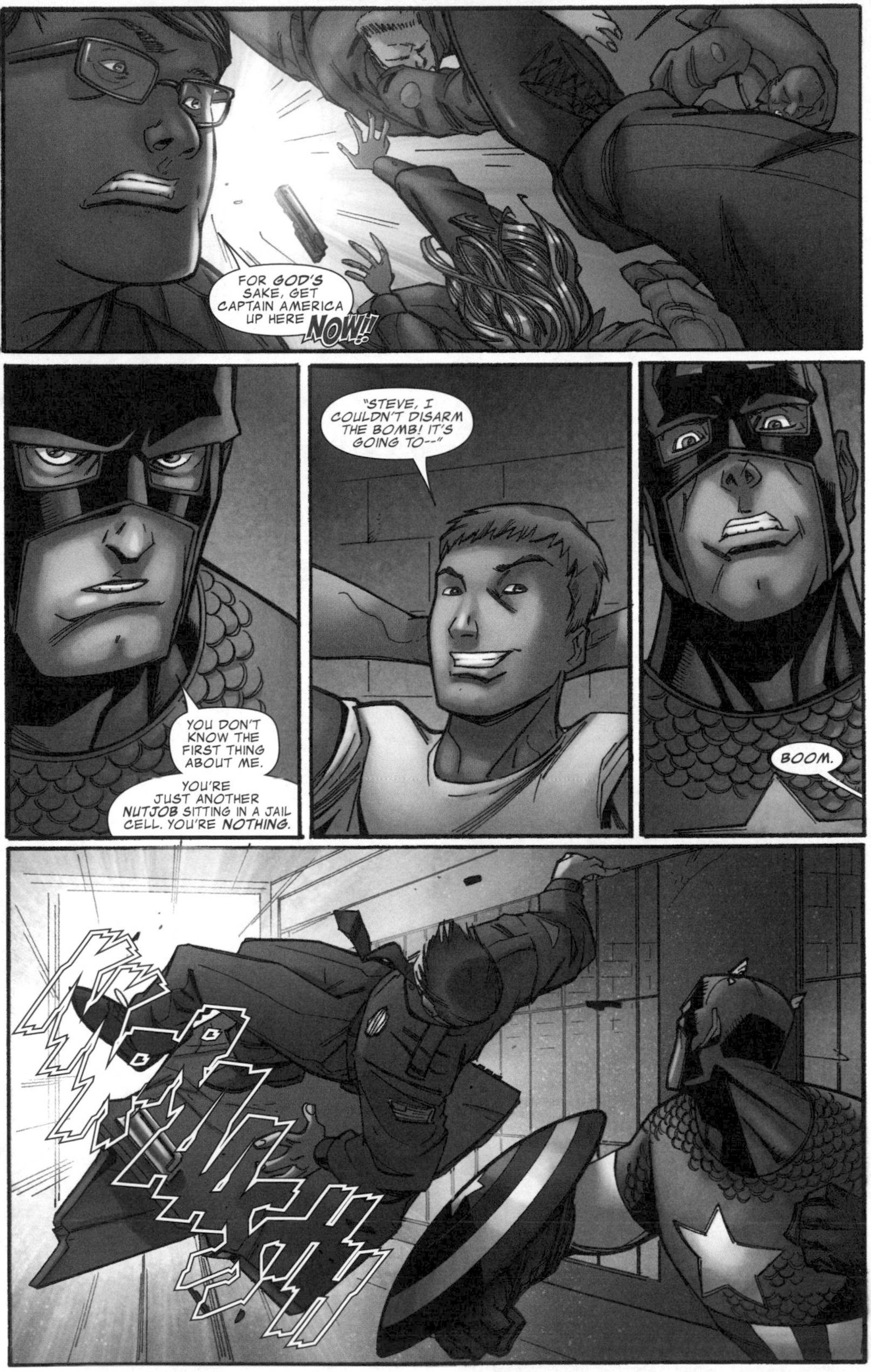
FOR GOD'S SAKE, GET CAPTAIN AMERICA UP HERE NOW!!
YOU DON'T KNOW THE FIRST THING ABOUT ME.
YOU'RE JUST ANOTHER NUTJOB SITTING IN A JAIL CELL. YOU'RE NOTHING.
"STEVE, I COULDN'T DISARM THE BOMB! IT'S GOING TO--"
BOOM.

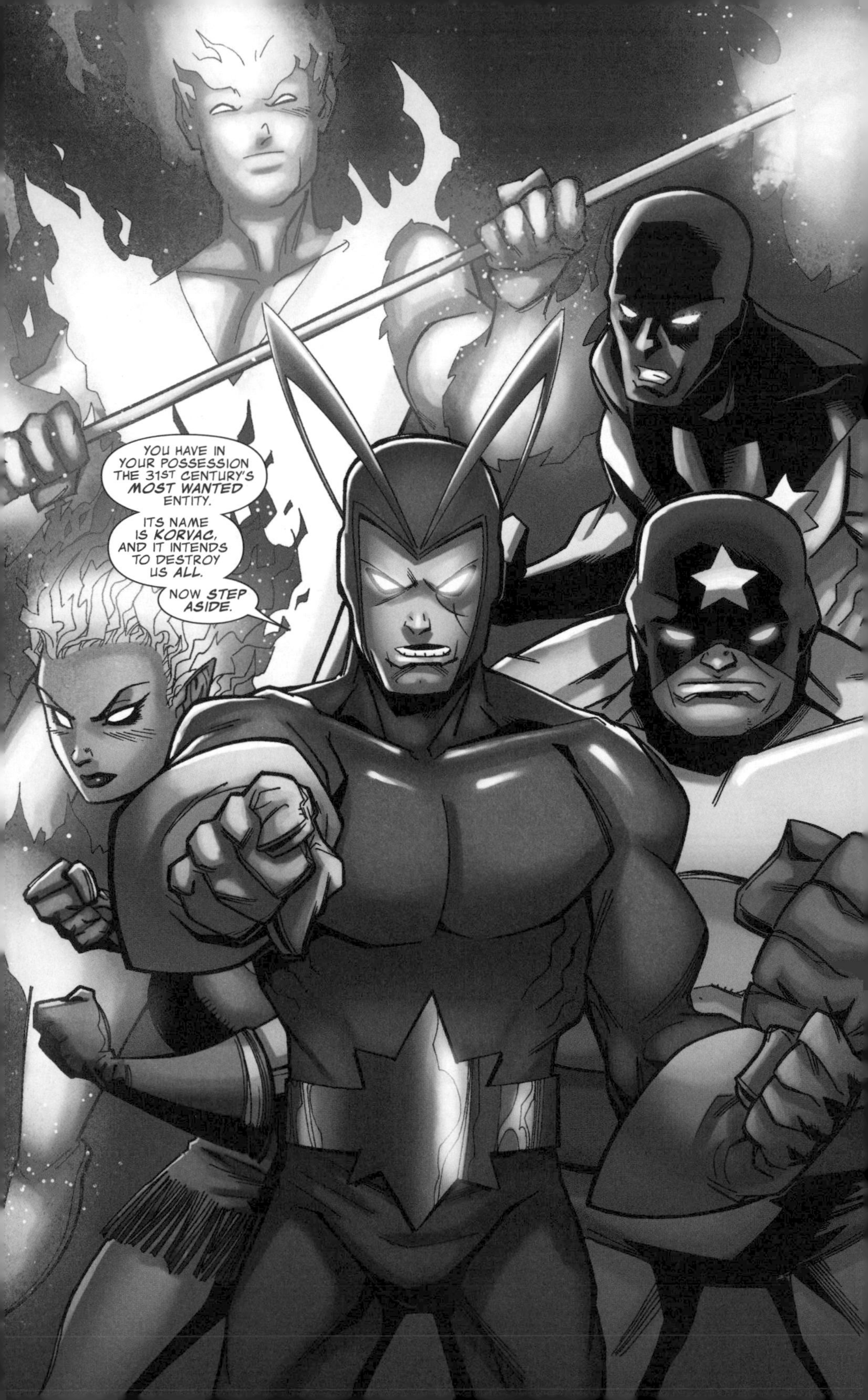
YOU HAVE IN YOUR POSSESSION THE 31ST CENTURY'S *MOST WANTED* ENTITY.
ITS NAME IS *KORVAC*, AND IT INTENDS TO DESTROY US *ALL*.
NOW *STEP ASIDE*.

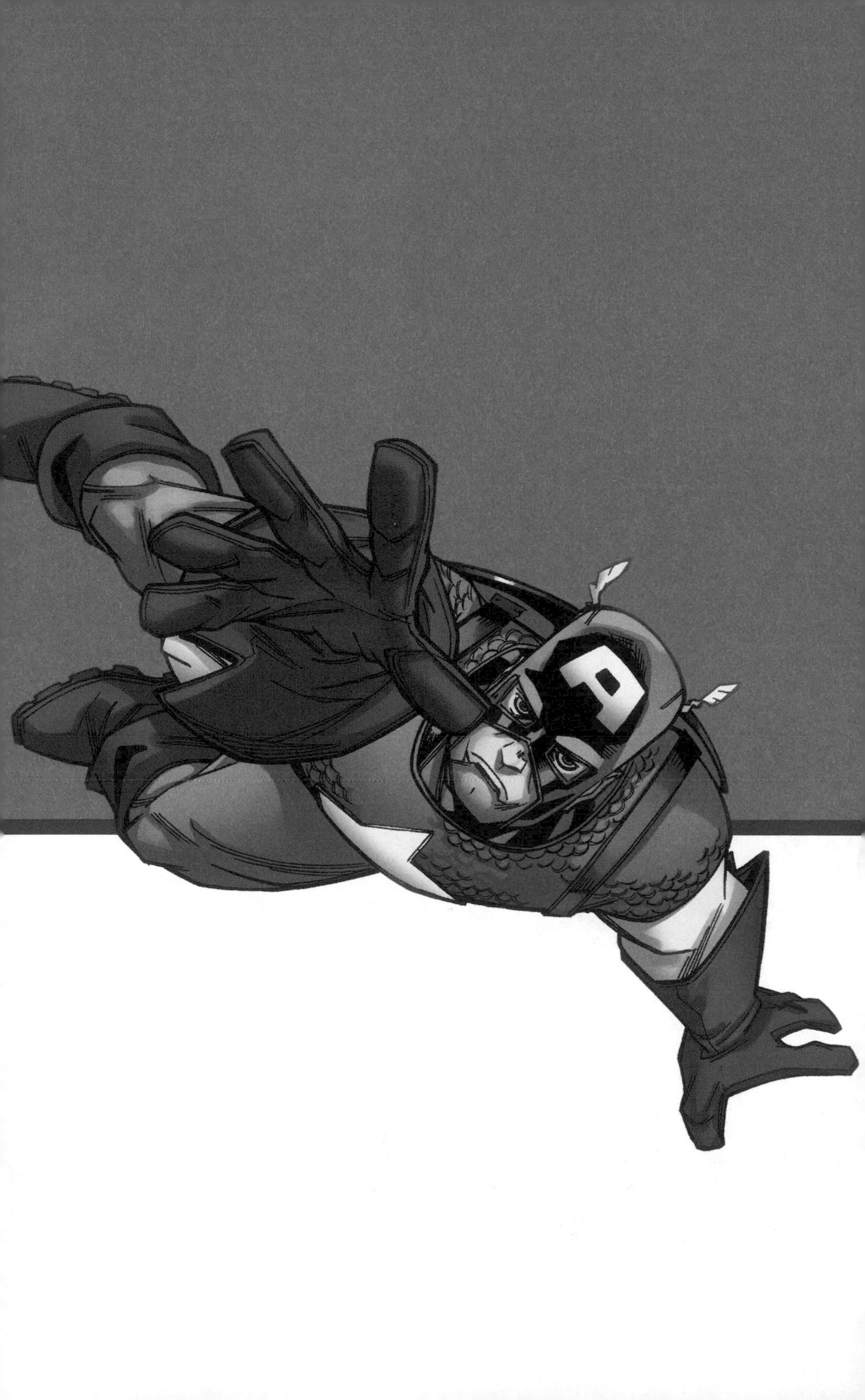

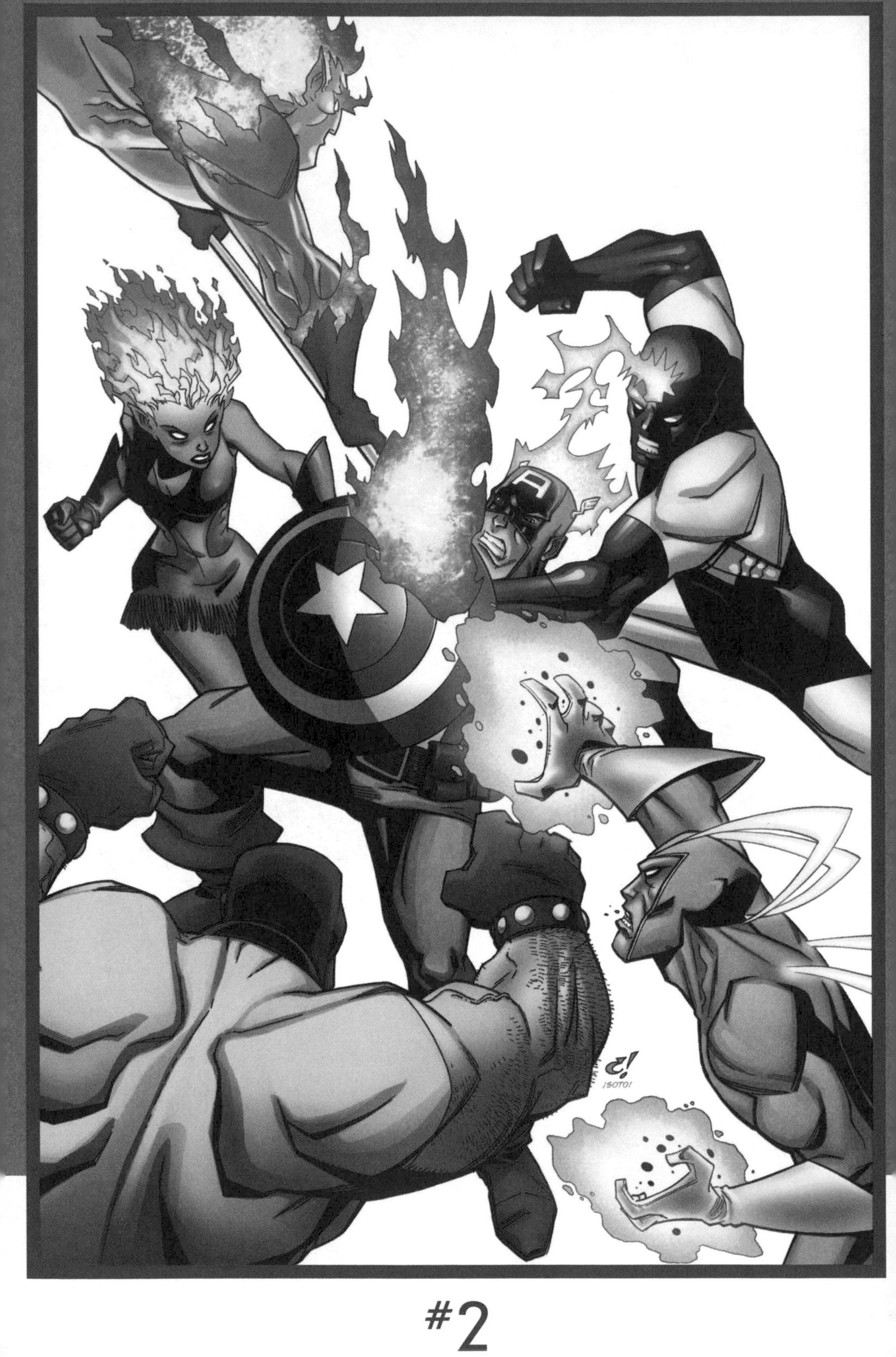

#2

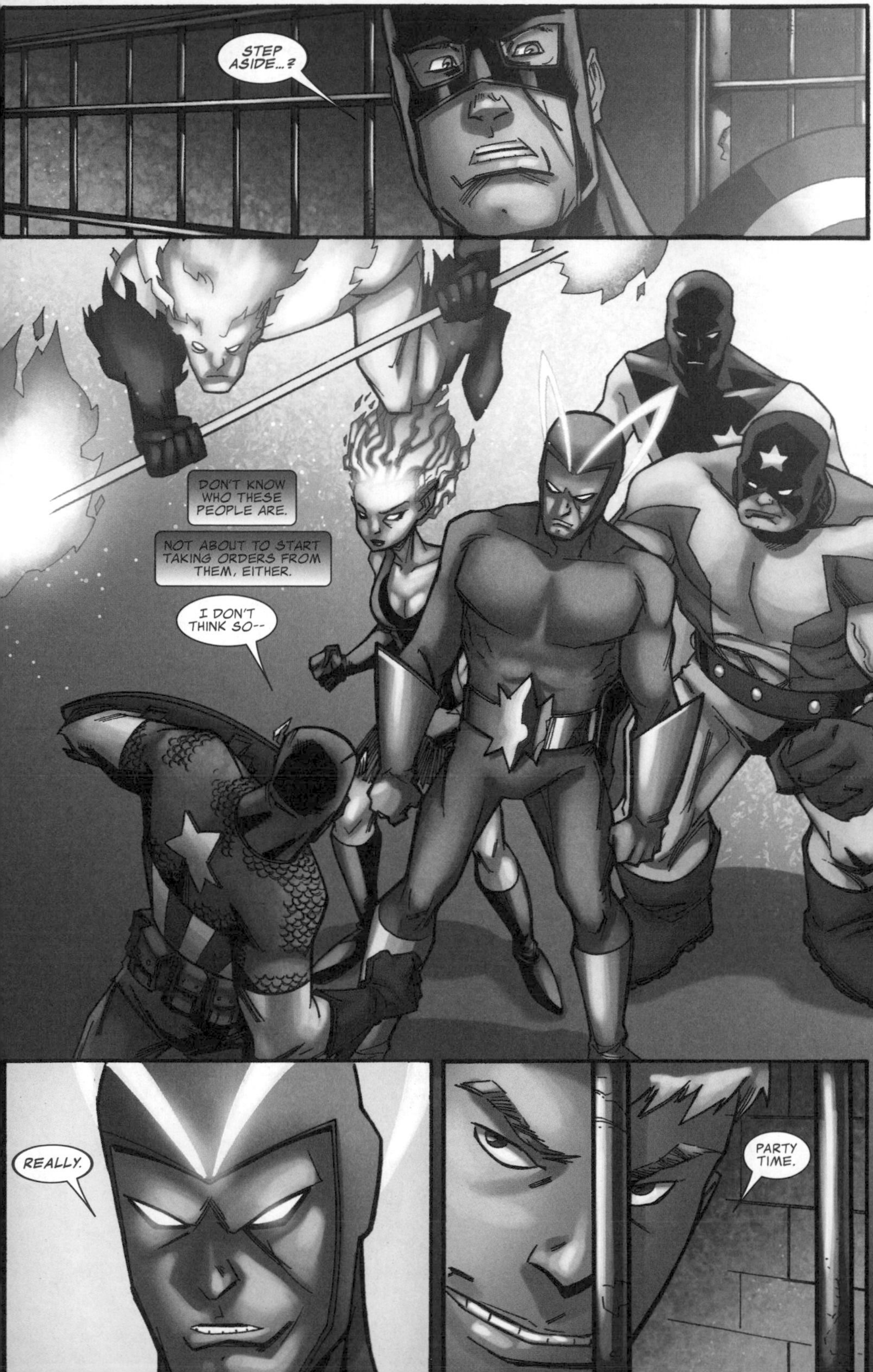
STEP ASIDE...?
DON'T KNOW WHO THESE PEOPLE ARE.
NOT ABOUT TO START TAKING ORDERS FROM THEM, EITHER.
I DON'T THINK SO--
REALLY.
PARTY TIME.

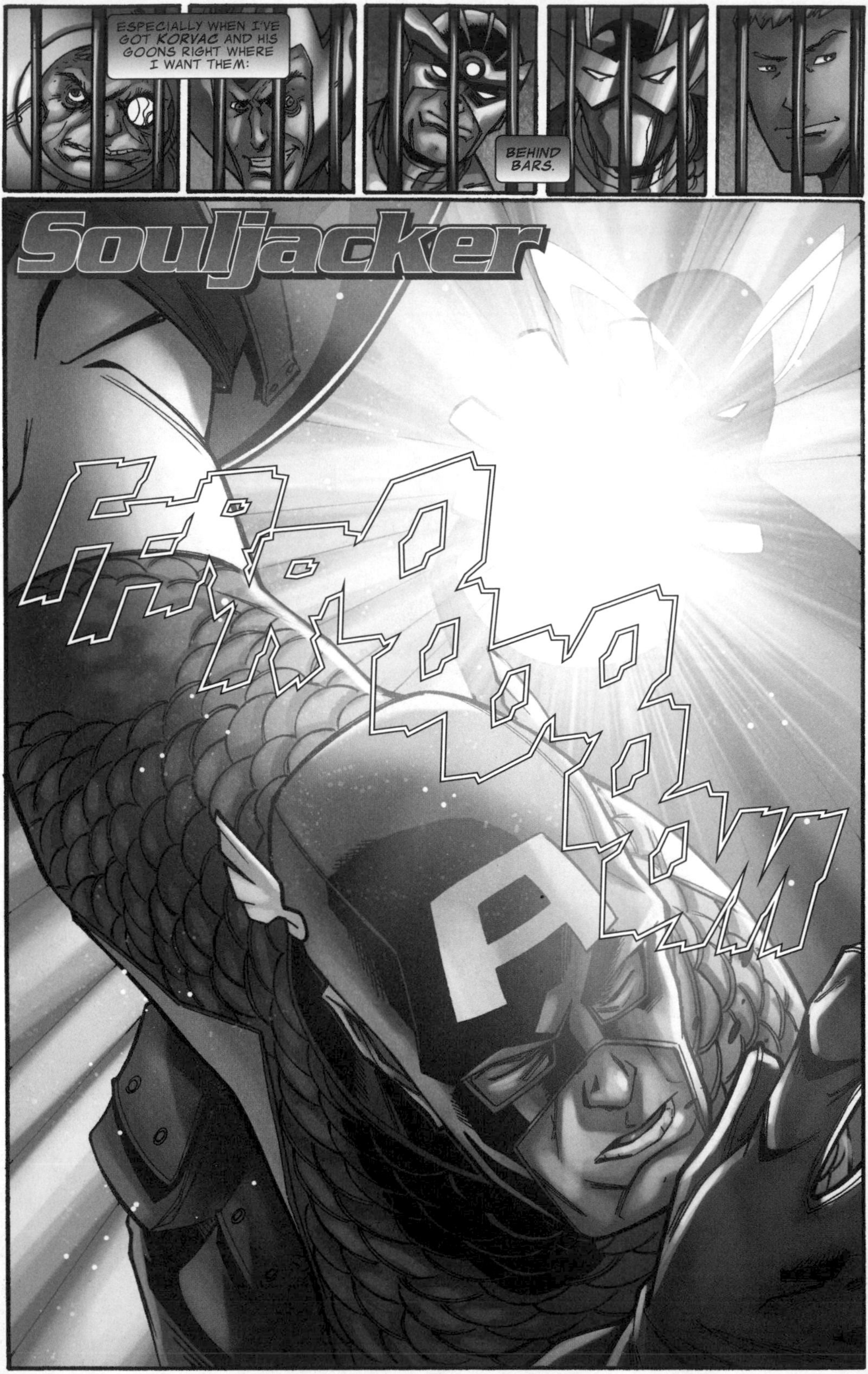
ESPECIALLY WHEN I'VE GOT KORVAC AND HIS GOONS RIGHT WHERE I WANT THEM:
BEHIND BARS.
Souljacker

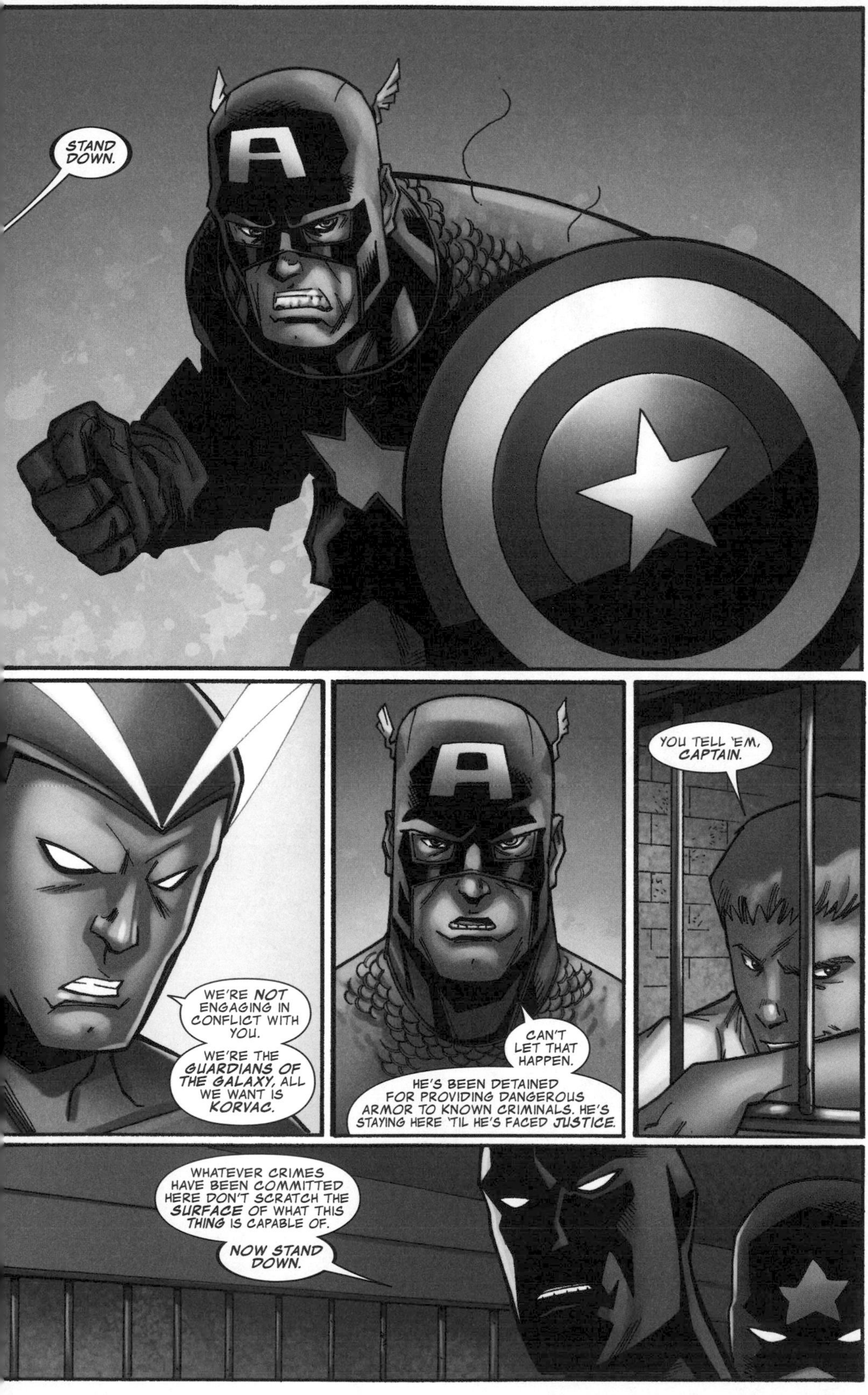
STAND DOWN.
WE'RE NOT ENGAGING IN CONFLICT WITH YOU.
WE'RE THE GUARDIANS OF THE GALAXY, ALL WE WANT IS KORVAC.
CAN'T LET THAT HAPPEN.
HE'S BEEN DETAINED FOR PROVIDING DANGEROUS ARMOR TO KNOWN CRIMINALS. HE'S STAYING HERE 'TIL HE'S FACED JUSTICE.
YOU TELL 'EM, CAPTAIN.
WHATEVER CRIMES HAVE BEEN COMMITTED HERE DON'T SCRATCH THE SURFACE OF WHAT THIS THING IS CAPABLE OF.
NOW STAND DOWN.

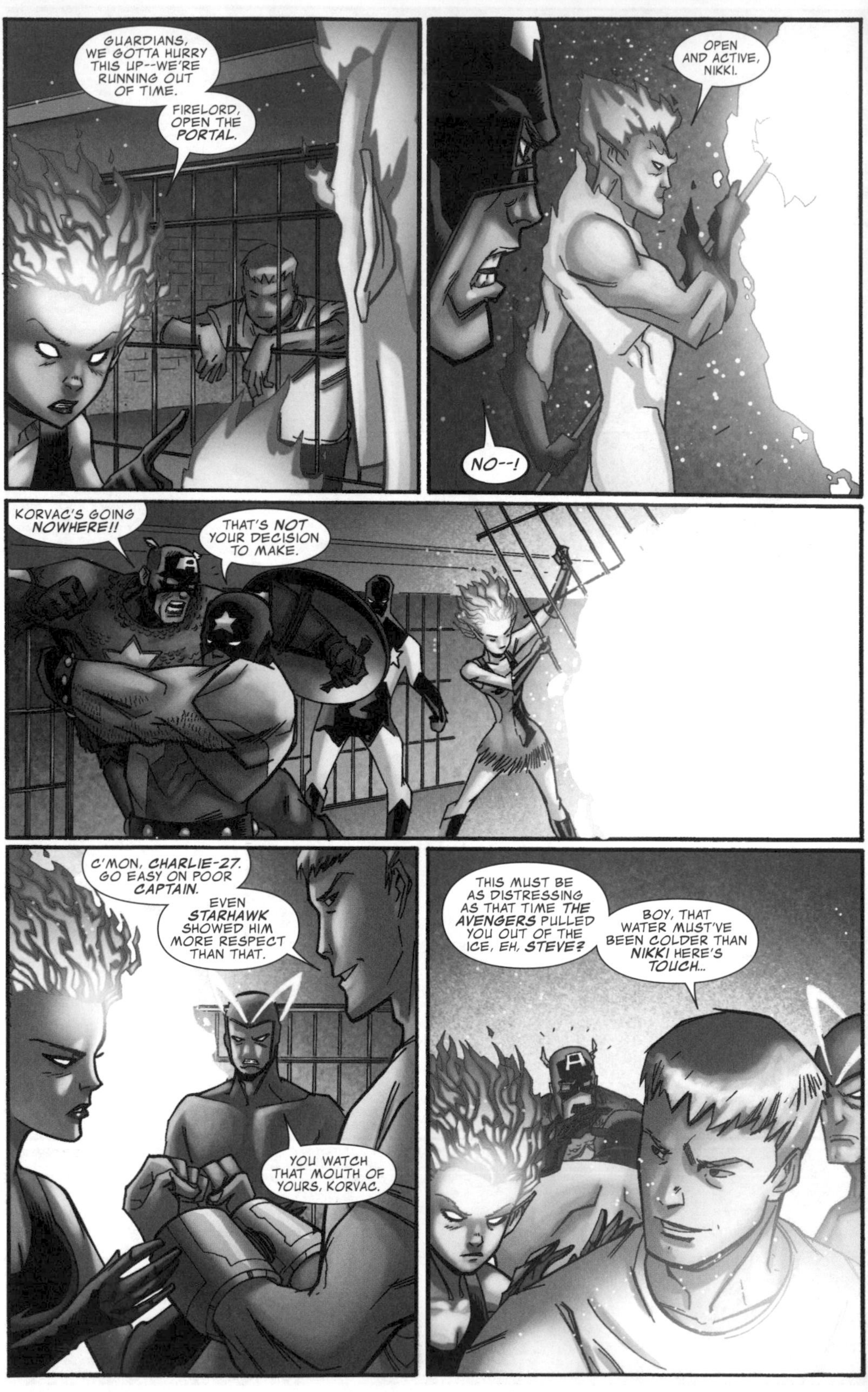
GUARDIANS, WE GOTTA HURRY THIS UP--WE'RE RUNNING OUT OF TIME.
FIRELORD, OPEN THE PORTAL.
OPEN AND ACTIVE, NIKKI.
NO--!
KORVAC'S GOING NOWHERE!!
THAT'S NOT YOUR DECISION TO MAKE.
C'MON, CHARLIE-27. GO EASY ON POOR CAPTAIN.
EVEN STARHAWK SHOWED HIM MORE RESPECT THAN THAT.
YOU WATCH THAT MOUTH OF YOURS, KORVAC.
THIS MUST BE AS DISTRESSING AS THAT TIME THE AVENGERS PULLED YOU OUT OF THE ICE, EH, STEVE?
BOY, THAT WATER MUST'VE BEEN COLDER THAN NIKKI HERE'S TOUCH...

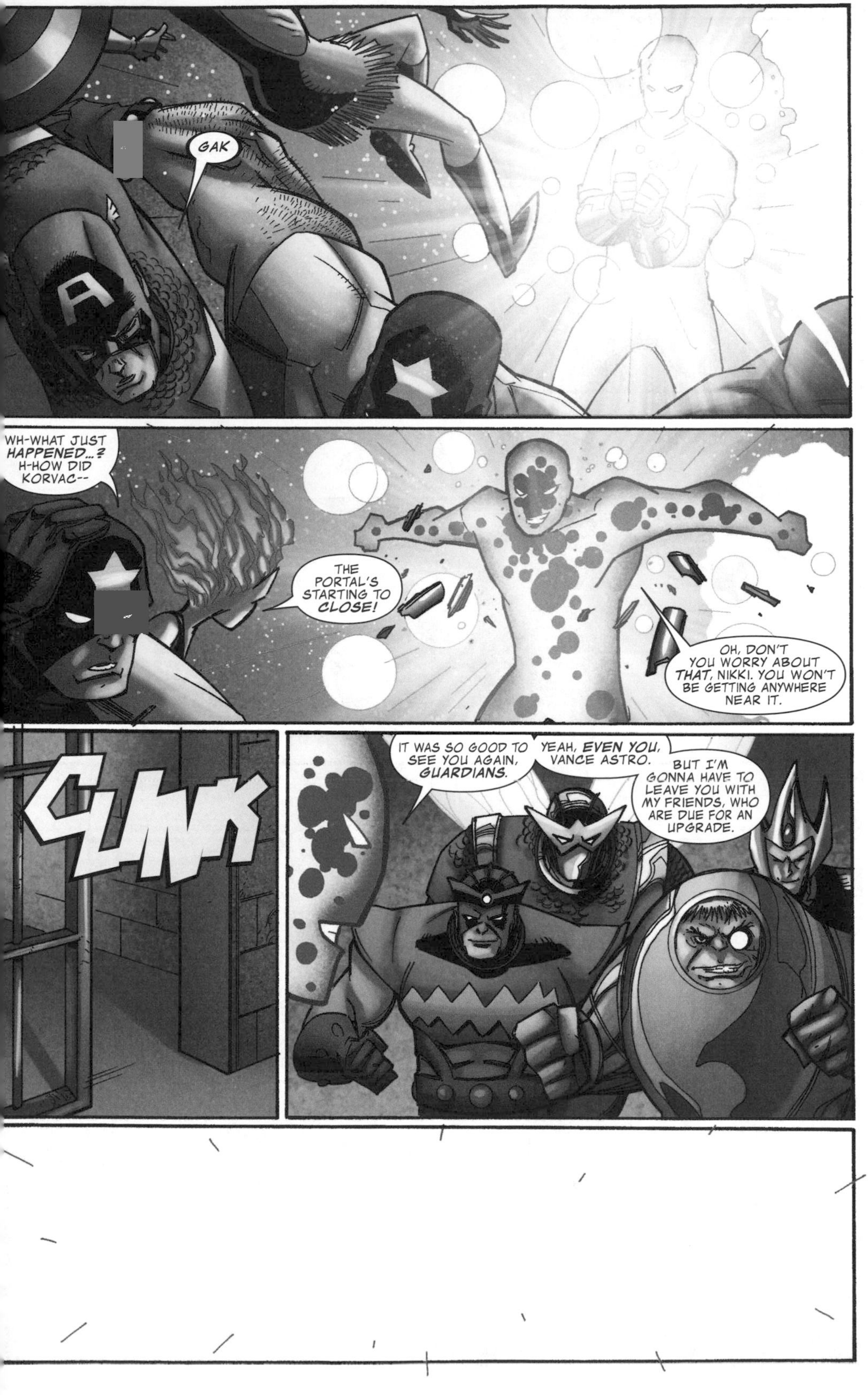
GAK
WH-WHAT JUST HAPPENED...? H-HOW DID KORVAC--
THE PORTAL'S STARTING TO CLOSE!
OH, DON'T YOU WORRY ABOUT THAT, NIKKI. YOU WON'T BE GETTING ANYWHERE NEAR IT.
CLINK
IT WAS SO GOOD TO SEE YOU AGAIN, GUARDIANS.
YEAH, EVEN YOU, VANCE ASTRO.
BUT I'M GONNA HAVE TO LEAVE YOU WITH MY FRIENDS, WHO ARE DUE FOR AN UPGRADE.

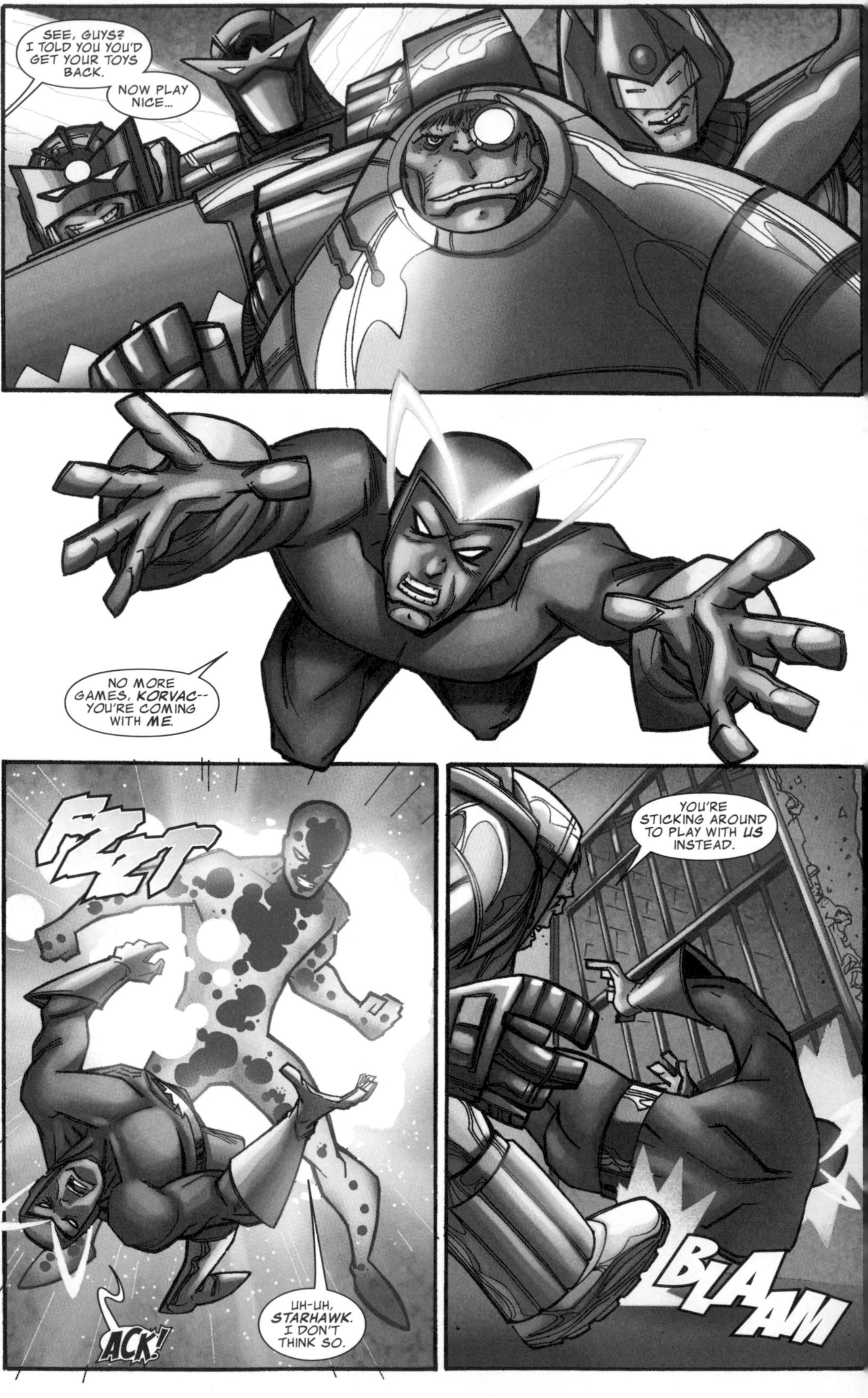
SEE, GUYS? I TOLD YOU YOU'D GET YOUR TOYS BACK.
NOW PLAY NICE...
NO MORE GAMES, KORVAC-- YOU'RE COMING WITH ME.
FZZT
ACK!
UH-UH, STARHAWK. I DON'T THINK SO.
YOU'RE STICKING AROUND TO PLAY WITH US INSTEAD.
BLAAM

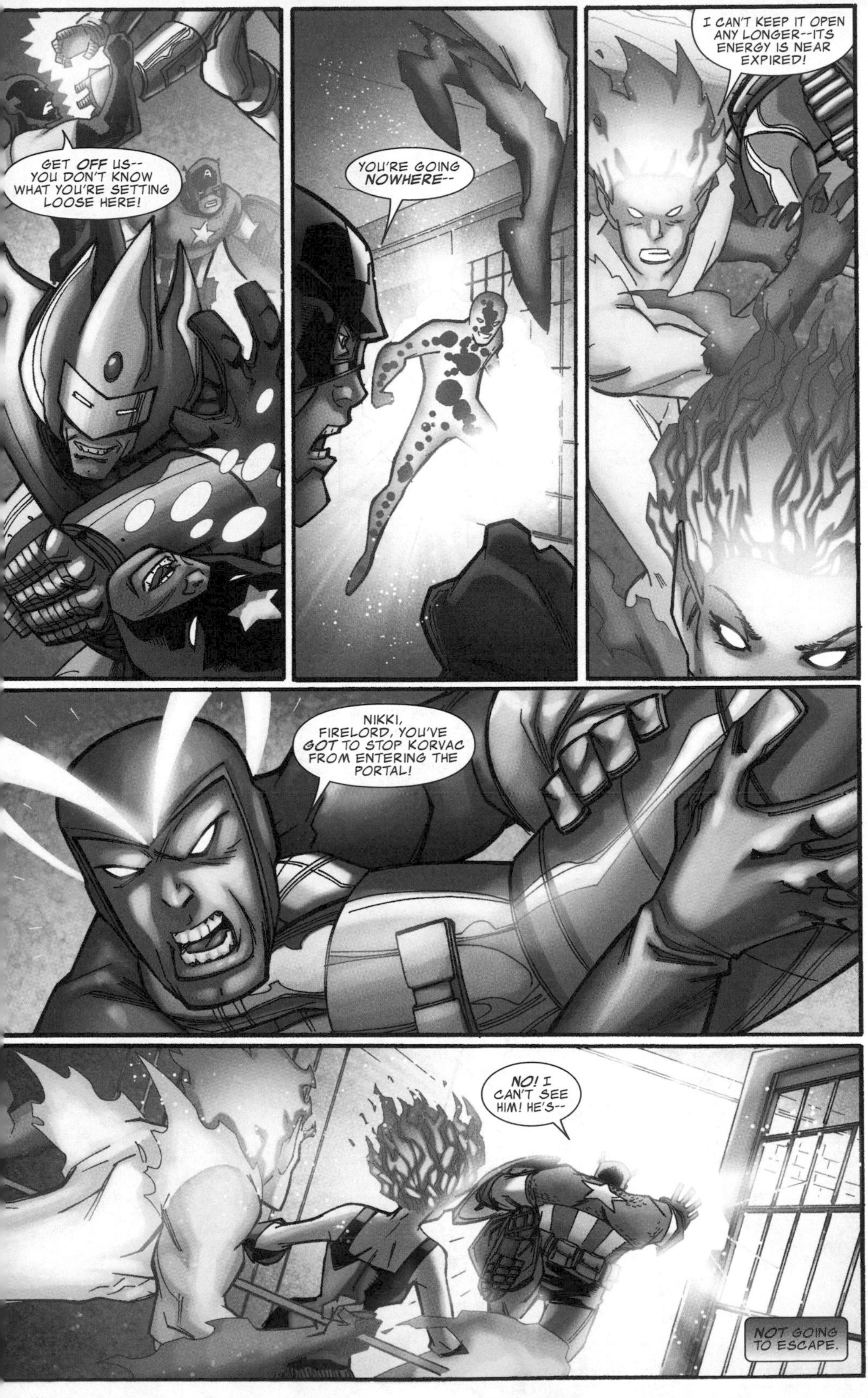
GET OFF US-- YOU DON'T KNOW WHAT YOU'RE SETTING LOOSE HERE!
YOU'RE GOING NOWHERE--
I CAN'T KEEP IT OPEN ANY LONGER--ITS ENERGY IS NEAR EXPIRED!
NIKKI, FIRELORD, YOU'VE GOT TO STOP KORVAC FROM ENTERING THE PORTAL!
NO! I CAN'T SEE HIM! HE'S--
NOT GOING TO ESCAPE.

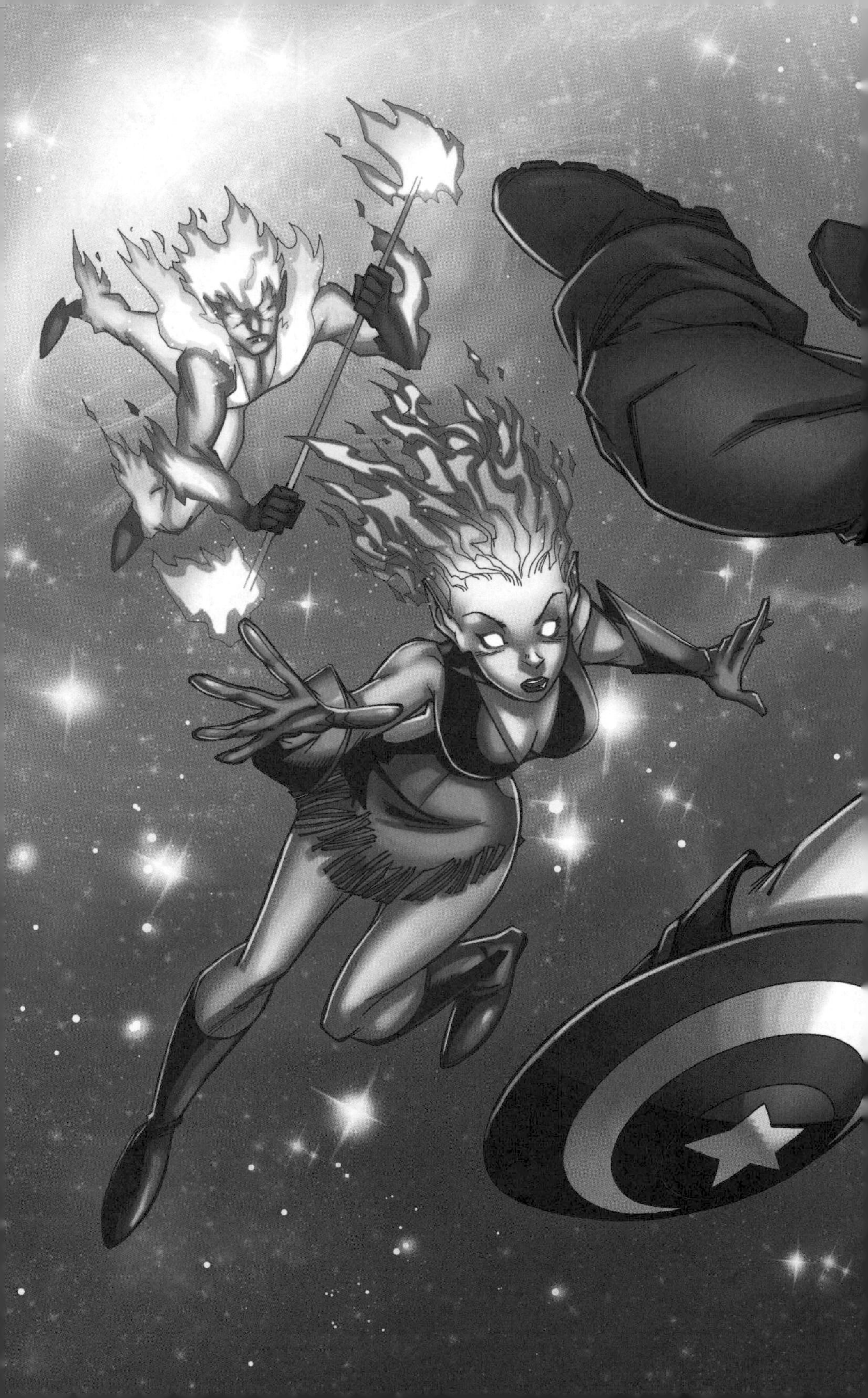

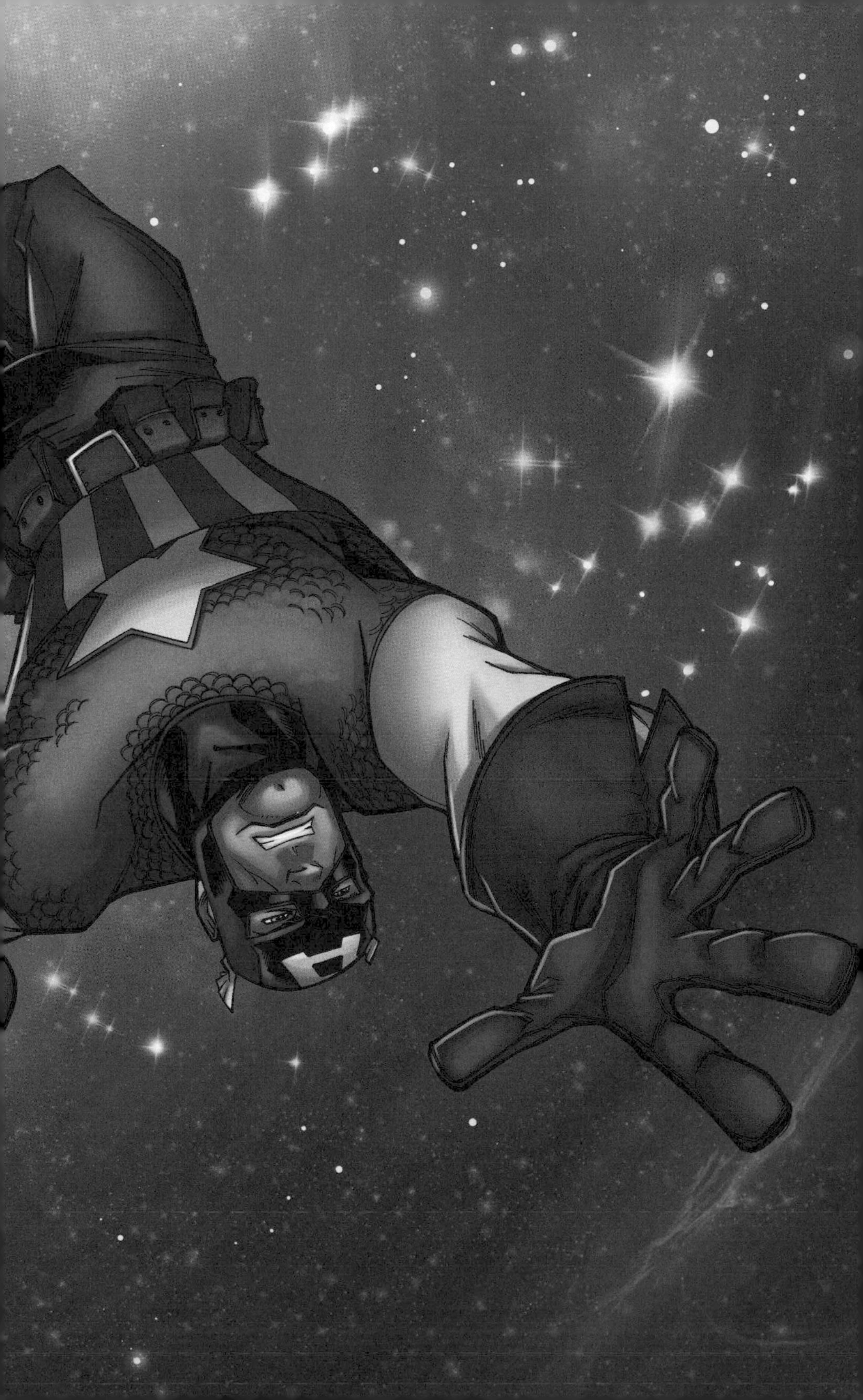

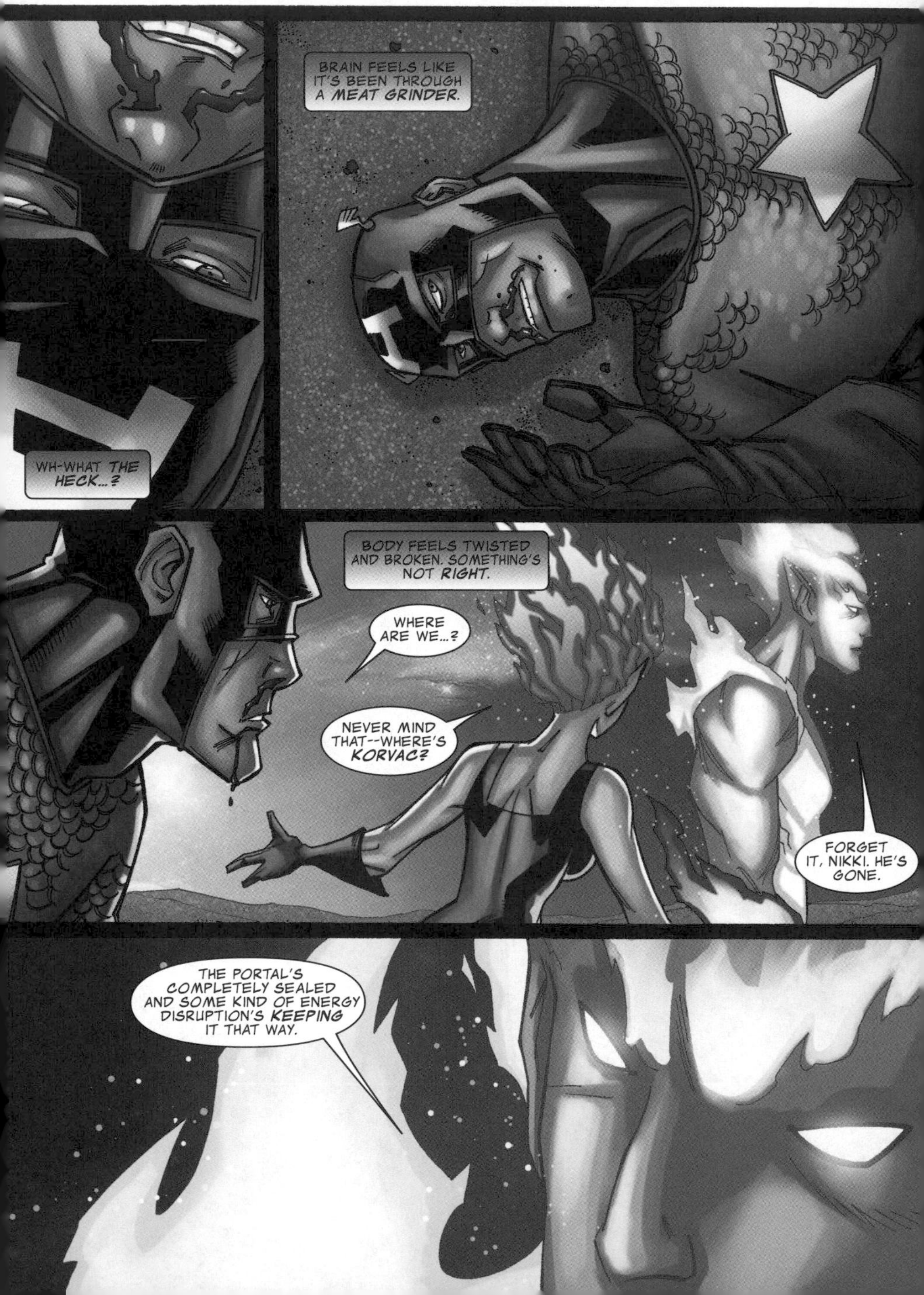
WH-WHAT THE HECK...?
BRAIN FEELS LIKE IT'S BEEN THROUGH A MEAT GRINDER.
BODY FEELS TWISTED AND BROKEN. SOMETHING'S NOT RIGHT.
WHERE ARE WE...?
NEVER MIND THAT--WHERE'S KORVAC?
FORGET IT, NIKKI. HE'S GONE.
THE PORTAL'S COMPLETELY SEALED AND SOME KIND OF ENERGY DISRUPTION'S KEEPING IT THAT WAY.

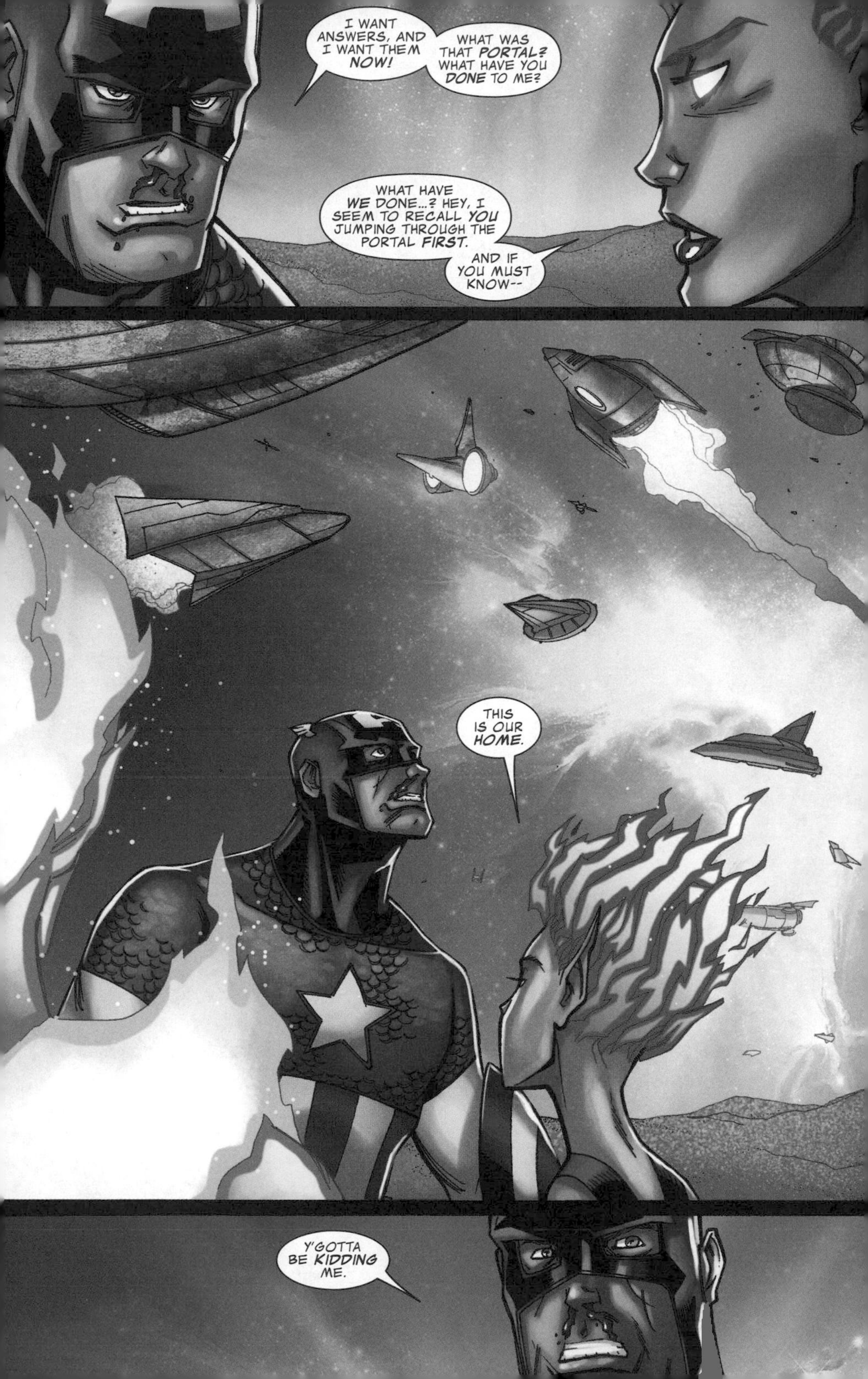
I WANT ANSWERS, AND I WANT THEM NOW!
WHAT WAS THAT PORTAL? WHAT HAVE YOU DONE TO ME?
WHAT HAVE WE DONE...? HEY, I SEEM TO RECALL YOU JUMPING THROUGH THE PORTAL FIRST.
AND IF YOU MUST KNOW--
THIS IS OUR HOME.
Y'GOTTA BE KIDDING ME.

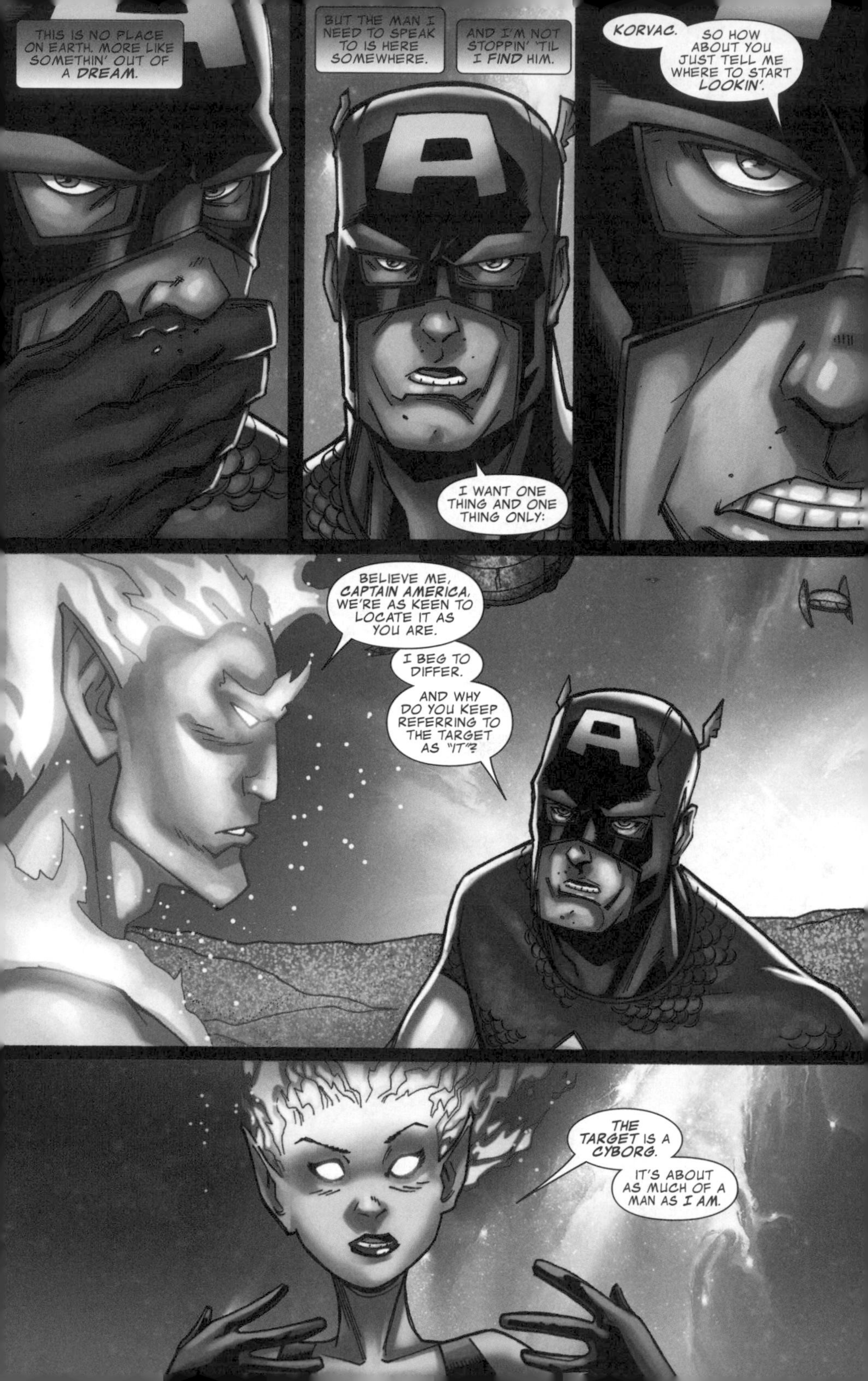

THIS IS NO PLACE ON EARTH. MORE LIKE SOMETHIN' OUT OF A DREAM.
BUT THE MAN I NEED TO SPEAK TO IS HERE SOMEWHERE.
AND I'M NOT STOPPIN' 'TIL I FIND HIM.
I WANT ONE THING AND ONE THING ONLY:
KORVAC.
SO HOW ABOUT YOU JUST TELL ME WHERE TO START LOOKIN'.
BELIEVE ME, CAPTAIN AMERICA, WE'RE AS KEEN TO LOCATE IT AS YOU ARE.
I BEG TO DIFFER.
AND WHY DO YOU KEEP REFERRING TO THE TARGET AS "IT"?
THE TARGET IS A CYBORG.
IT'S ABOUT AS MUCH OF A MAN AS I AM.

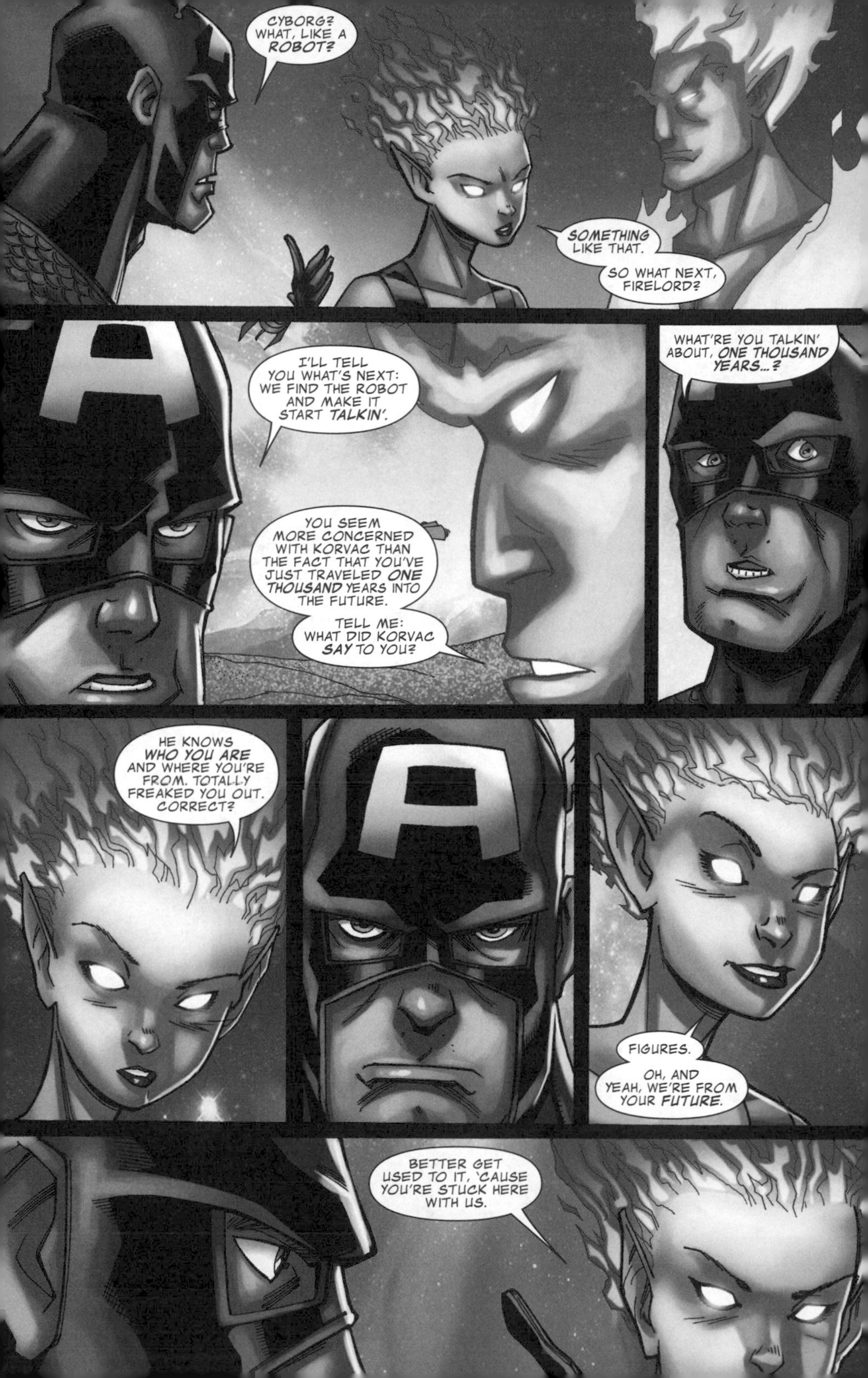
CYBORG? WHAT, LIKE A ROBOT?
SOMETHING LIKE THAT.
SO WHAT NEXT, FIRELORD?
I'LL TELL YOU WHAT'S NEXT: WE FIND THE ROBOT AND MAKE IT START TALKIN'.
YOU SEEM MORE CONCERNED WITH KORVAC THAN THE FACT THAT YOU'VE JUST TRAVELED ONE THOUSAND YEARS INTO THE FUTURE.
TELL ME: WHAT DID KORVAC SAY TO YOU?
WHAT'RE YOU TALKIN' ABOUT, ONE THOUSAND YEARS...?
HE KNOWS WHO YOU ARE AND WHERE YOU'RE FROM. TOTALLY FREAKED YOU OUT. CORRECT?
FIGURES.
OH, AND YEAH, WE'RE FROM YOUR FUTURE.
BETTER GET USED TO IT, 'CAUSE YOU'RE STUCK HERE WITH US.

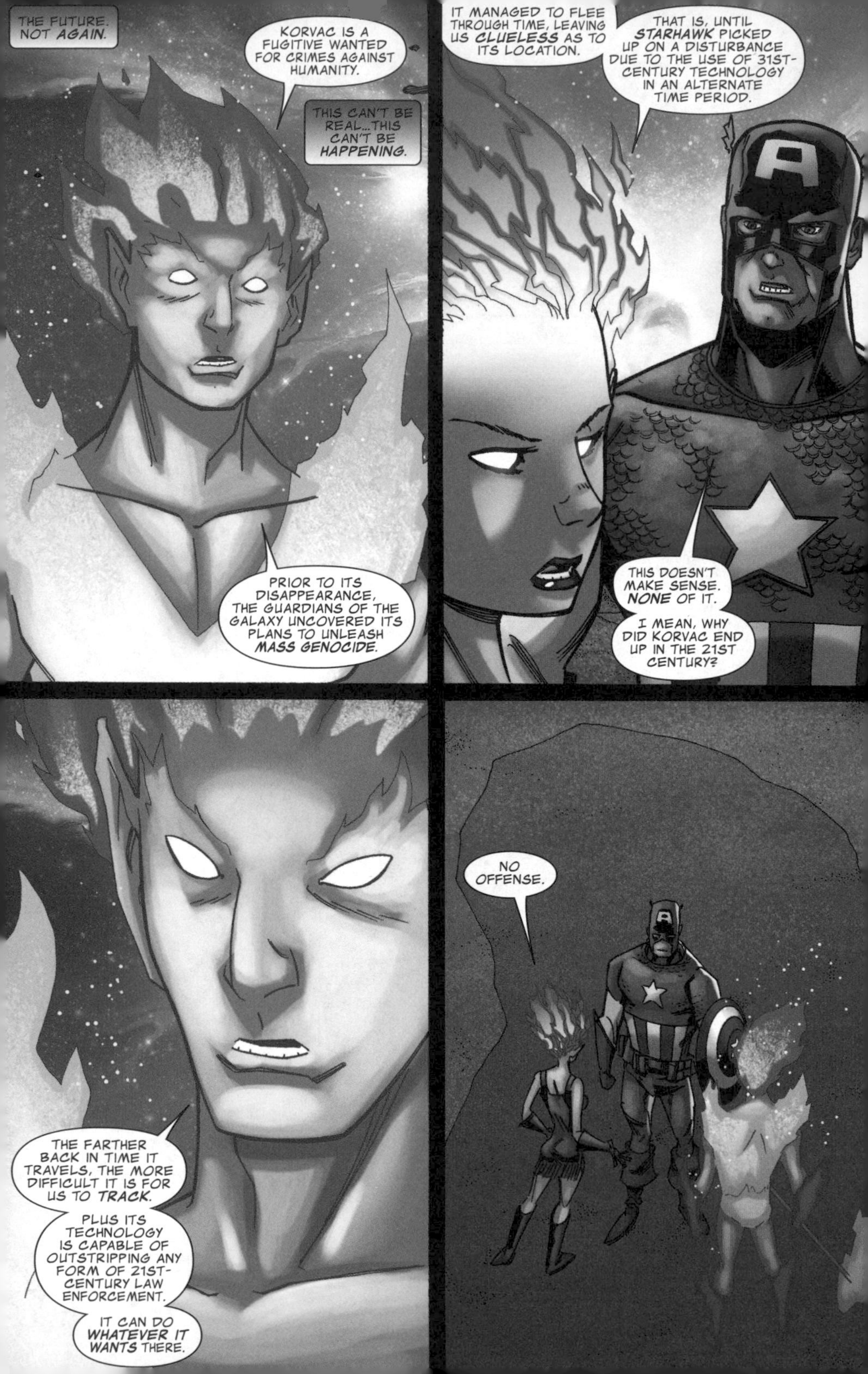
THE FUTURE. NOT AGAIN.
KORVAC IS A FUGITIVE WANTED FOR CRIMES AGAINST HUMANITY.
THIS CAN'T BE REAL...THIS CAN'T BE HAPPENING.
PRIOR TO ITS DISAPPEARANCE, THE GUARDIANS OF THE GALAXY UNCOVERED ITS PLANS TO UNLEASH MASS GENOCIDE.
IT MANAGED TO FLEE THROUGH TIME, LEAVING US CLUELESS AS TO ITS LOCATION.
THAT IS, UNTIL STARHAWK PICKED UP ON A DISTURBANCE DUE TO THE USE OF 31ST-CENTURY TECHNOLOGY IN AN ALTERNATE TIME PERIOD.
THIS DOESN'T MAKE SENSE. NONE OF IT.
I MEAN, WHY DID KORVAC END UP IN THE 21ST CENTURY?
THE FARTHER BACK IN TIME IT TRAVELS, THE MORE DIFFICULT IT IS FOR US TO TRACK.
PLUS ITS TECHNOLOGY IS CAPABLE OF OUTSTRIPPING ANY FORM OF 21ST-CENTURY LAW ENFORCEMENT.
IT CAN DO WHATEVER IT WANTS THERE.
NO OFFENSE.

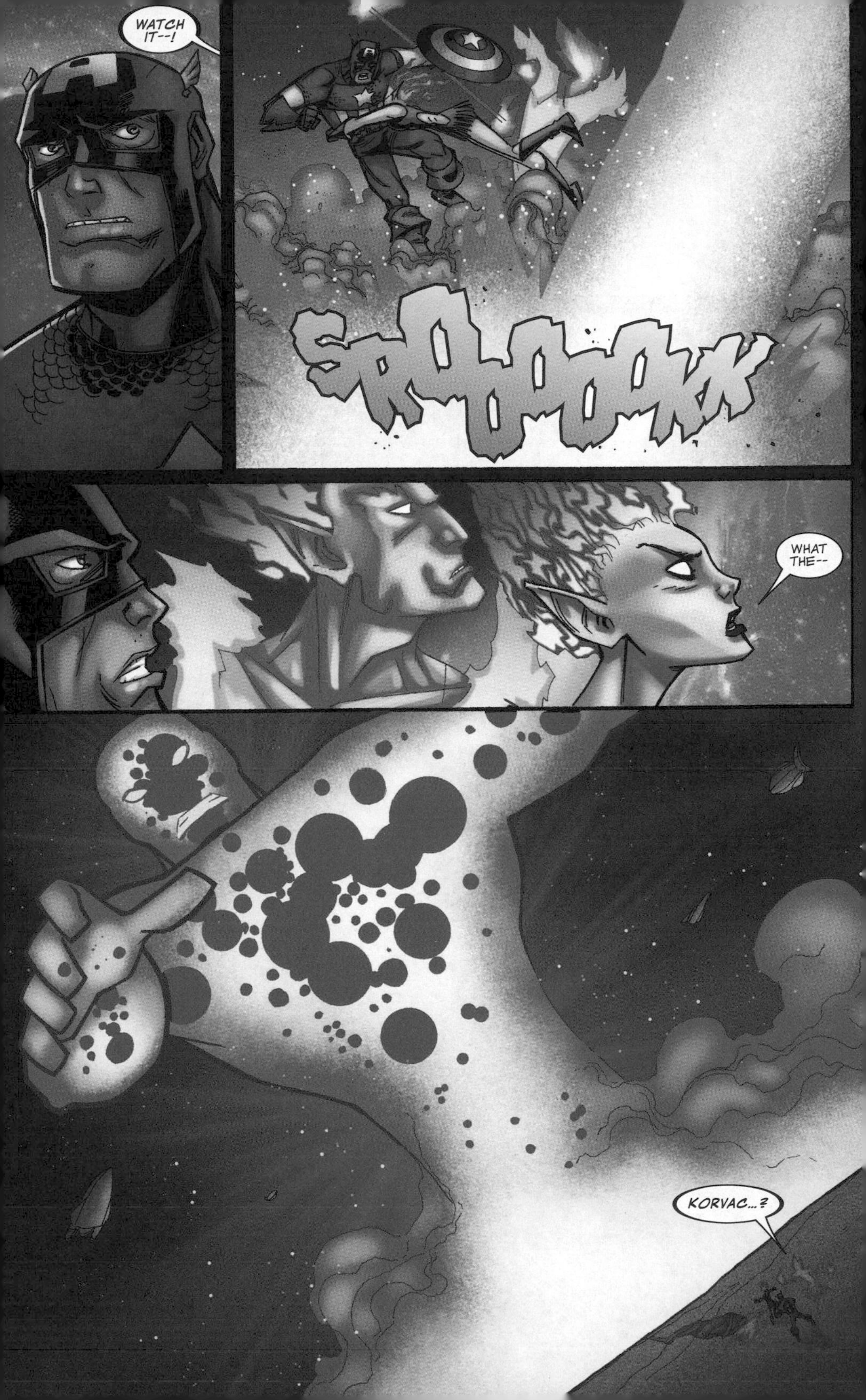
WATCH IT--!
SPROOOOKK
WHAT THE--
KORVAC...?

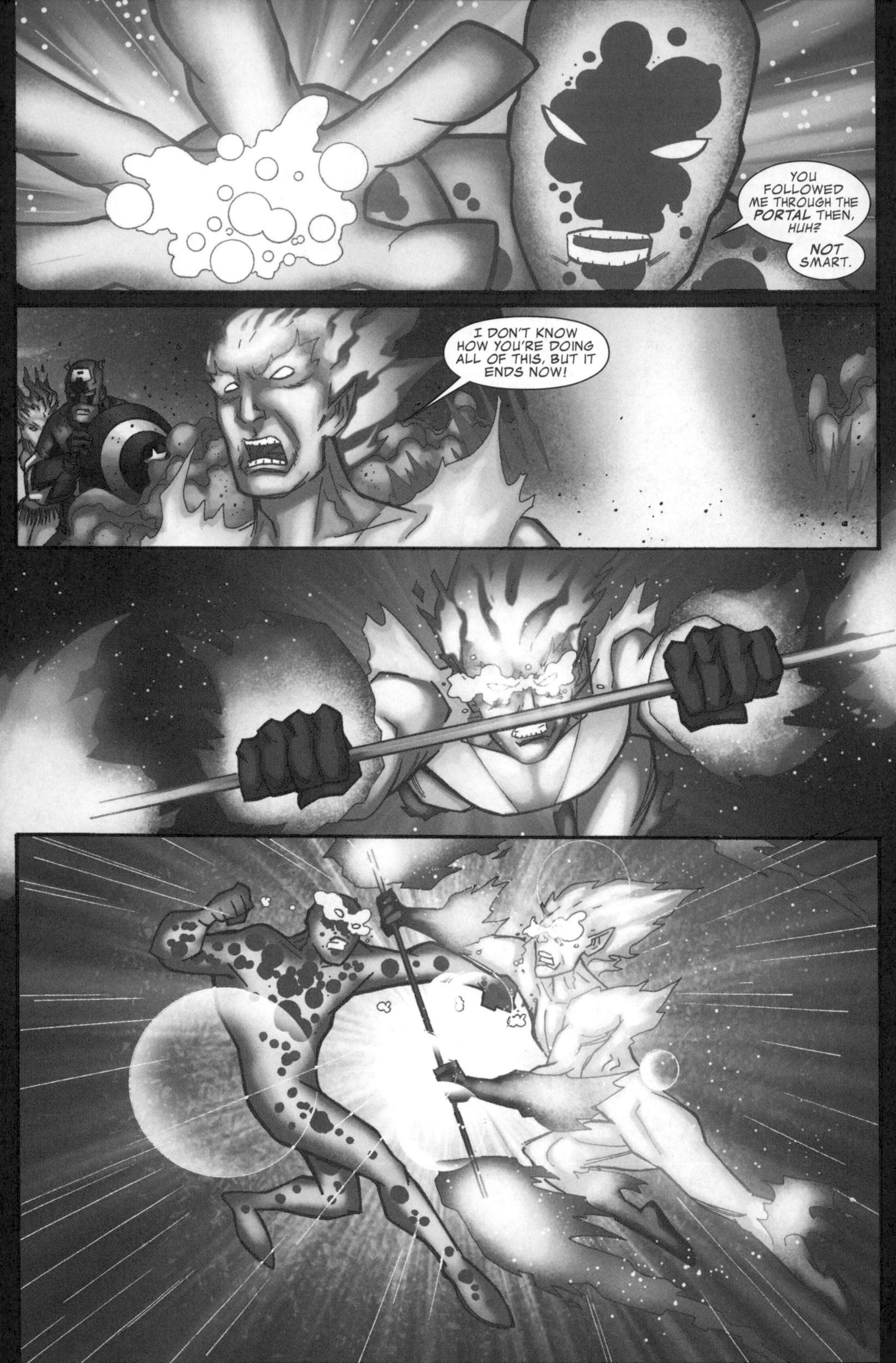
YOU FOLLOWED ME THROUGH THE PORTAL THEN, HUH?
NOT SMART.
I DON'T KNOW HOW YOU'RE DOING ALL OF THIS, BUT IT ENDS NOW!

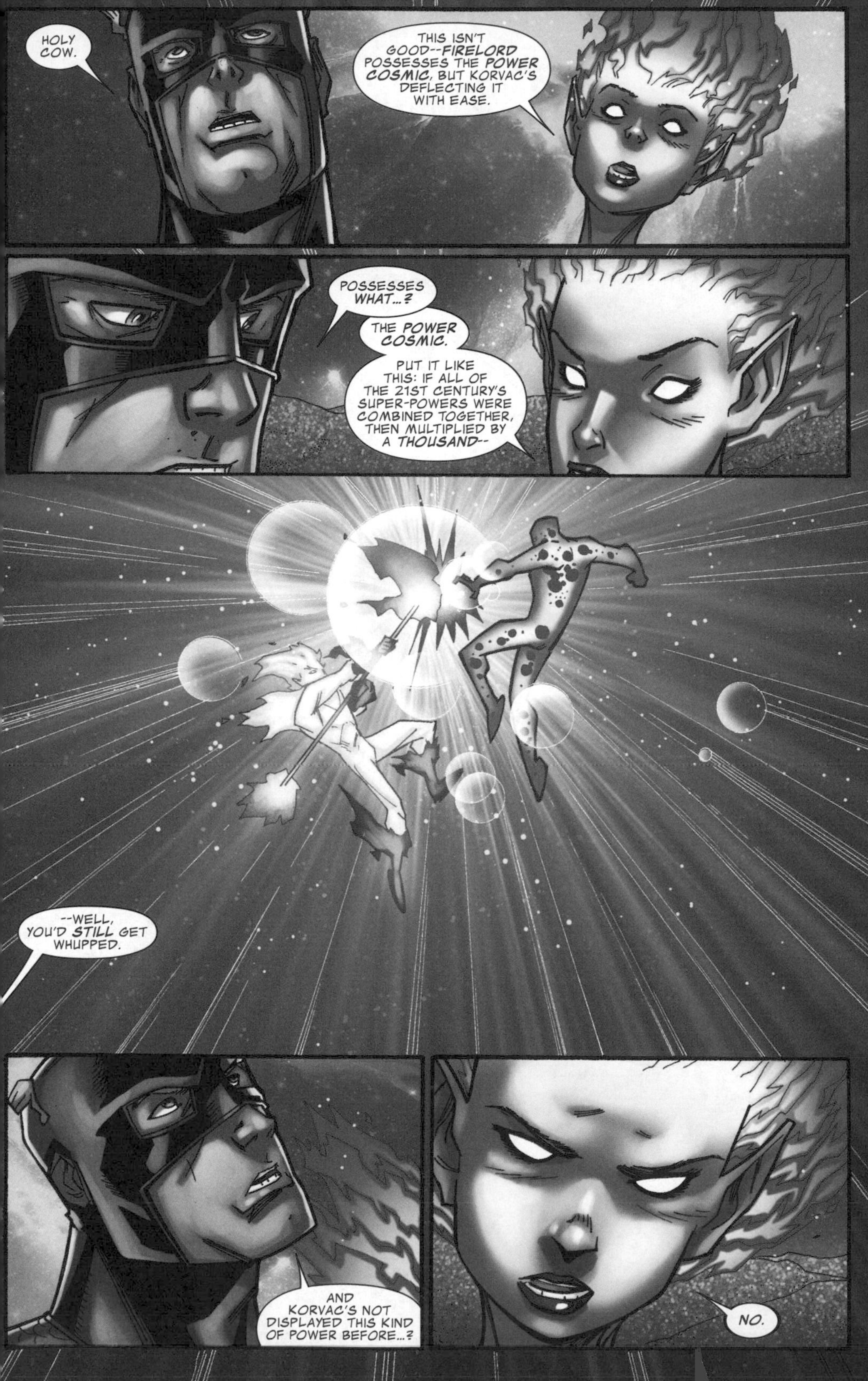
HOLY COW.
THIS ISN'T GOOD--FIRELORD POSSESSES THE POWER COSMIC, BUT KORVAC'S DEFLECTING IT WITH EASE.
POSSESSES WHAT...?
THE POWER COSMIC.
PUT IT LIKE THIS: IF ALL OF THE 21ST CENTURY'S SUPER-POWERS WERE COMBINED TOGETHER, THEN MULTIPLIED BY A THOUSAND--
--WELL, YOU'D STILL GET WHUPPED.
AND KORVAC'S NOT DISPLAYED THIS KIND OF POWER BEFORE...?
NO.

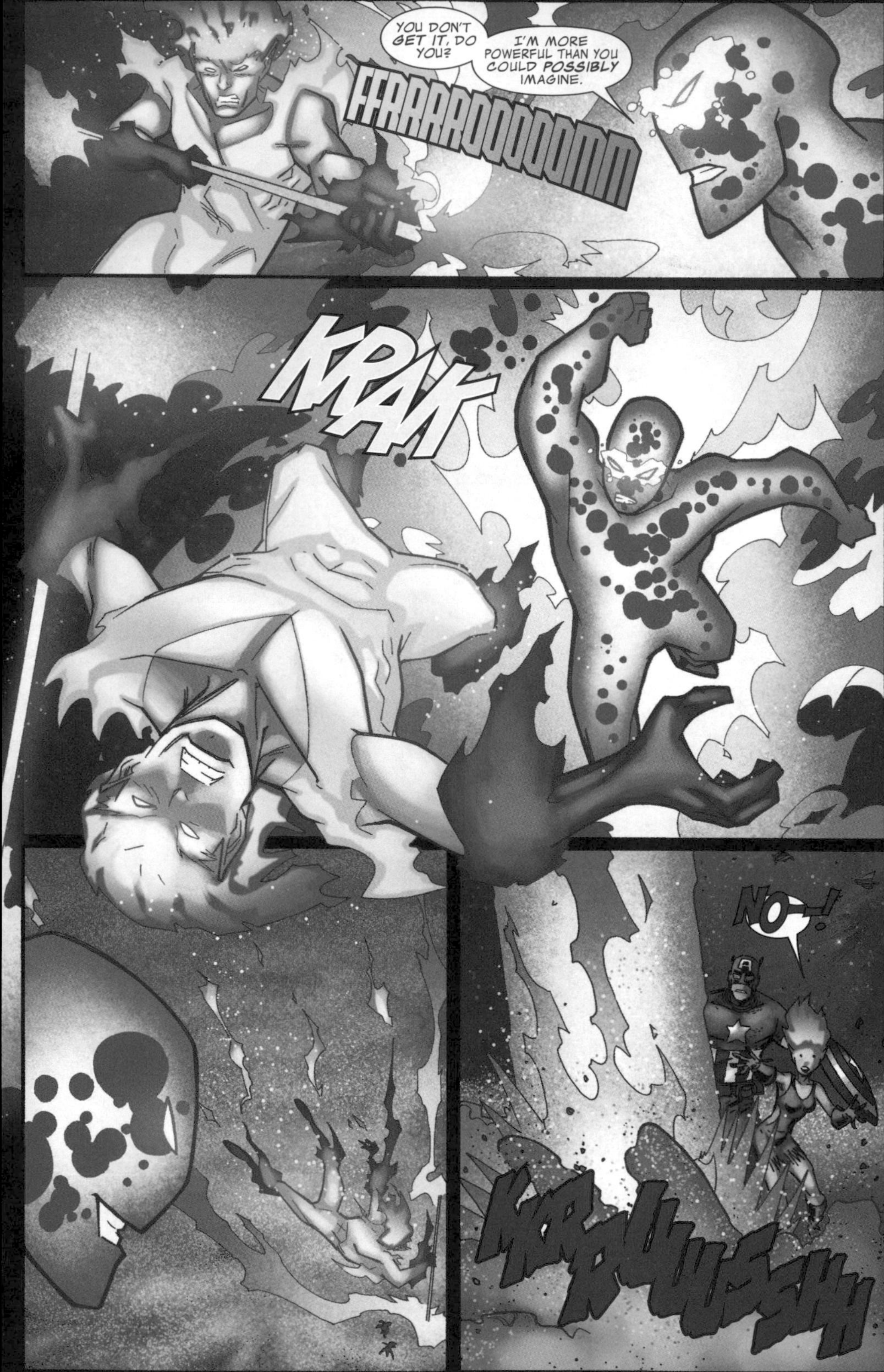
YOU DON'T GET IT, DO YOU?
I'M MORE POWERFUL THAN YOU COULD POSSIBLY IMAGINE.
FFRRRRROOOOOOMM
KRAK
NO--!
KORBUUUSHH

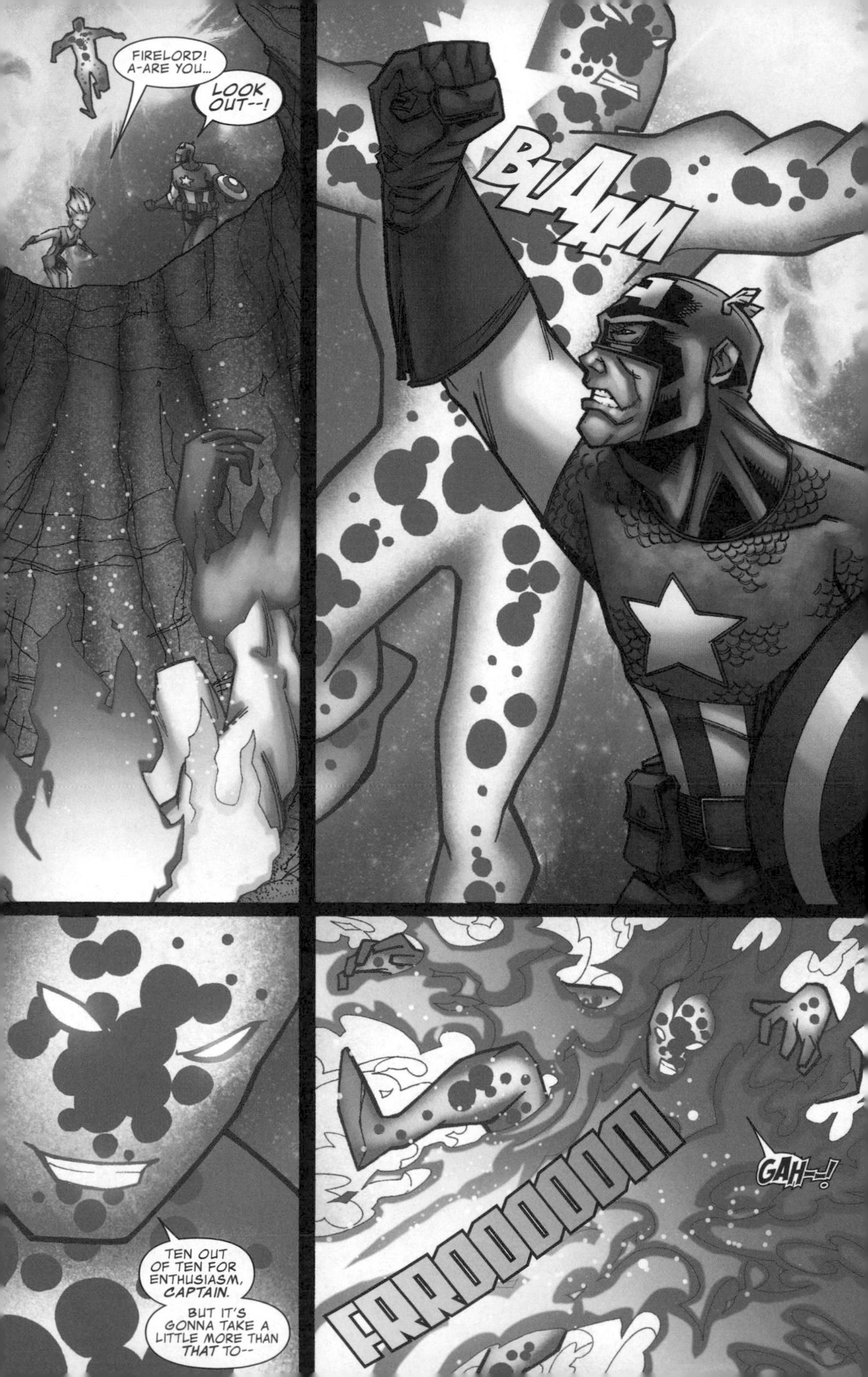
FIRELORD! A-ARE YOU...
LOOK OUT--!
BLAAMM
TEN OUT OF TEN FOR ENTHUSIASM, CAPTAIN.
BUT IT'S GONNA TAKE A LITTLE MORE THAN THAT TO--
FRROOOOOOM
GAH--!

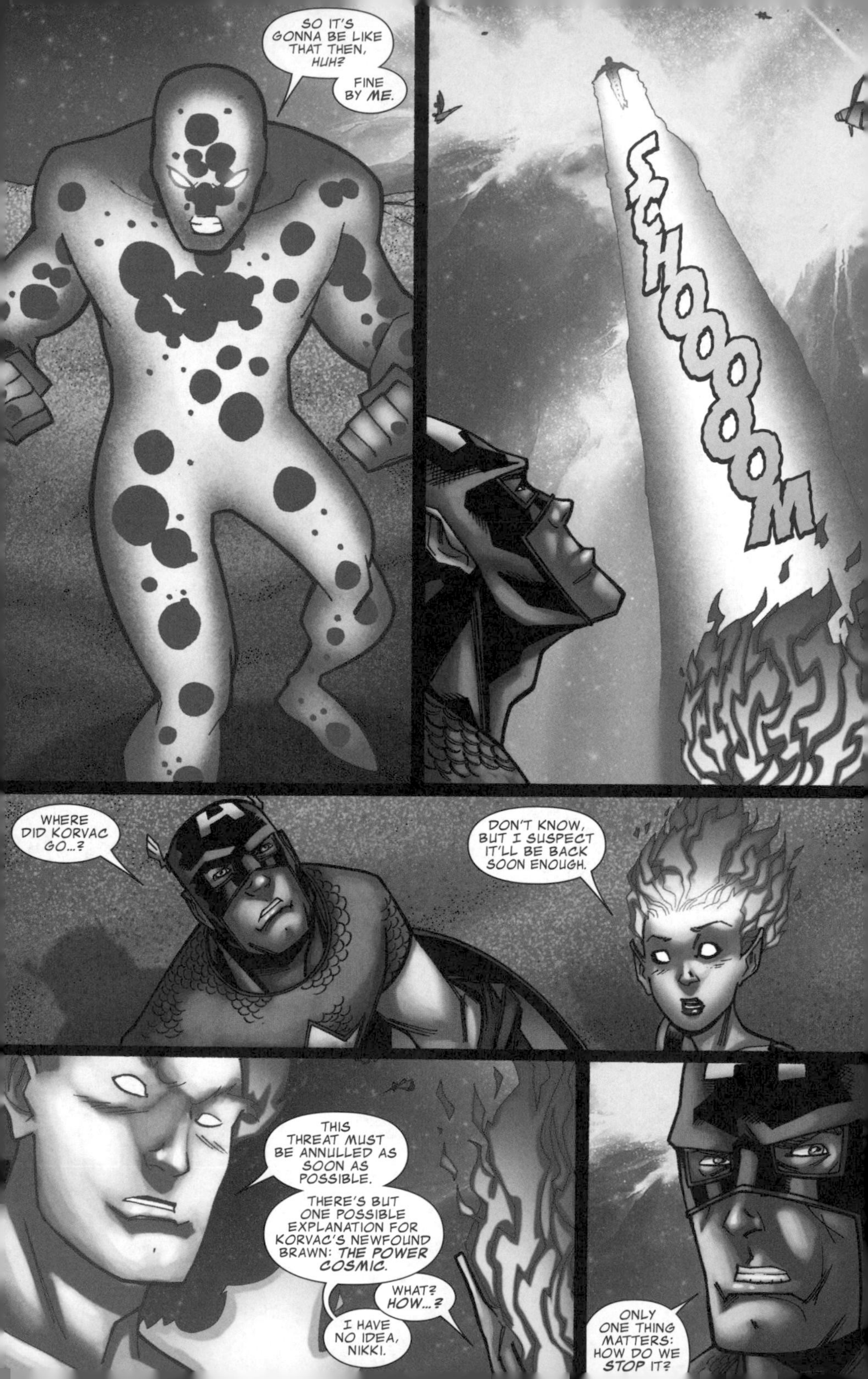
SO IT'S GONNA BE LIKE THAT THEN, HUH?
FINE BY ME.
WHOOOOOM
WHERE DID KORVAC GO...?
DON'T KNOW, BUT I SUSPECT IT'LL BE BACK SOON ENOUGH.
THIS THREAT MUST BE ANNULLED AS SOON AS POSSIBLE.
THERE'S BUT ONE POSSIBLE EXPLANATION FOR KORVAC'S NEWFOUND BRAWN: THE POWER COSMIC.
WHAT? HOW...?
I HAVE NO IDEA, NIKKI.
ONLY ONE THING MATTERS: HOW DO WE STOP IT?

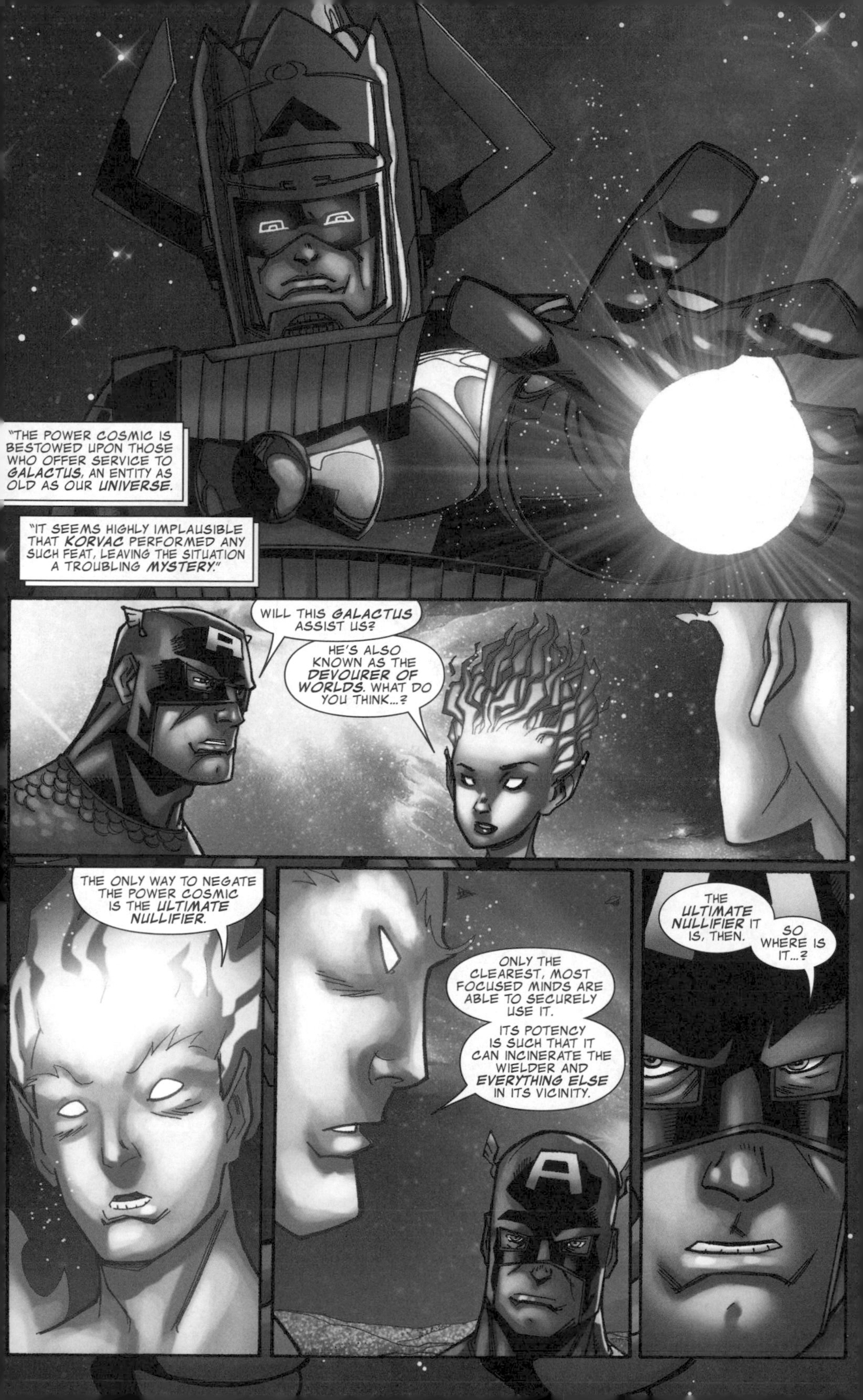
"THE POWER COSMIC IS BESTOWED UPON THOSE WHO OFFER SERVICE TO GALACTUS, AN ENTITY AS OLD AS OUR UNIVERSE.
"IT SEEMS HIGHLY IMPLAUSIBLE THAT KORVAC PERFORMED ANY SUCH FEAT, LEAVING THE SITUATION A TROUBLING MYSTERY."
WILL THIS GALACTUS ASSIST US?
HE'S ALSO KNOWN AS THE DEVOURER OF WORLDS. WHAT DO YOU THINK...?
THE ONLY WAY TO NEGATE THE POWER COSMIC IS THE ULTIMATE NULLIFIER.
ONLY THE CLEAREST, MOST FOCUSED MINDS ARE ABLE TO SECURELY USE IT.
ITS POTENCY IS SUCH THAT IT CAN INCINERATE THE WIELDER AND EVERYTHING ELSE IN ITS VICINITY.
THE ULTIMATE NULLIFIER IT IS, THEN.
SO WHERE IS IT...?

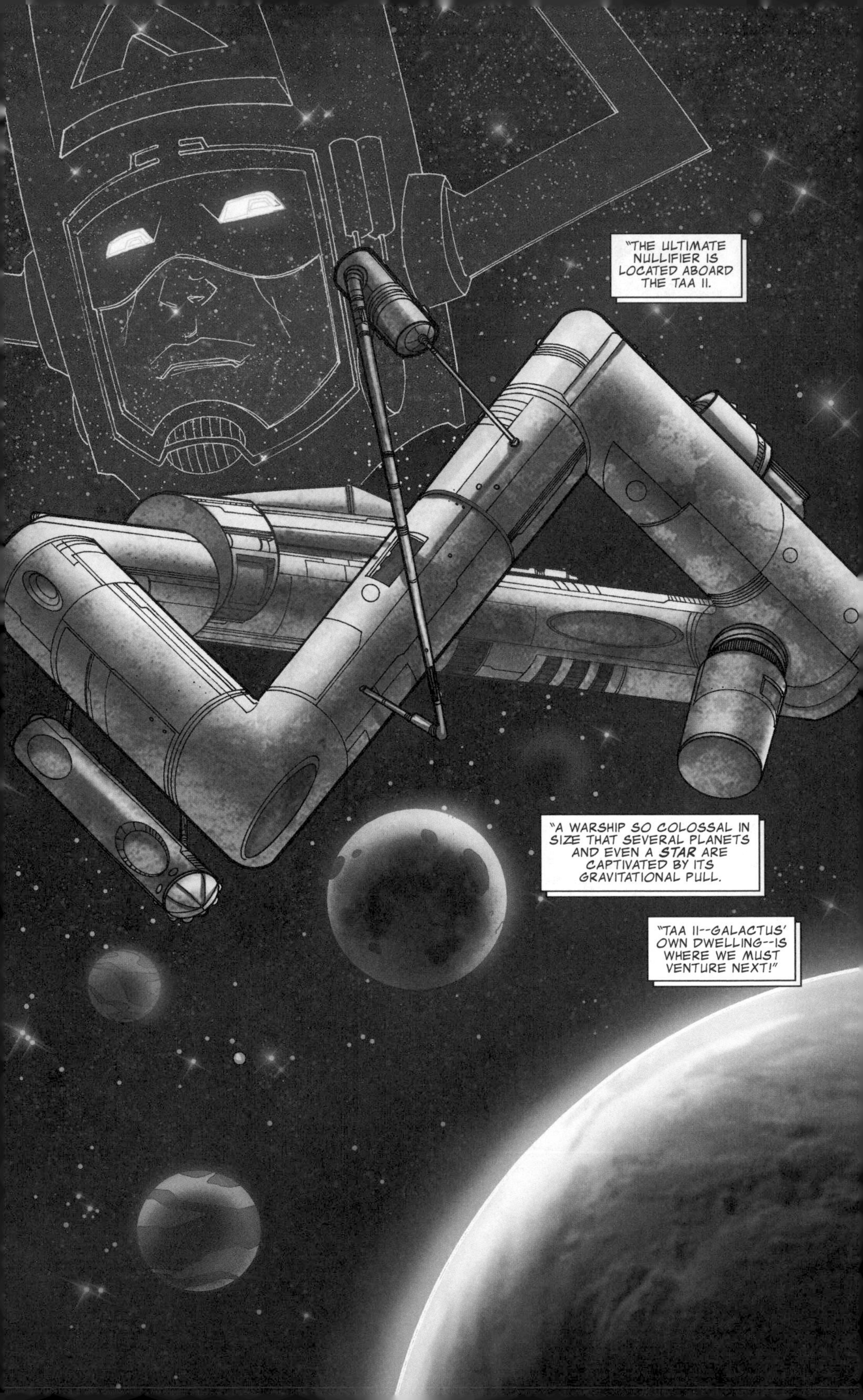
"THE ULTIMATE NULLIFIER IS LOCATED ABOARD THE TAA II.
"A WARSHIP SO COLOSSAL IN SIZE THAT SEVERAL PLANETS AND EVEN A STAR ARE CAPTIVATED BY ITS GRAVITATIONAL PULL.
"TAA II--GALACTUS' OWN DWELLING--IS WHERE WE MUST VENTURE NEXT!"

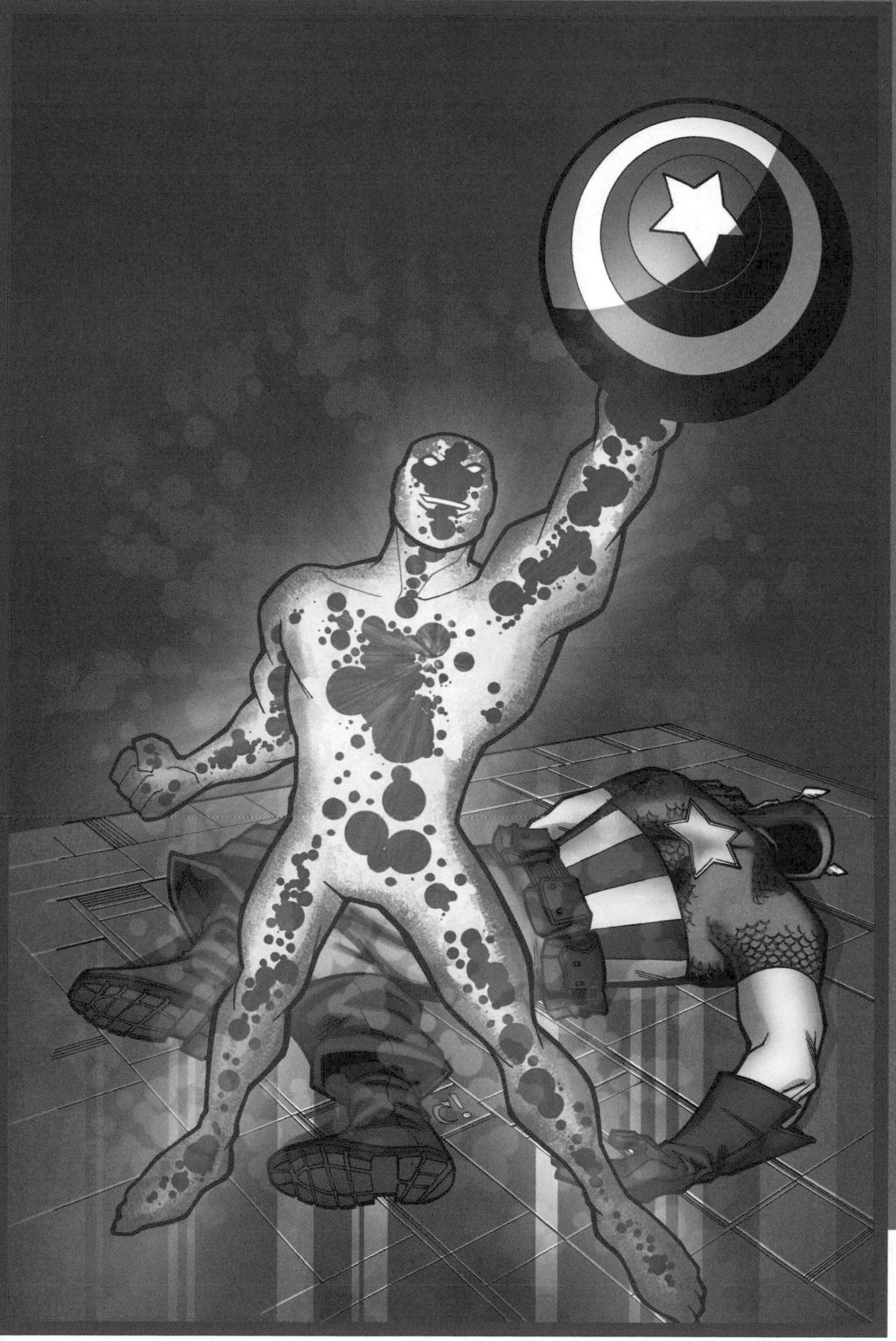

#3

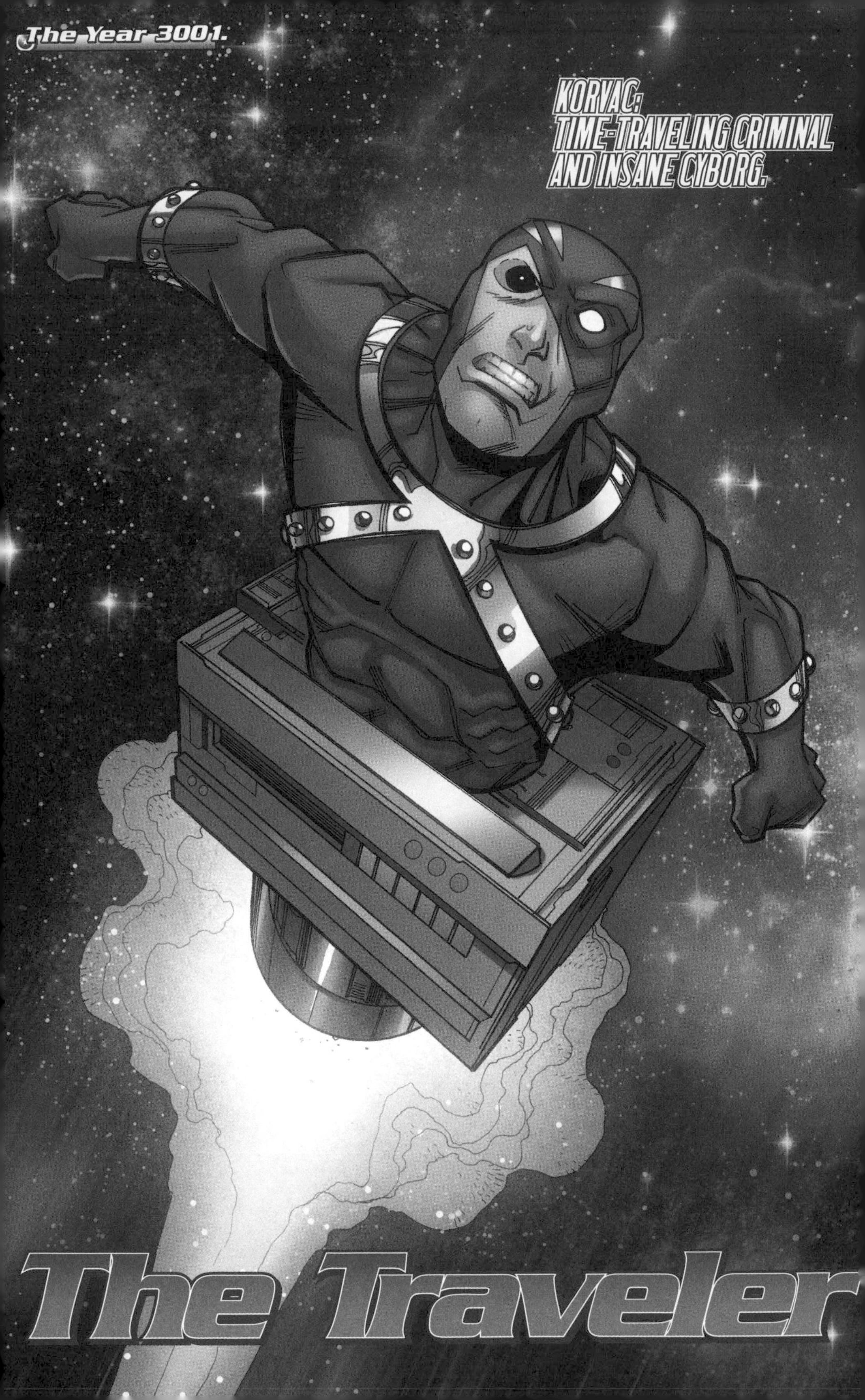
The Year 3001.
KORVAC:
TIME-TRAVELING CRIMINAL
AND INSANE CYBORG.
The Traveler

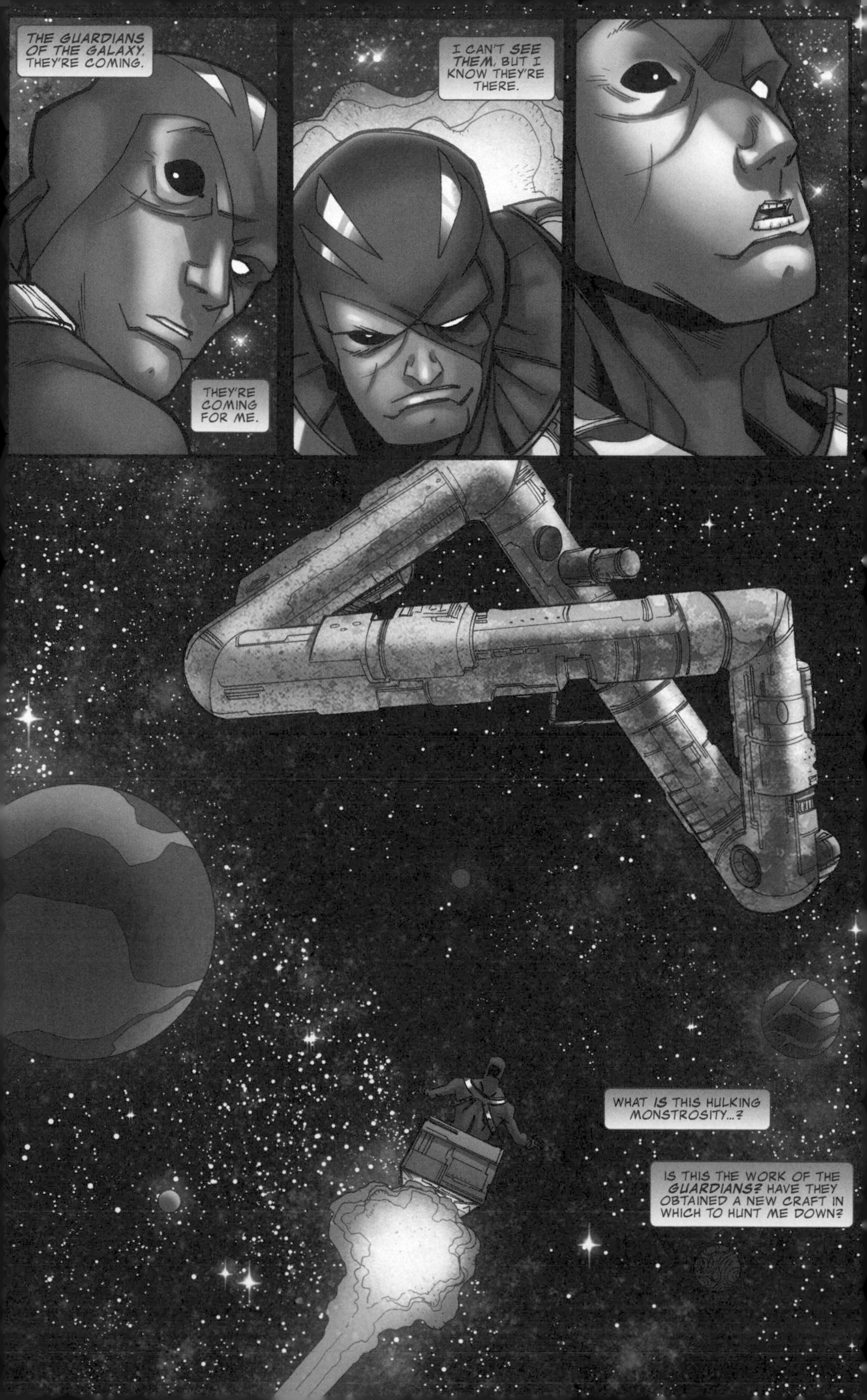
THE GUARDIANS OF THE GALAXY. THEY'RE COMING.
THEY'RE COMING FOR ME.
I CAN'T SEE THEM, BUT I KNOW THEY'RE THERE.
WHAT IS THIS HULKING MONSTROSITY...?
IS THIS THE WORK OF THE GUARDIANS? HAVE THEY OBTAINED A NEW CRAFT IN WHICH TO HUNT ME DOWN?

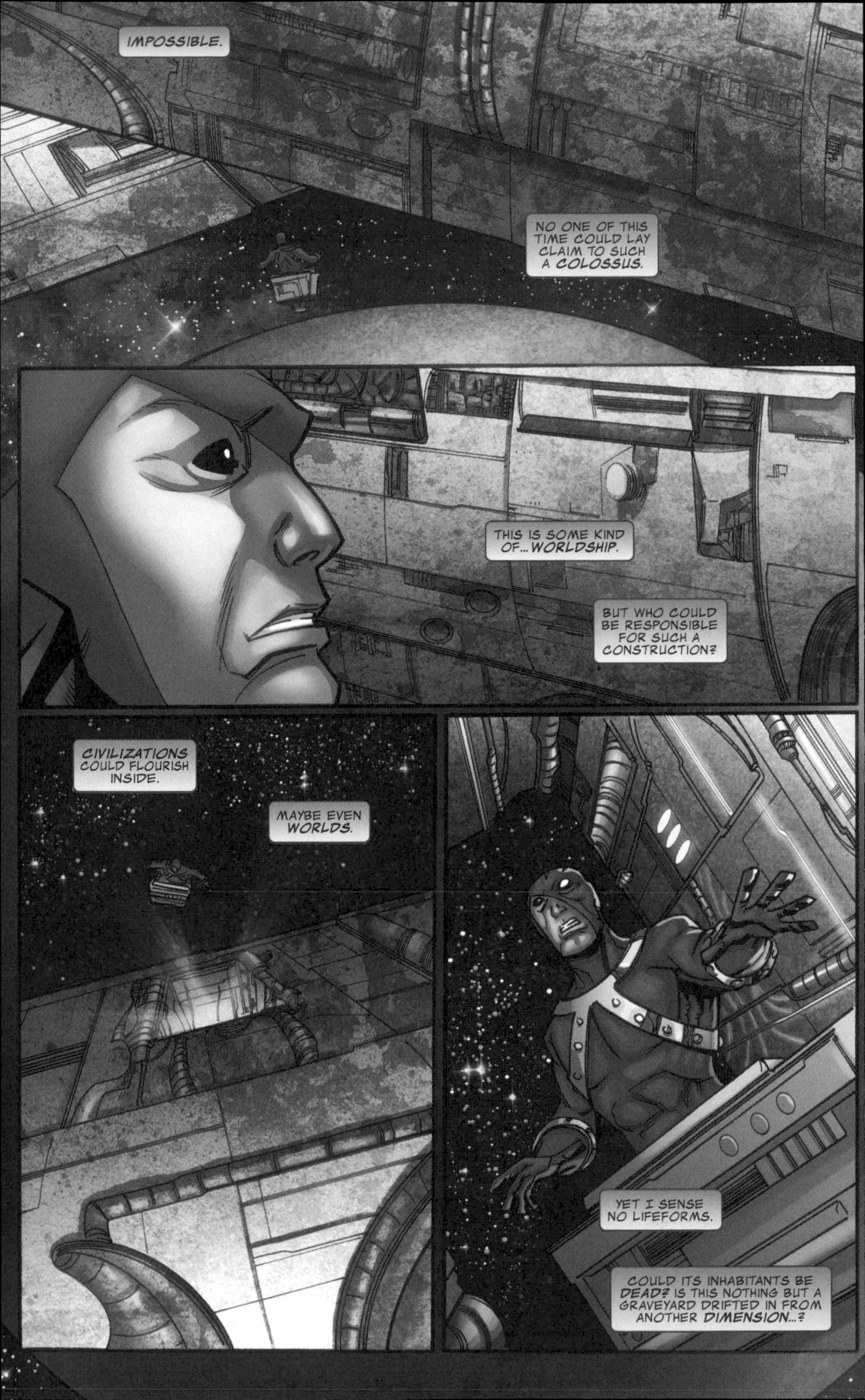
IMPOSSIBLE.
NO ONE OF THIS TIME COULD LAY CLAIM TO SUCH A COLOSSUS.
THIS IS SOME KIND OF... WORLDSHIP.
BUT WHO COULD BE RESPONSIBLE FOR SUCH A CONSTRUCTION?
CIVILIZATIONS COULD FLOURISH INSIDE.
MAYBE EVEN WORLDS.
YET I SENSE NO LIFEFORMS.
COULD ITS INHABITANTS BE DEAD? IS THIS NOTHING BUT A GRAVEYARD DRIFTED IN FROM ANOTHER DIMENSION...?

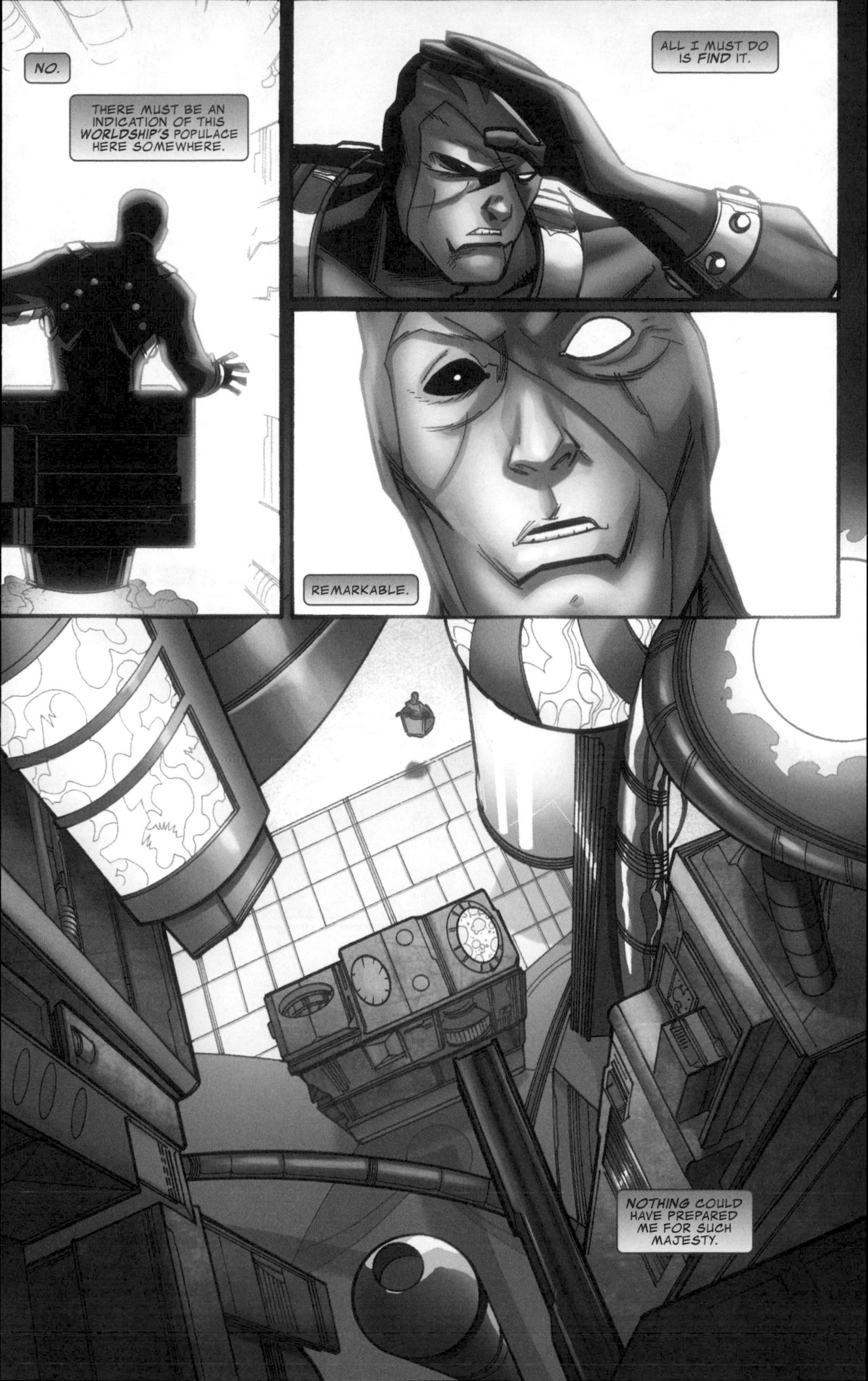
NO.
THERE MUST BE AN INDICATION OF THIS WORLDSHIP'S POPULACE HERE SOMEWHERE.
ALL I MUST DO IS FIND IT.
REMARKABLE.
NOTHING COULD HAVE PREPARED ME FOR SUCH MAJESTY.

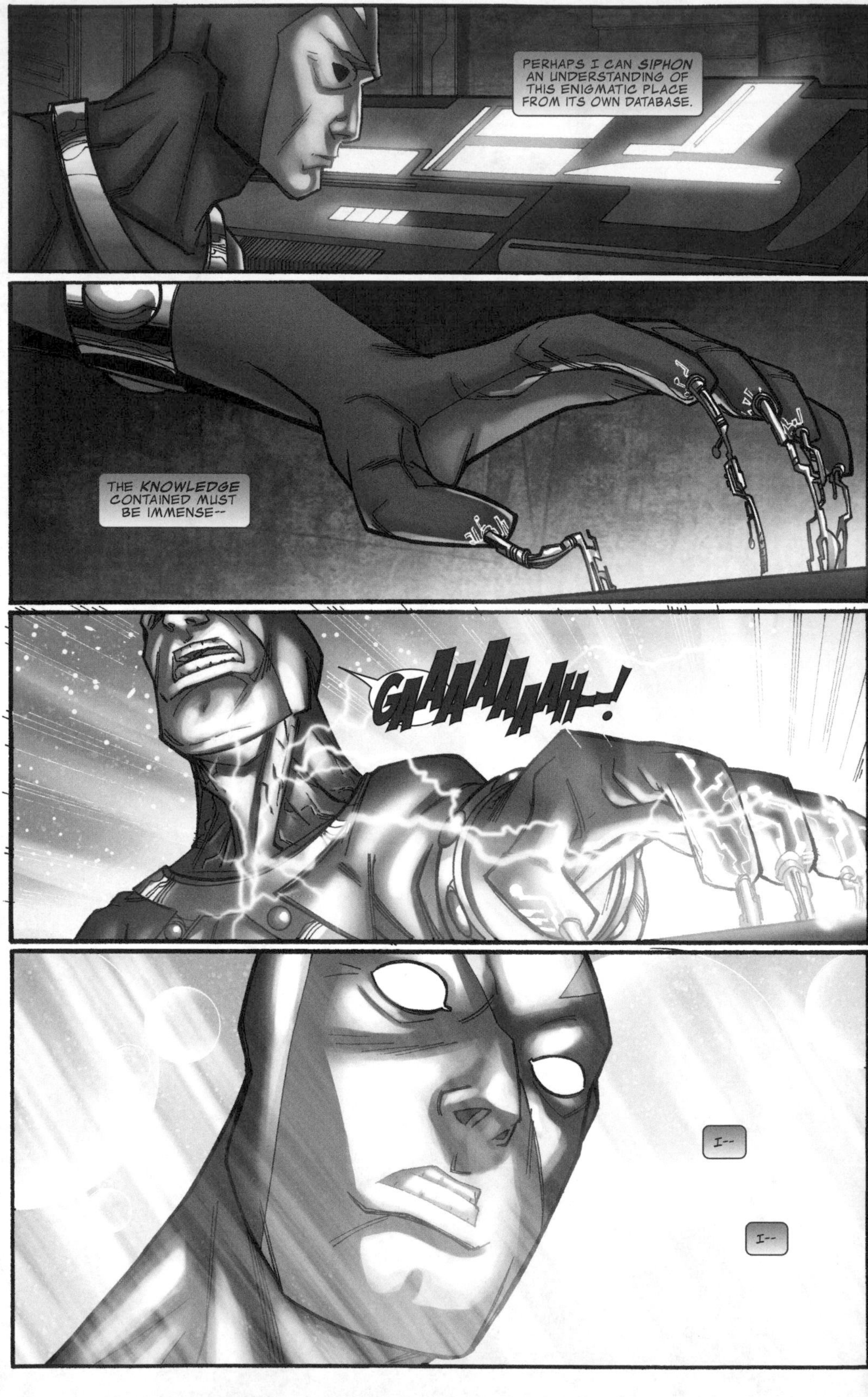
PERHAPS I CAN SIPHON AN UNDERSTANDING OF THIS ENIGMATIC PLACE FROM ITS OWN DATABASE.
THE KNOWLEDGE CONTAINED MUST BE IMMENSE--
GAAAAAAAAH--!
I--
I--

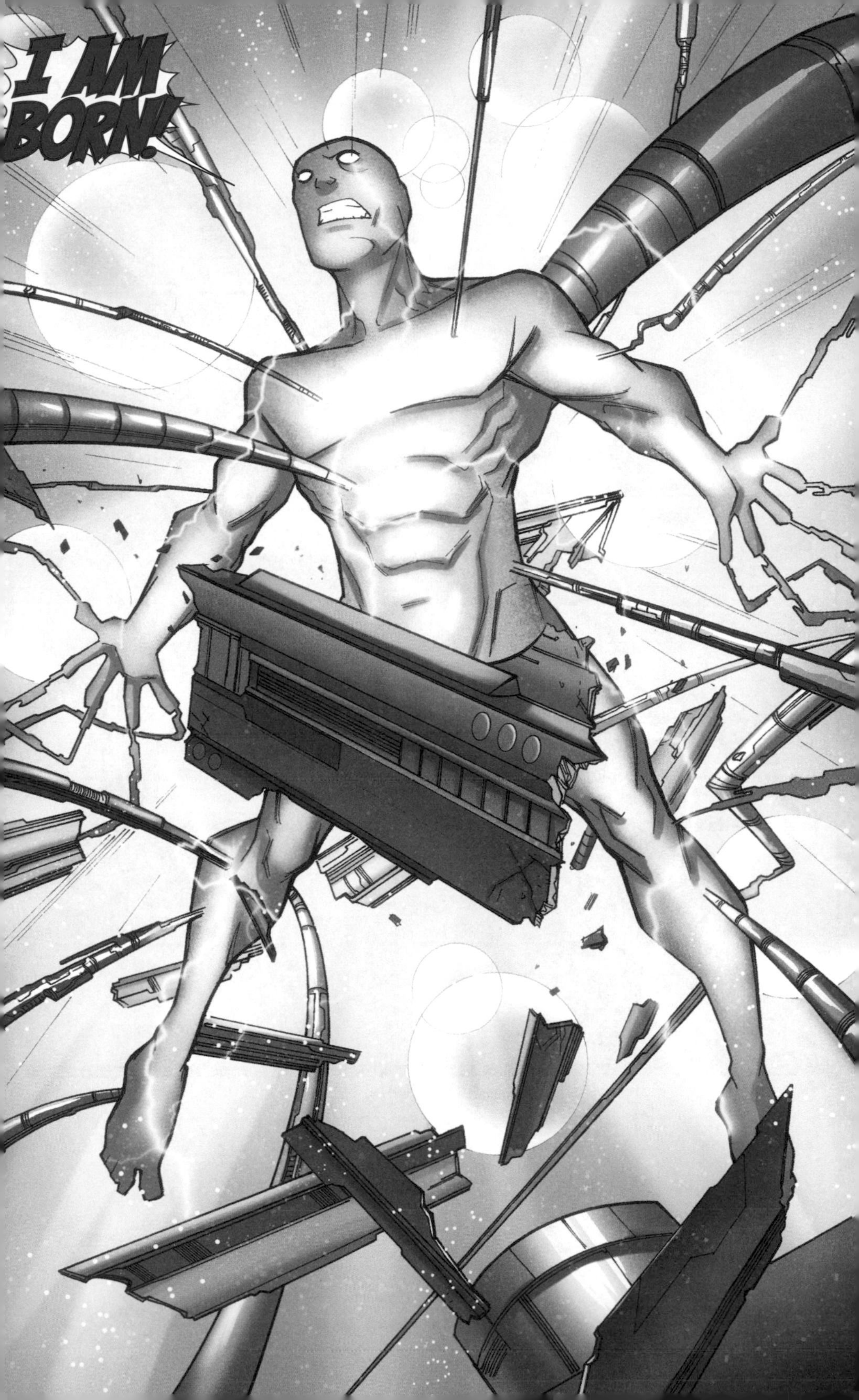
I AM BORN!

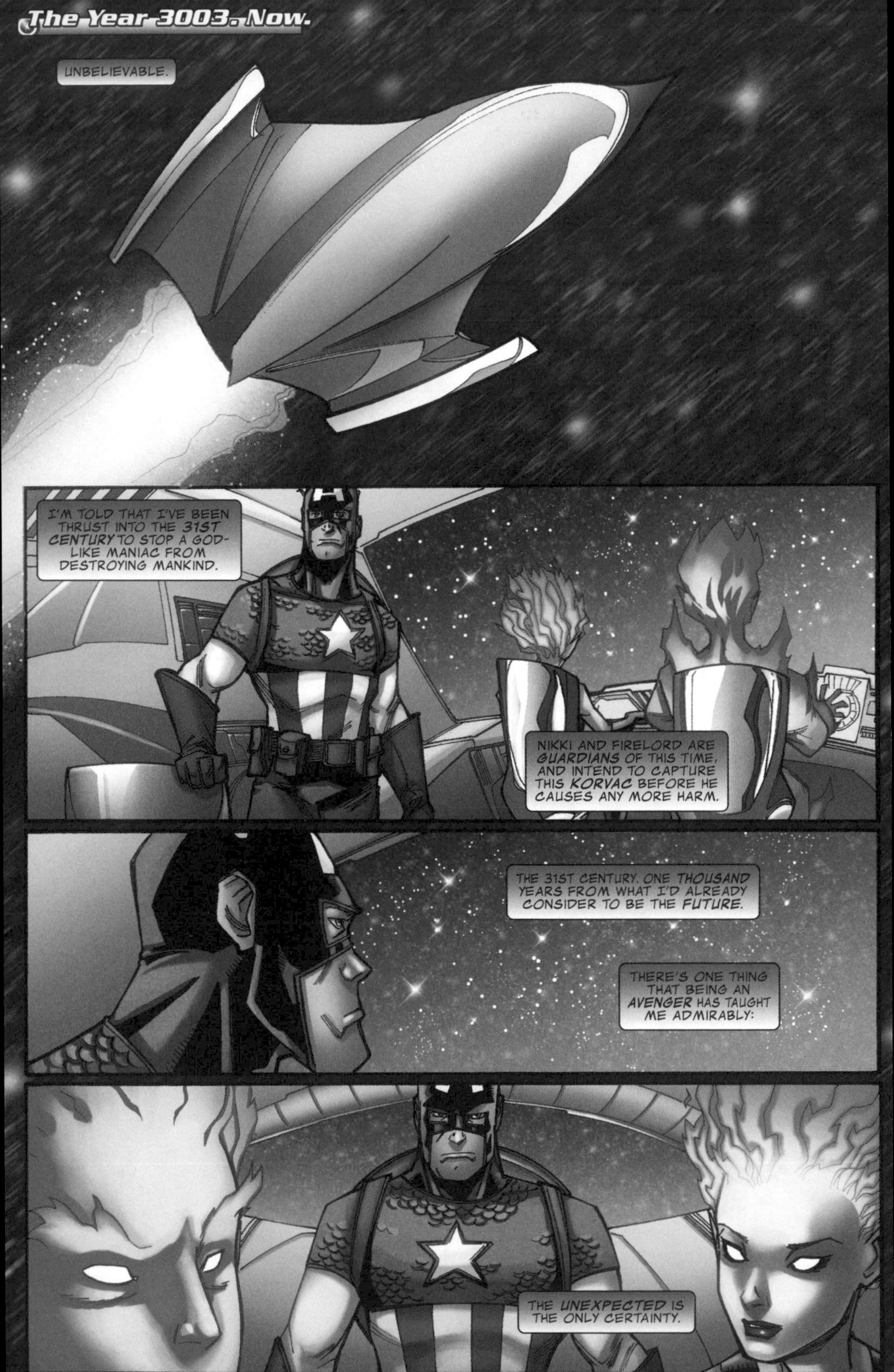
The Year 3003. Now.
UNBELIEVABLE.
I'M TOLD THAT I'VE BEEN THRUST INTO THE 31ST CENTURY TO STOP A GOD-LIKE MANIAC FROM DESTROYING MANKIND.
NIKKI AND FIRELORD ARE GUARDIANS OF THIS TIME, AND INTEND TO CAPTURE THIS KORVAC BEFORE HE CAUSES ANY MORE HARM.
THE 31ST CENTURY. ONE THOUSAND YEARS FROM WHAT I'D ALREADY CONSIDER TO BE THE FUTURE.
THERE'S ONE THING THAT BEING AN AVENGER HAS TAUGHT ME ADMIRABLY:
THE UNEXPECTED IS THE ONLY CERTAINTY.

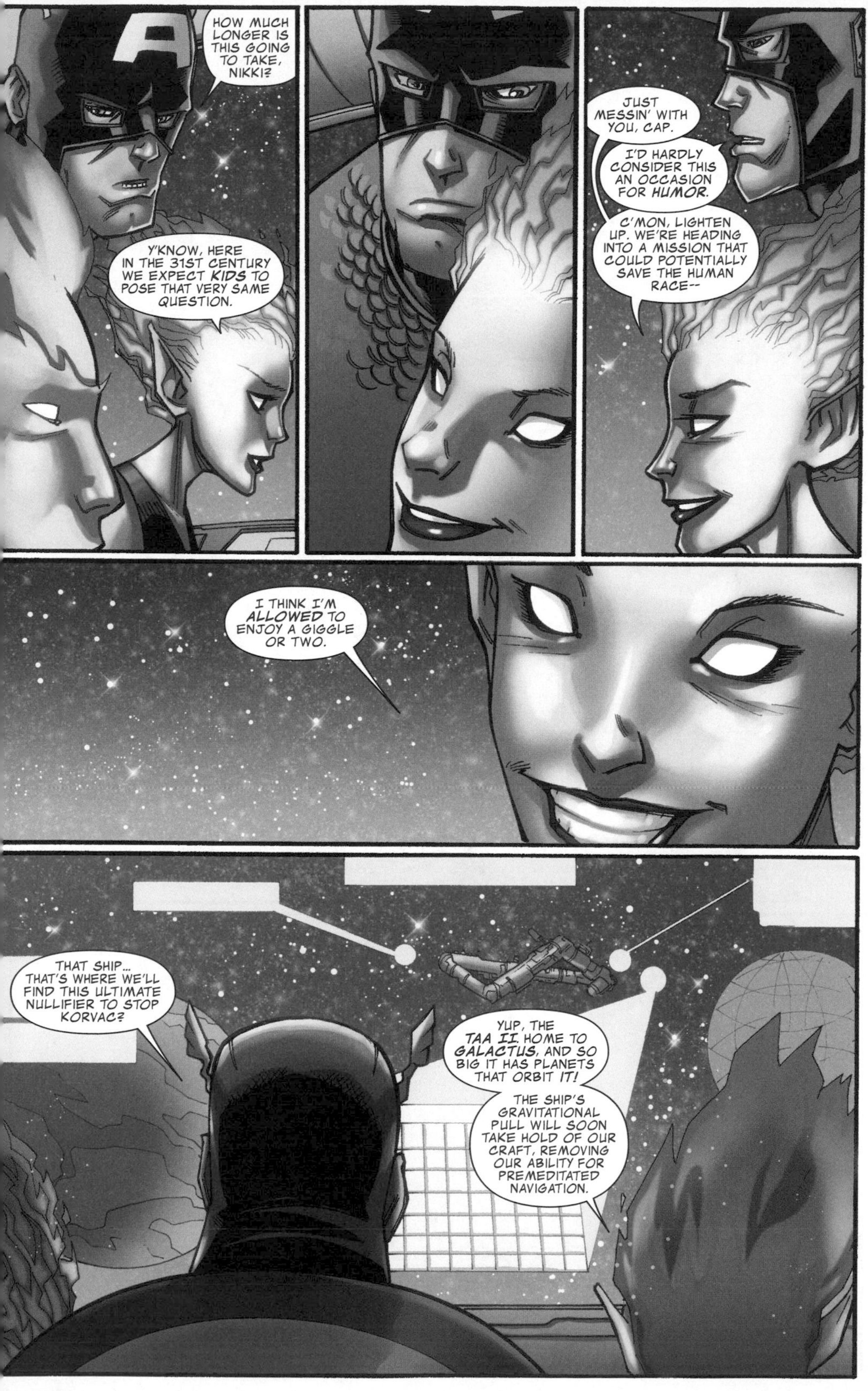
HOW MUCH LONGER IS THIS GOING TO TAKE, NIKKI?
Y'KNOW, HERE IN THE 31ST CENTURY WE EXPECT KIDS TO POSE THAT VERY SAME QUESTION.
JUST MESSIN' WITH YOU, CAP.
I'D HARDLY CONSIDER THIS AN OCCASION FOR HUMOR.
C'MON, LIGHTEN UP. WE'RE HEADING INTO A MISSION THAT COULD POTENTIALLY SAVE THE HUMAN RACE--
I THINK I'M ALLOWED TO ENJOY A GIGGLE OR TWO.
THAT SHIP... THAT'S WHERE WE'LL FIND THIS ULTIMATE NULLIFIER TO STOP KORVAC?
YUP, THE TAA II. HOME TO GALACTUS, AND SO BIG IT HAS PLANETS THAT ORBIT IT!
THE SHIP'S GRAVITATIONAL PULL WILL SOON TAKE HOLD OF OUR CRAFT, REMOVING OUR ABILITY FOR PREMEDITATED NAVIGATION.

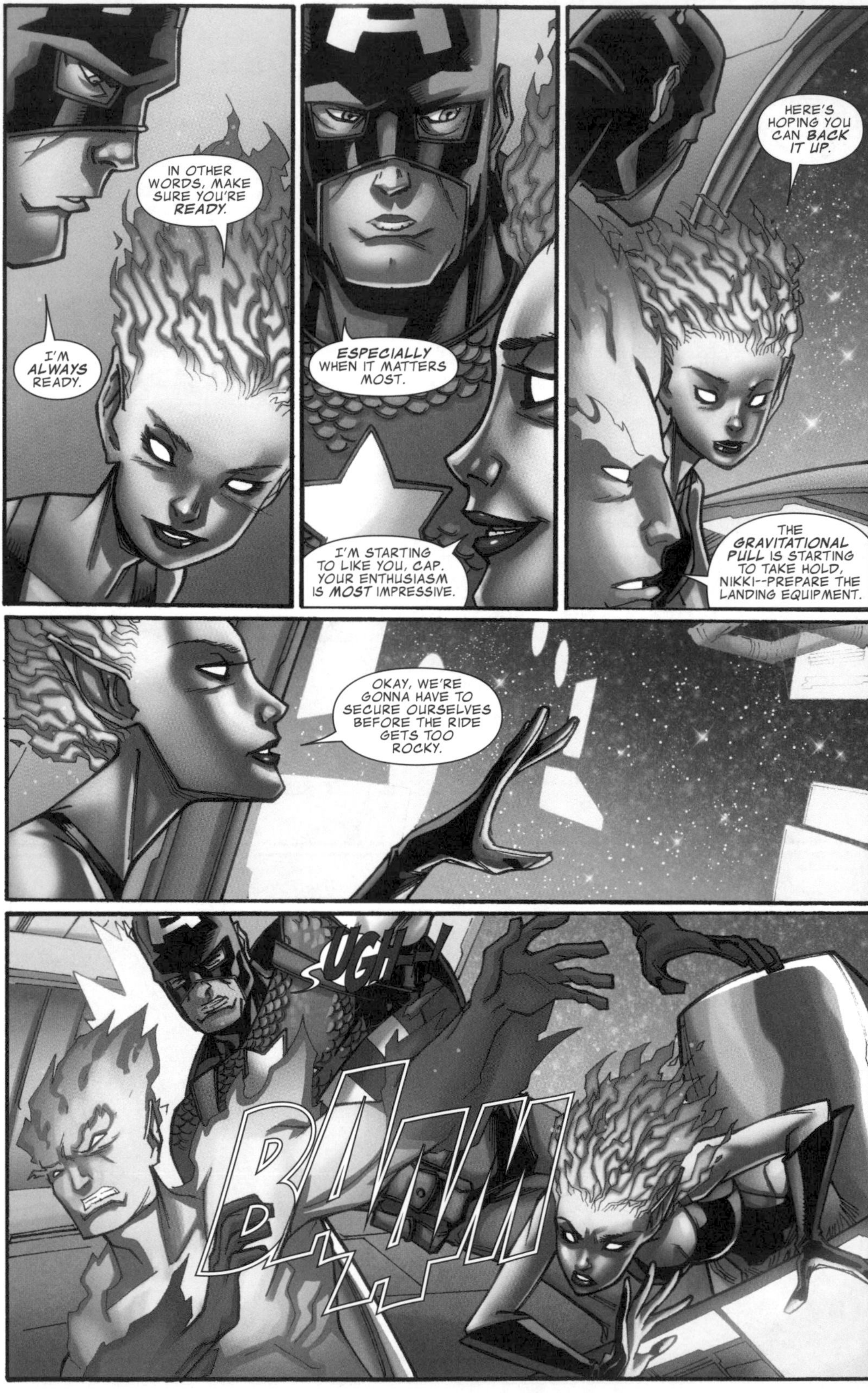
IN OTHER WORDS, MAKE SURE YOU'RE READY.
I'M ALWAYS READY.
ESPECIALLY WHEN IT MATTERS MOST.
I'M STARTING TO LIKE YOU, CAP. YOUR ENTHUSIASM IS MOST IMPRESSIVE.
HERE'S HOPING YOU CAN BACK IT UP.
THE GRAVITATIONAL PULL IS STARTING TO TAKE HOLD, NIKKI--PREPARE THE LANDING EQUIPMENT.
OKAY, WE'RE GONNA HAVE TO SECURE OURSELVES BEFORE THE RIDE GETS TOO ROCKY.
UGH--!
BLAM

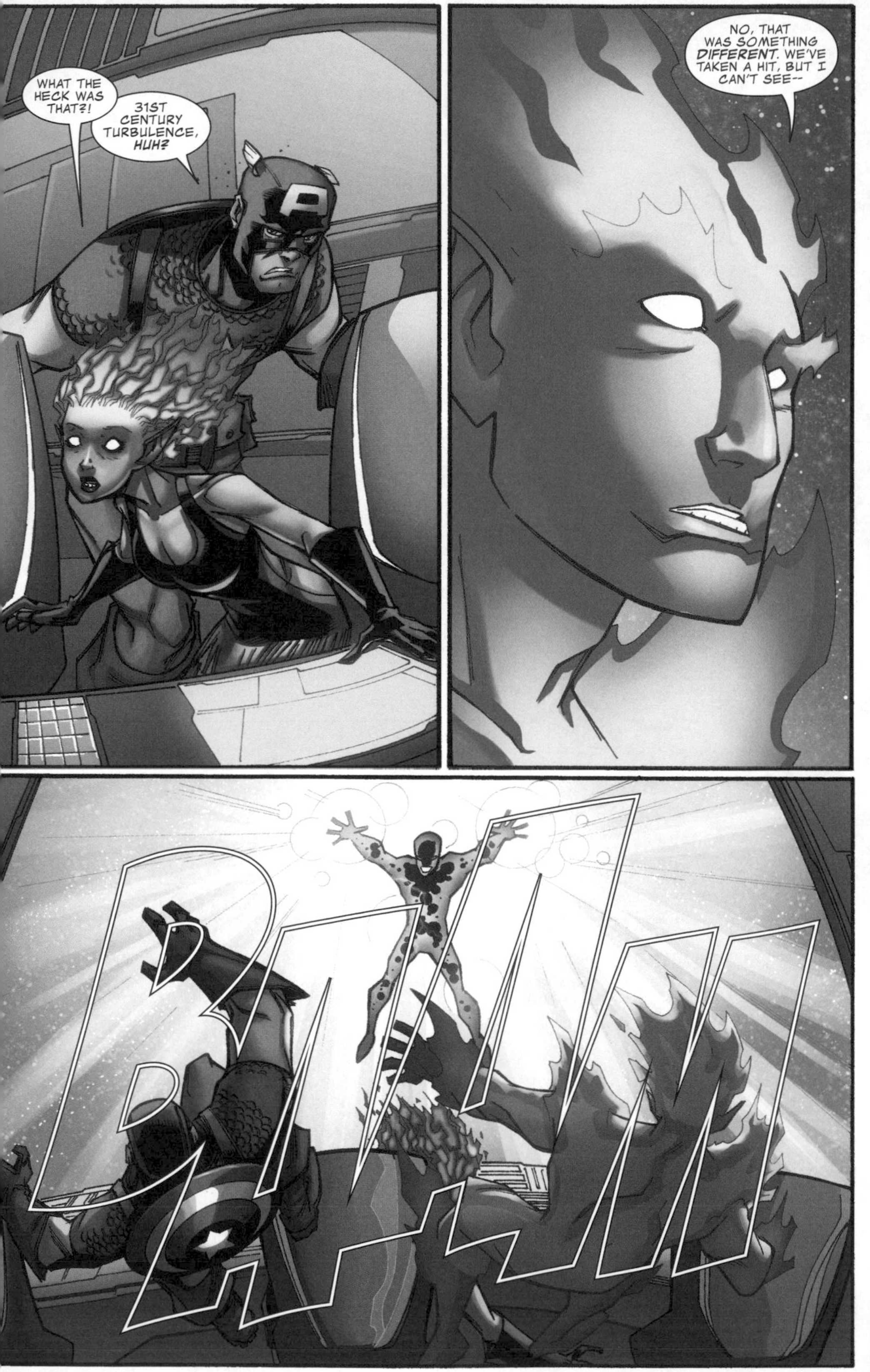
WHAT THE HECK WAS THAT?!
31ST CENTURY TURBULENCE, HUH?
NO, THAT WAS SOMETHING DIFFERENT. WE'VE TAKEN A HIT, BUT I CAN'T SEE--
BLAM

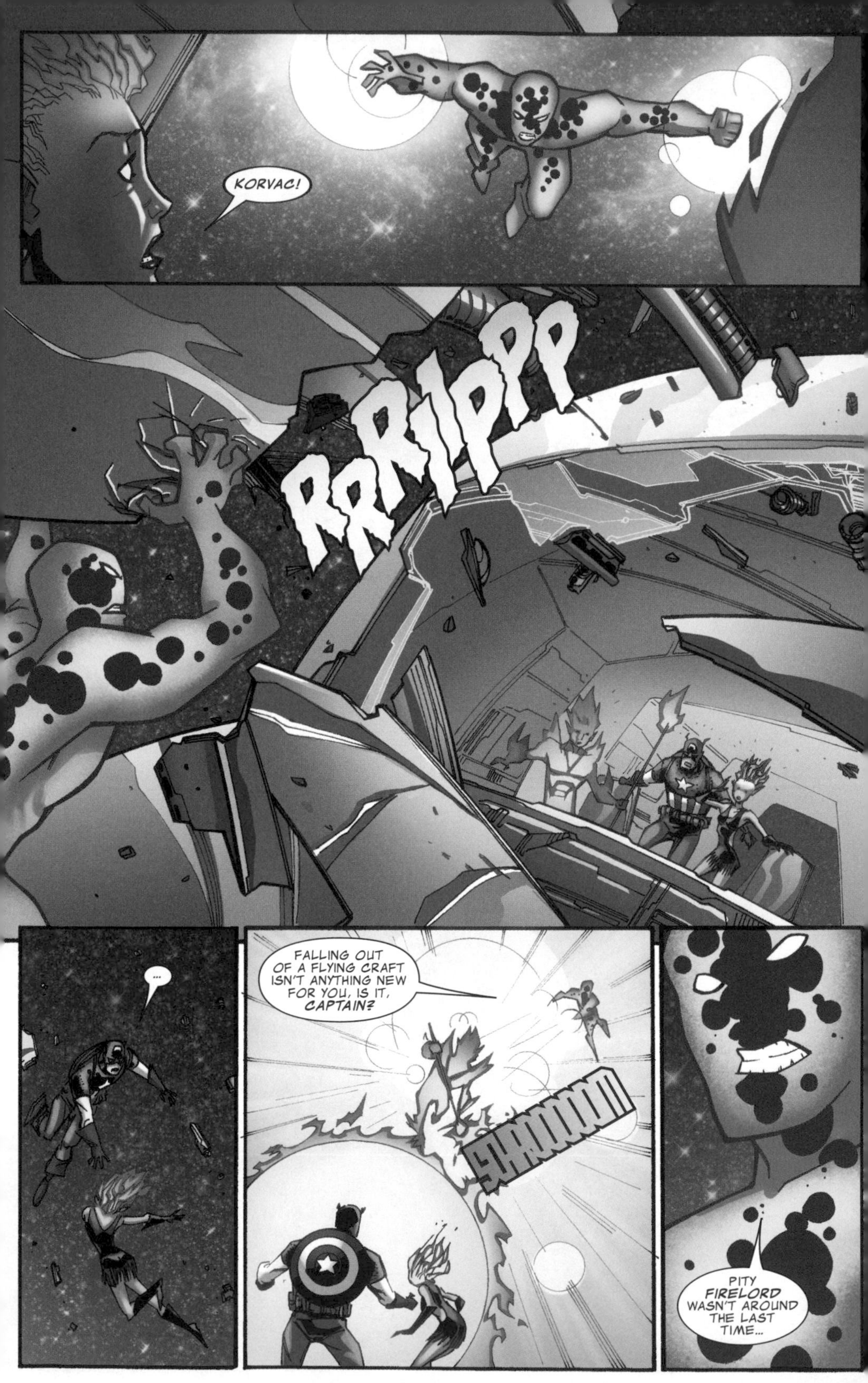
KORVAC!
RRRIPPP
...
FALLING OUT OF A FLYING CRAFT ISN'T ANYTHING NEW FOR YOU, IS IT, CAPTAIN?
SHHOOOOOM
PITY FIRELORD WASN'T AROUND THE LAST TIME...

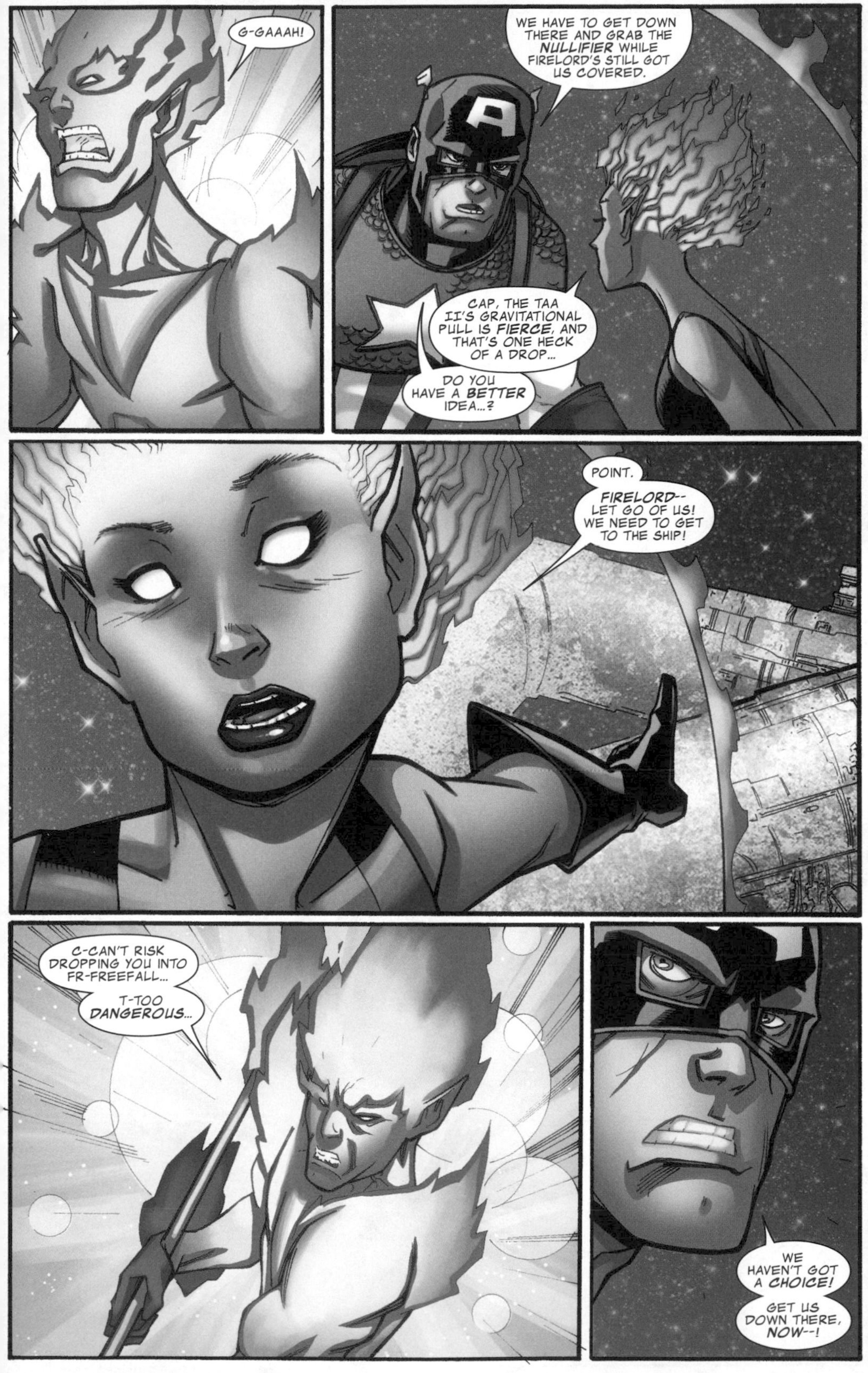
G-GAAAH!
WE HAVE TO GET DOWN THERE AND GRAB THE NULLIFIER WHILE FIRELORD'S STILL GOT US COVERED.
CAP, THE TAA II'S GRAVITATIONAL PULL IS FIERCE, AND THAT'S ONE HECK OF A DROP...
DO YOU HAVE A BETTER IDEA...?
POINT.
FIRELORD-- LET GO OF US! WE NEED TO GET TO THE SHIP!
C-CAN'T RISK DROPPING YOU INTO FR-FREEFALL...
T-TOO DANGEROUS...
WE HAVEN'T GOT A CHOICE!
GET US DOWN THERE, NOW--!

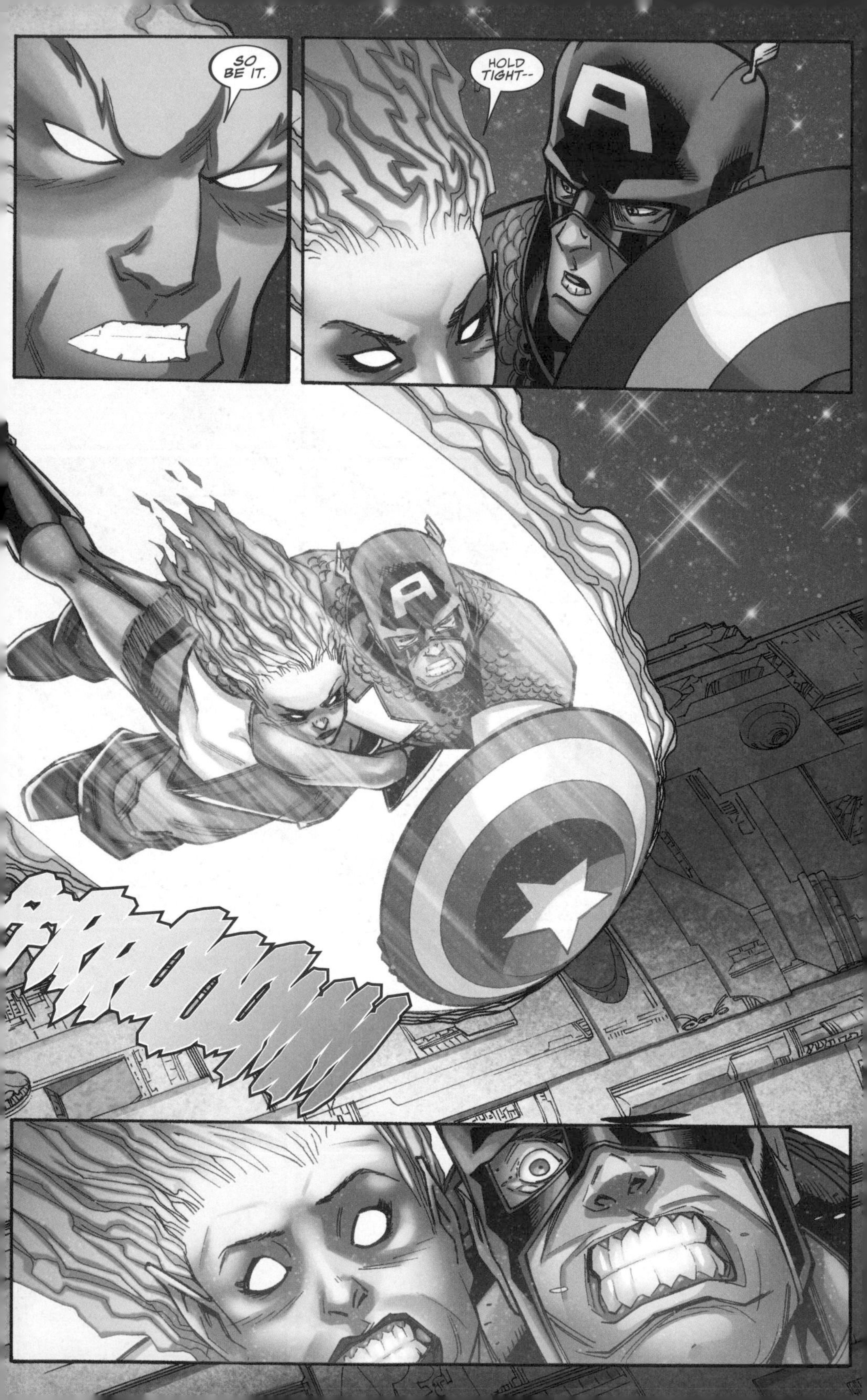
SO BE IT.
HOLD TIGHT--

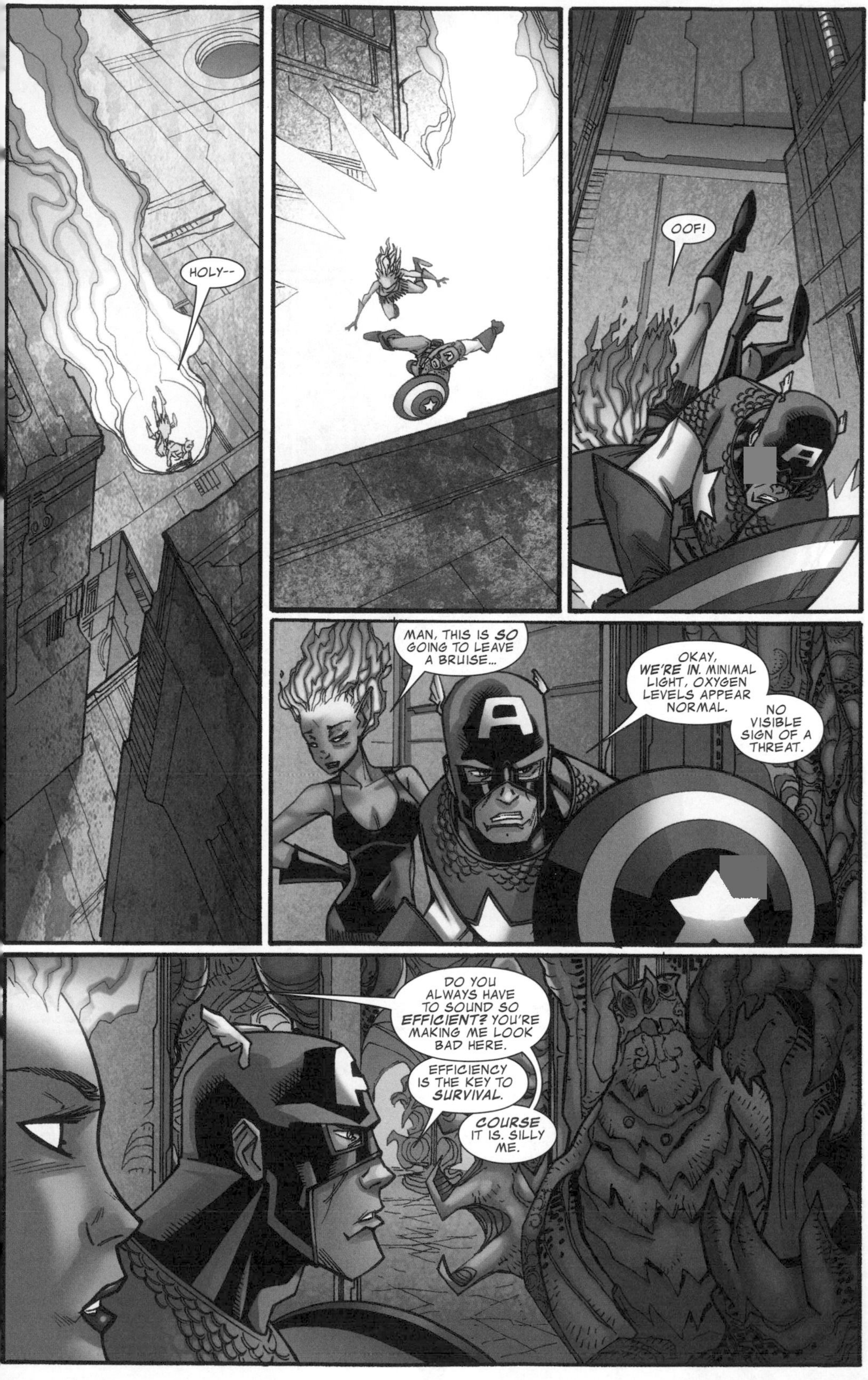
HOLY--
OOF!
MAN, THIS IS SO GOING TO LEAVE A BRUISE...
OKAY, WE'RE IN. MINIMAL LIGHT, OXYGEN LEVELS APPEAR NORMAL.
NO VISIBLE SIGN OF A THREAT.
DO YOU ALWAYS HAVE TO SOUND SO EFFICIENT? YOU'RE MAKING ME LOOK BAD HERE.
EFFICIENCY IS THE KEY TO SURVIVAL.
COURSE IT IS. SILLY ME.

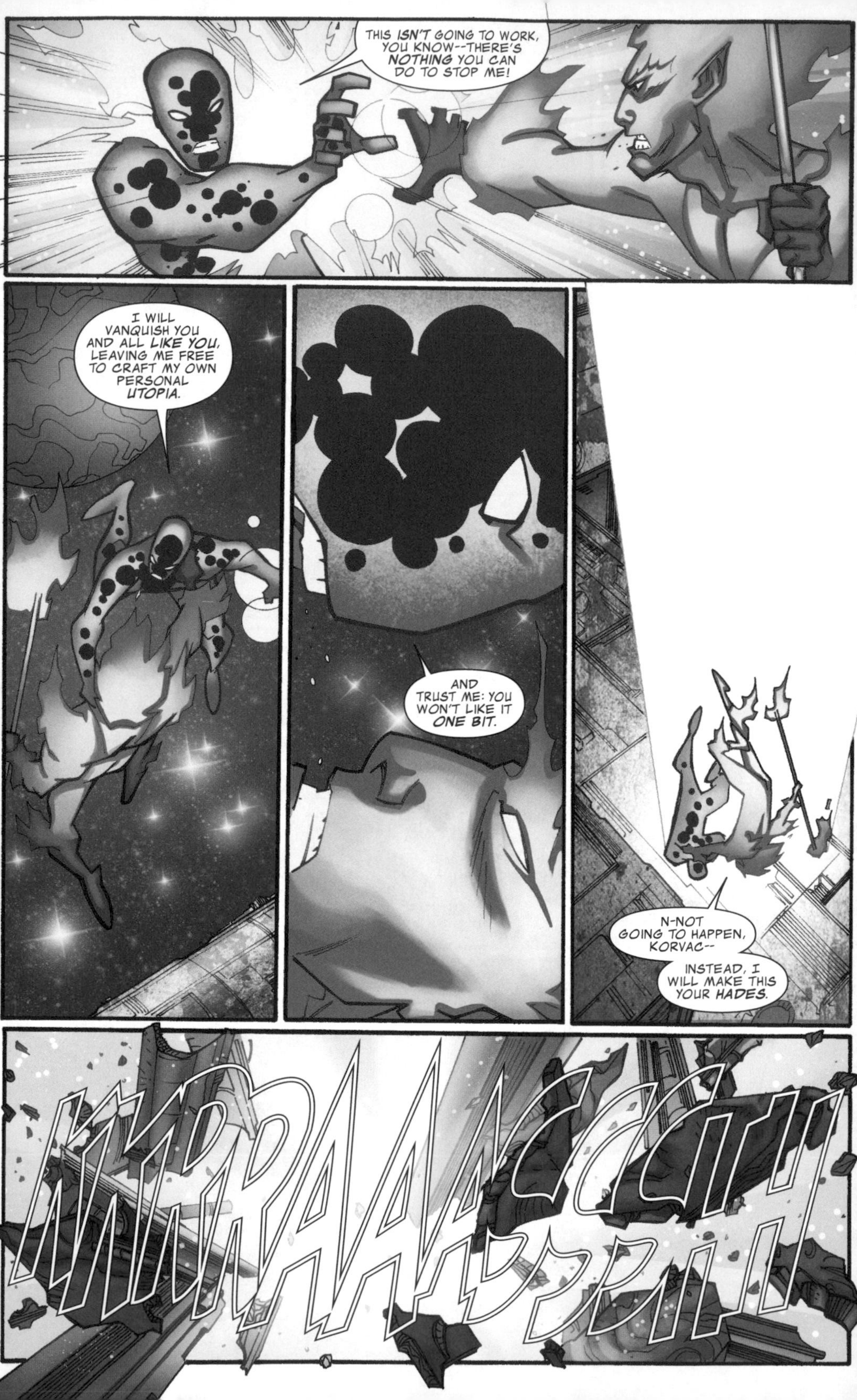
THIS ISN'T GOING TO WORK, YOU KNOW--THERE'S NOTHING YOU CAN DO TO STOP ME!
I WILL VANQUISH YOU AND ALL LIKE YOU, LEAVING ME FREE TO CRAFT MY OWN PERSONAL UTOPIA.
AND TRUST ME: YOU WON'T LIKE IT ONE BIT.
N-NOT GOING TO HAPPEN, KORVAC--
INSTEAD, I WILL MAKE THIS YOUR HADES.

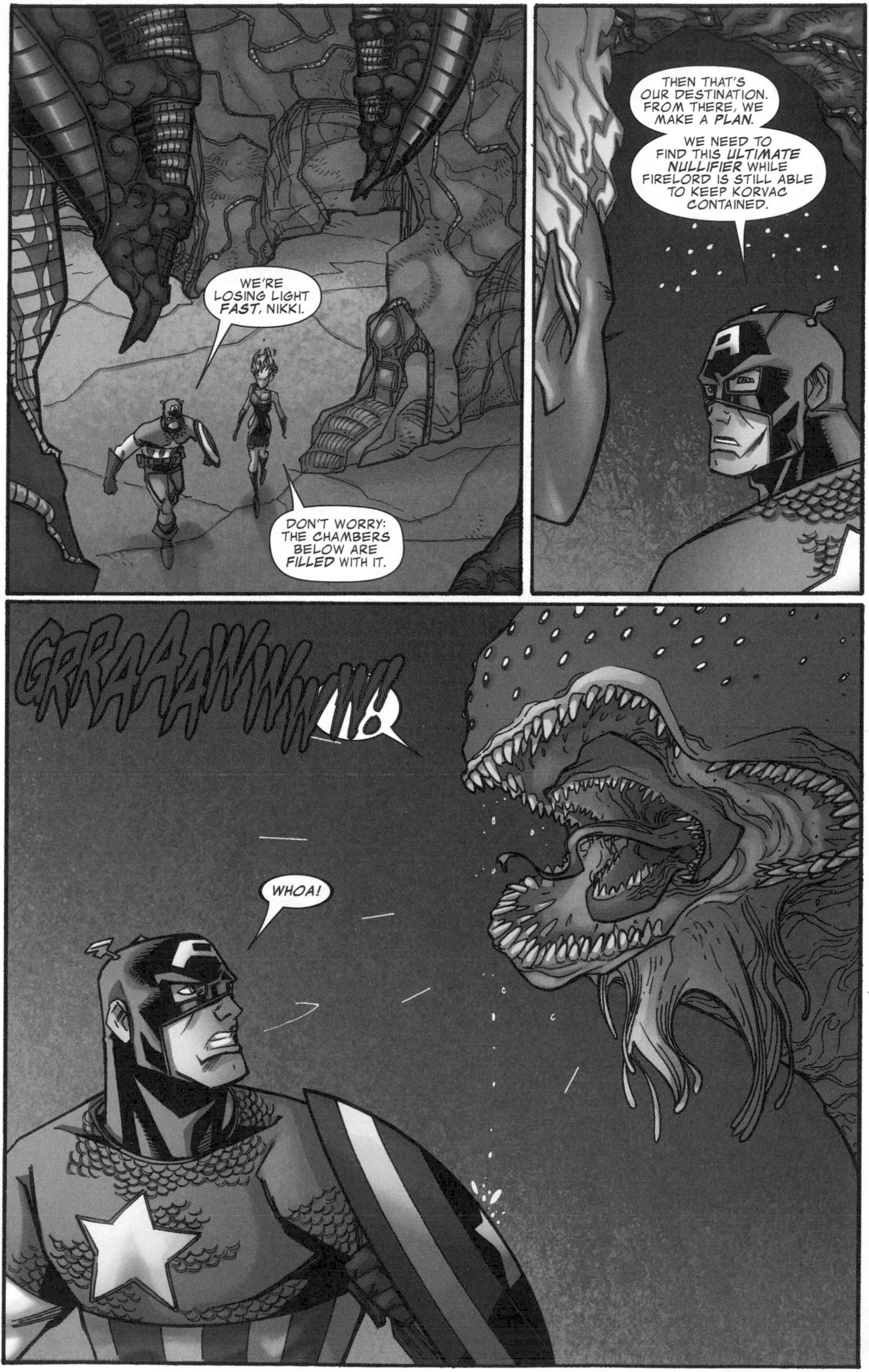
WE'RE LOSING LIGHT FAST, NIKKI.
DON'T WORRY: THE CHAMBERS BELOW ARE FILLED WITH IT.
THEN THAT'S OUR DESTINATION. FROM THERE, WE MAKE A PLAN.
WE NEED TO FIND THIS ULTIMATE NULLIFIER WHILE FIRELORD IS STILL ABLE TO KEEP KORVAC CONTAINED.
GRRAAWWWWN!
WHOA!

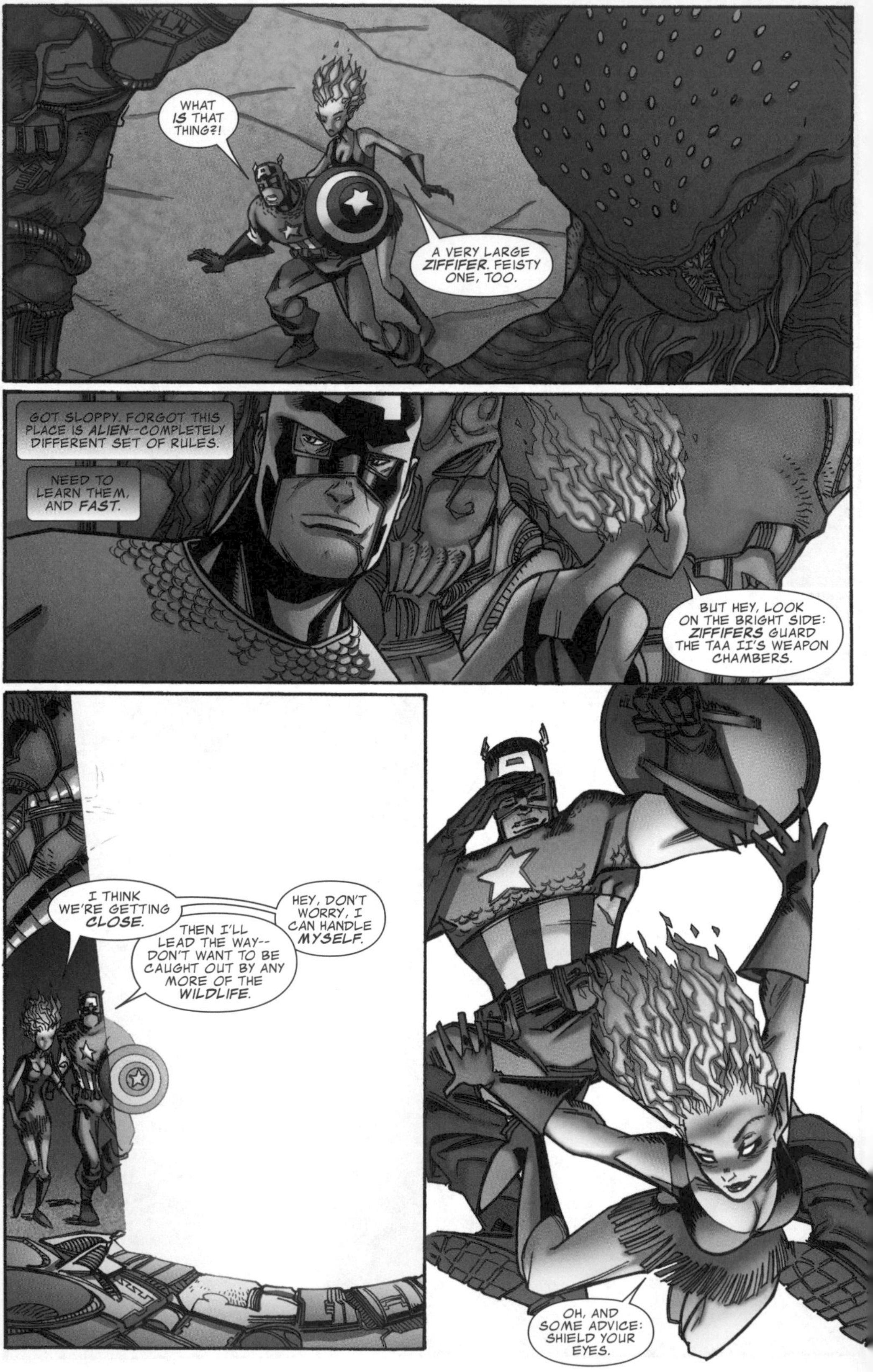
WHAT IS THAT THING?!
A VERY LARGE ZIFFIFER. FEISTY ONE, TOO.
GOT SLOPPY. FORGOT THIS PLACE IS ALIEN--COMPLETELY DIFFERENT SET OF RULES.
NEED TO LEARN THEM, AND FAST.
BUT HEY, LOOK ON THE BRIGHT SIDE: ZIFFIFERS GUARD THE TAA II'S WEAPON CHAMBERS.
I THINK WE'RE GETTING CLOSE.
HEY, DON'T WORRY, I CAN HANDLE MYSELF.
THEN I'LL LEAD THE WAY-- DON'T WANT TO BE CAUGHT OUT BY ANY MORE OF THE WILDLIFE.
OH, AND SOME ADVICE: SHIELD YOUR EYES.

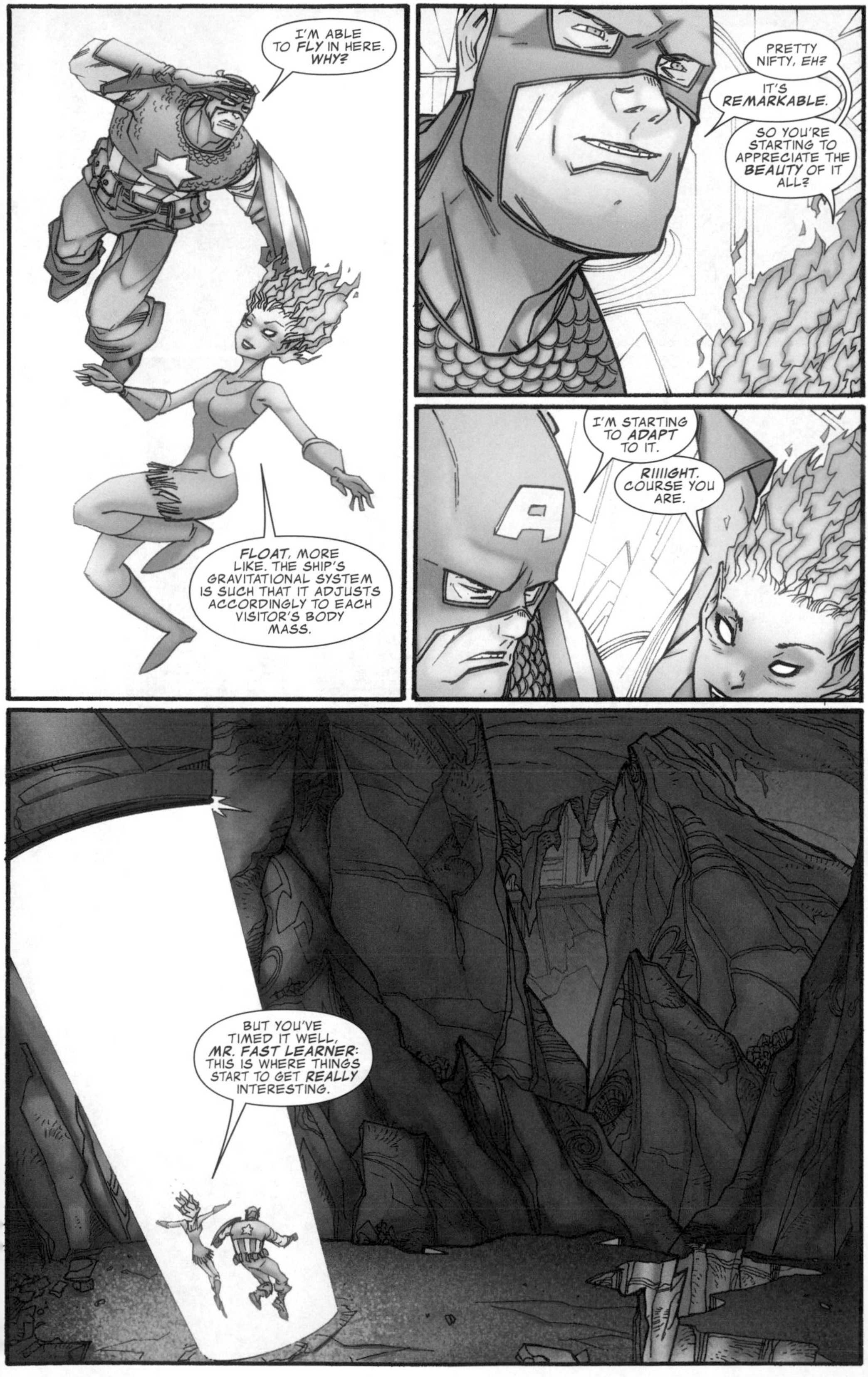
I'M ABLE TO FLY IN HERE. WHY?
FLOAT, MORE LIKE. THE SHIP'S GRAVITATIONAL SYSTEM IS SUCH THAT IT ADJUSTS ACCORDINGLY TO EACH VISITOR'S BODY MASS.
PRETTY NIFTY, EH?
IT'S REMARKABLE.
SO YOU'RE STARTING TO APPRECIATE THE BEAUTY OF IT ALL?
I'M STARTING TO ADAPT TO IT.
RIIIIGHT. COURSE YOU ARE.
BUT YOU'VE TIMED IT WELL, MR. FAST LEARNER: THIS IS WHERE THINGS START TO GET REALLY INTERESTING.

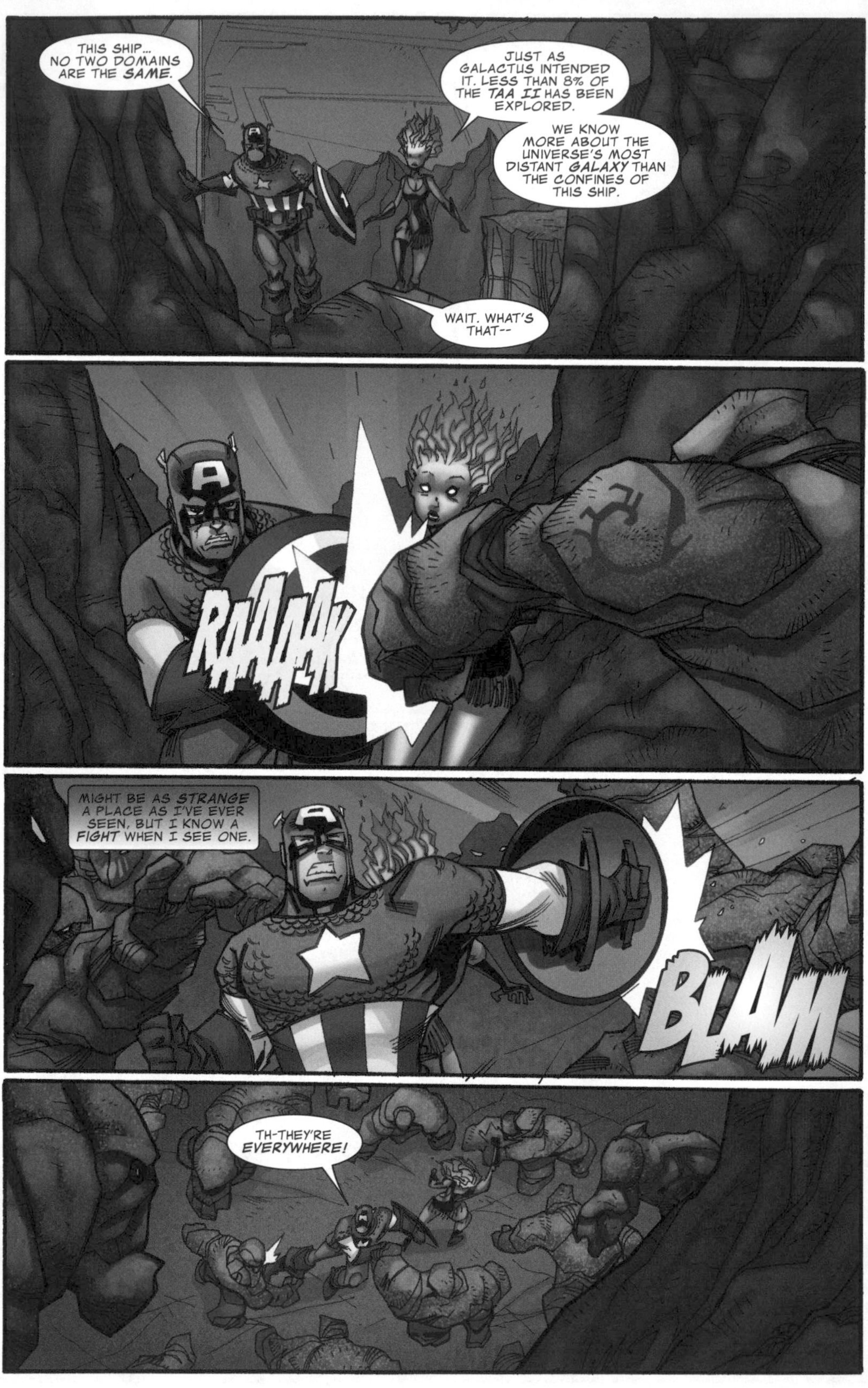
THIS SHIP... NO TWO DOMAINS ARE THE SAME.
JUST AS GALACTUS INTENDED IT. LESS THAN 8% OF THE TAA II HAS BEEN EXPLORED.
WE KNOW MORE ABOUT THE UNIVERSE'S MOST DISTANT GALAXY THAN THE CONFINES OF THIS SHIP.
WAIT. WHAT'S THAT--
RAAAAK
MIGHT BE AS STRANGE A PLACE AS I'VE EVER SEEN, BUT I KNOW A FIGHT WHEN I SEE ONE.
BLAM
TH-THEY'RE EVERYWHERE!

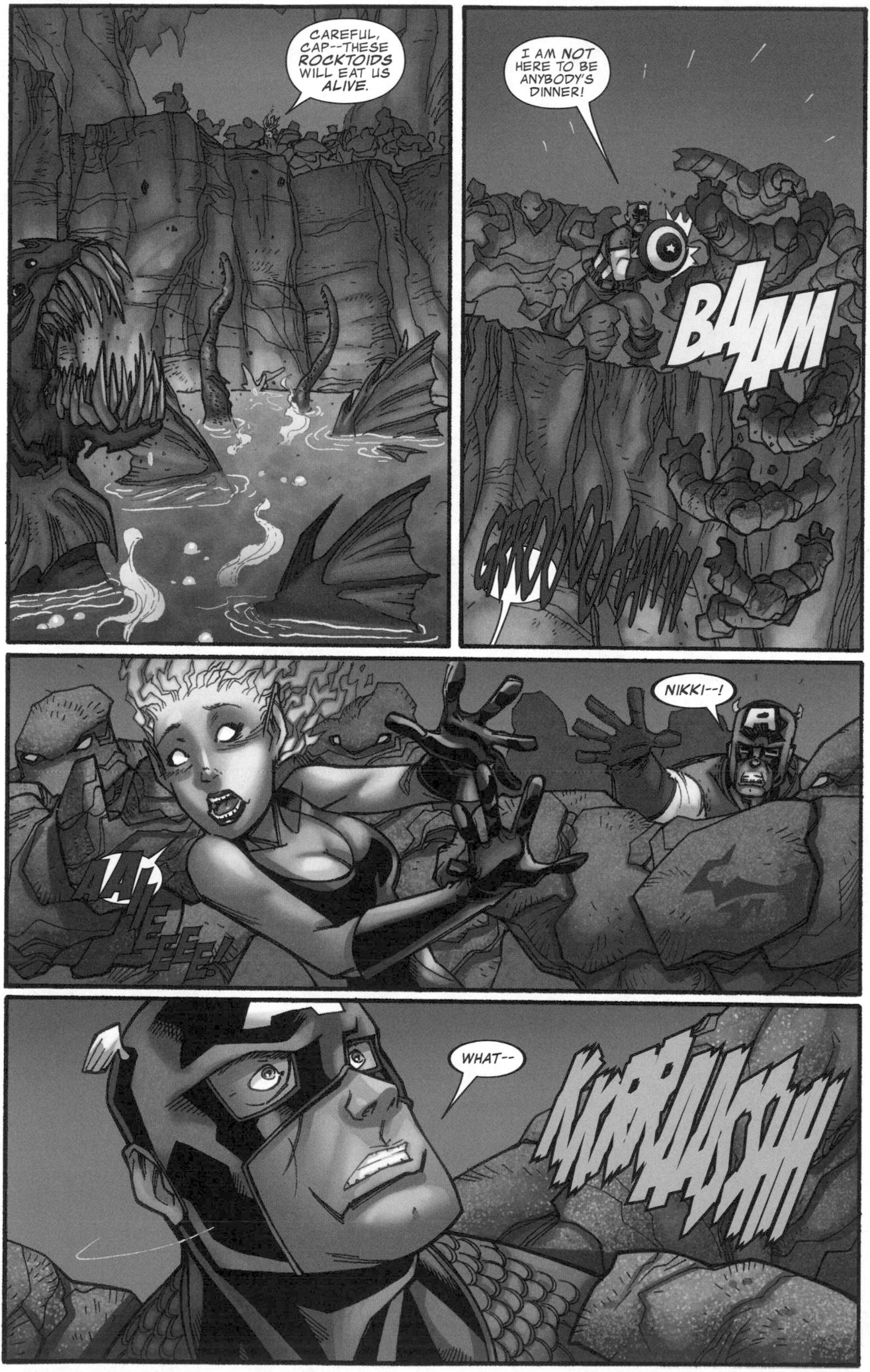
CAREFUL, CAP--THESE ROCKTOIDS WILL EAT US ALIVE.
I AM NOT HERE TO BE ANYBODY'S DINNER!
BAAM
GRROOOAAWW
NIKKI--!
AAIEEEEE!
WHAT--
KKRRAKSSH

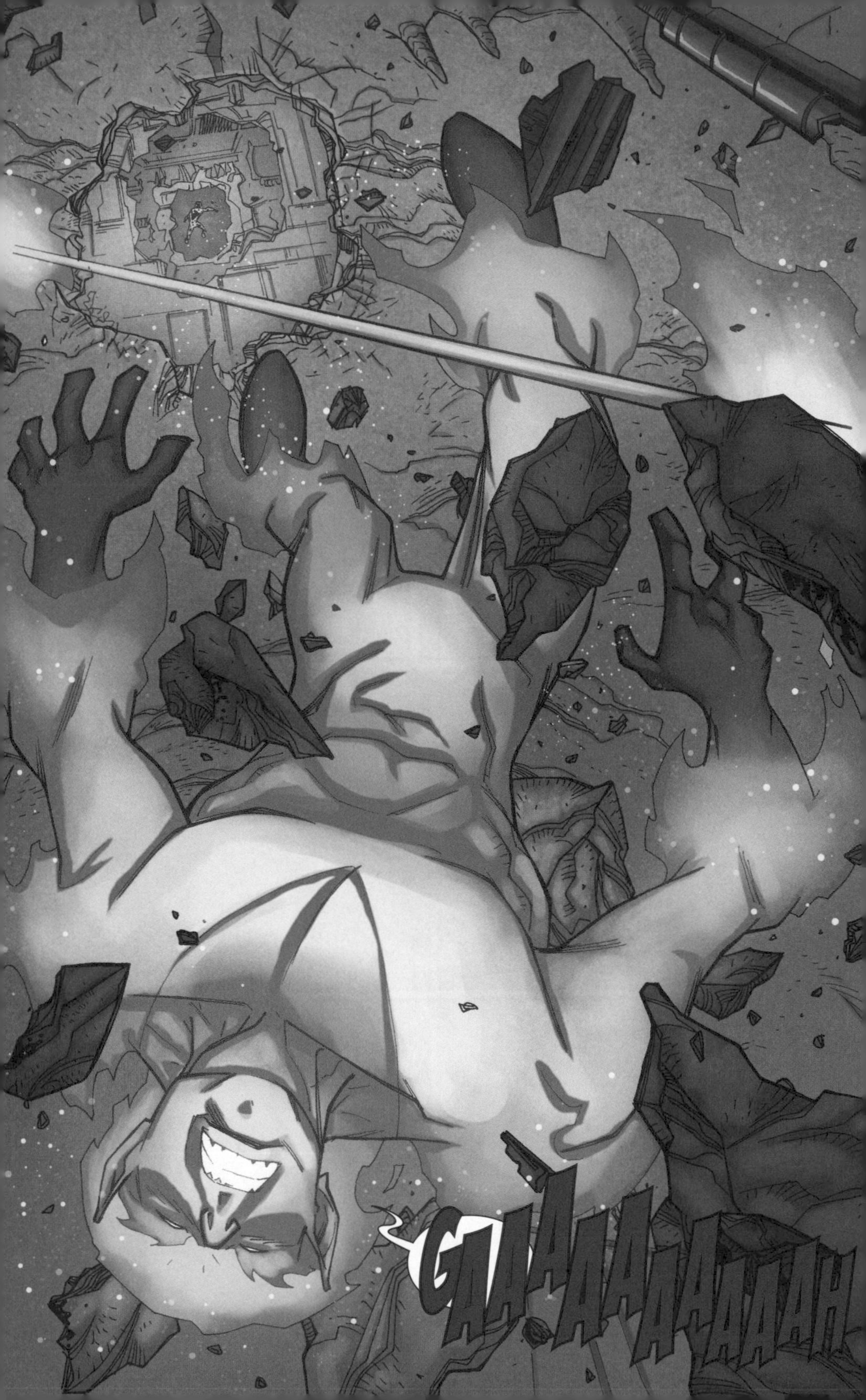
GAAAAAAAAAAH

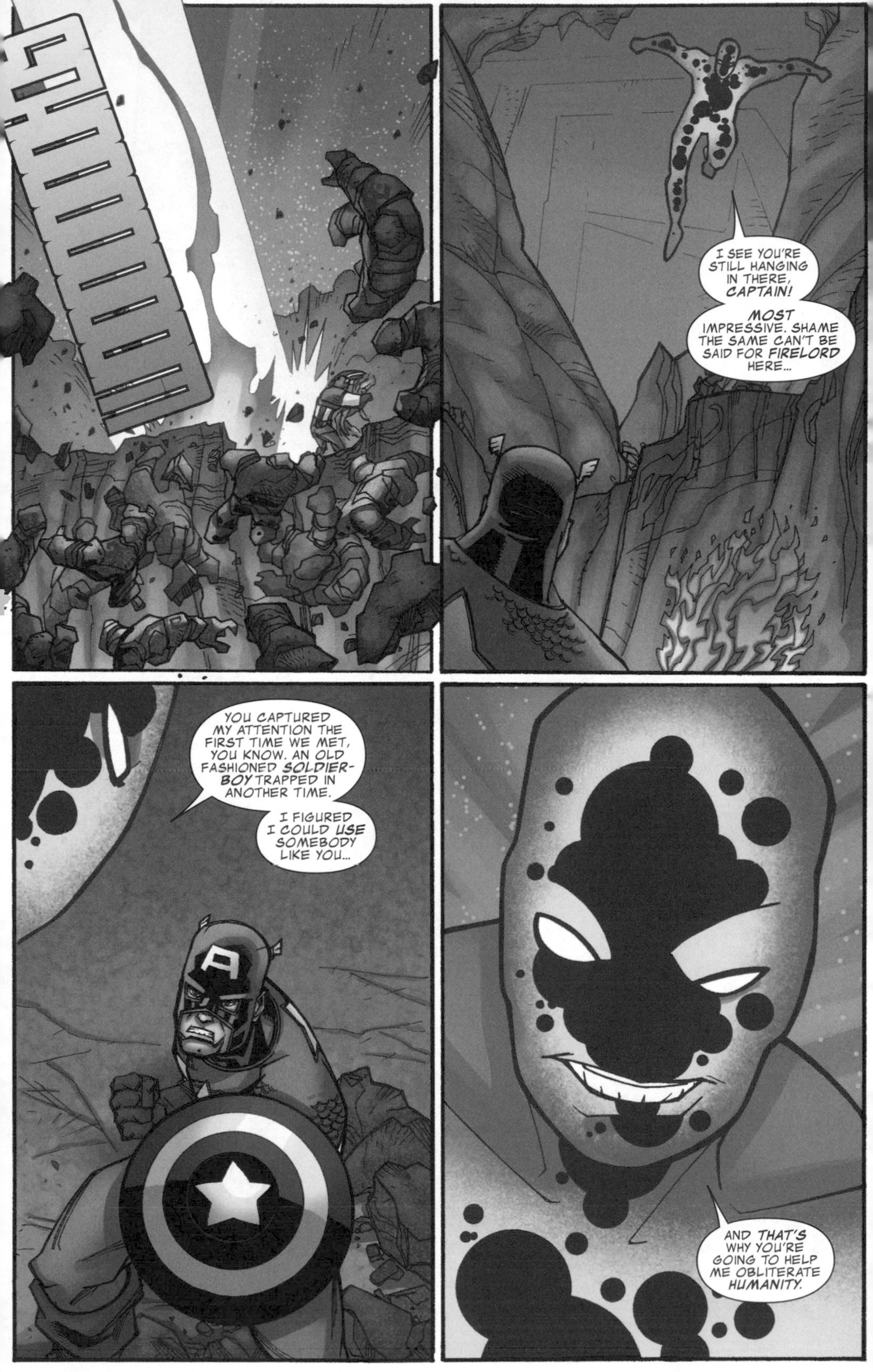
I SEE YOU'RE STILL HANGING IN THERE, CAPTAIN!
MOST IMPRESSIVE. SHAME THE SAME CAN'T BE SAID FOR FIRELORD HERE...
YOU CAPTURED MY ATTENTION THE FIRST TIME WE MET, YOU KNOW. AN OLD FASHIONED SOLDIER-BOY TRAPPED IN ANOTHER TIME.
I FIGURED I COULD USE SOMEBODY LIKE YOU...
AND THAT'S WHY YOU'RE GOING TO HELP ME OBLITERATE HUMANITY.

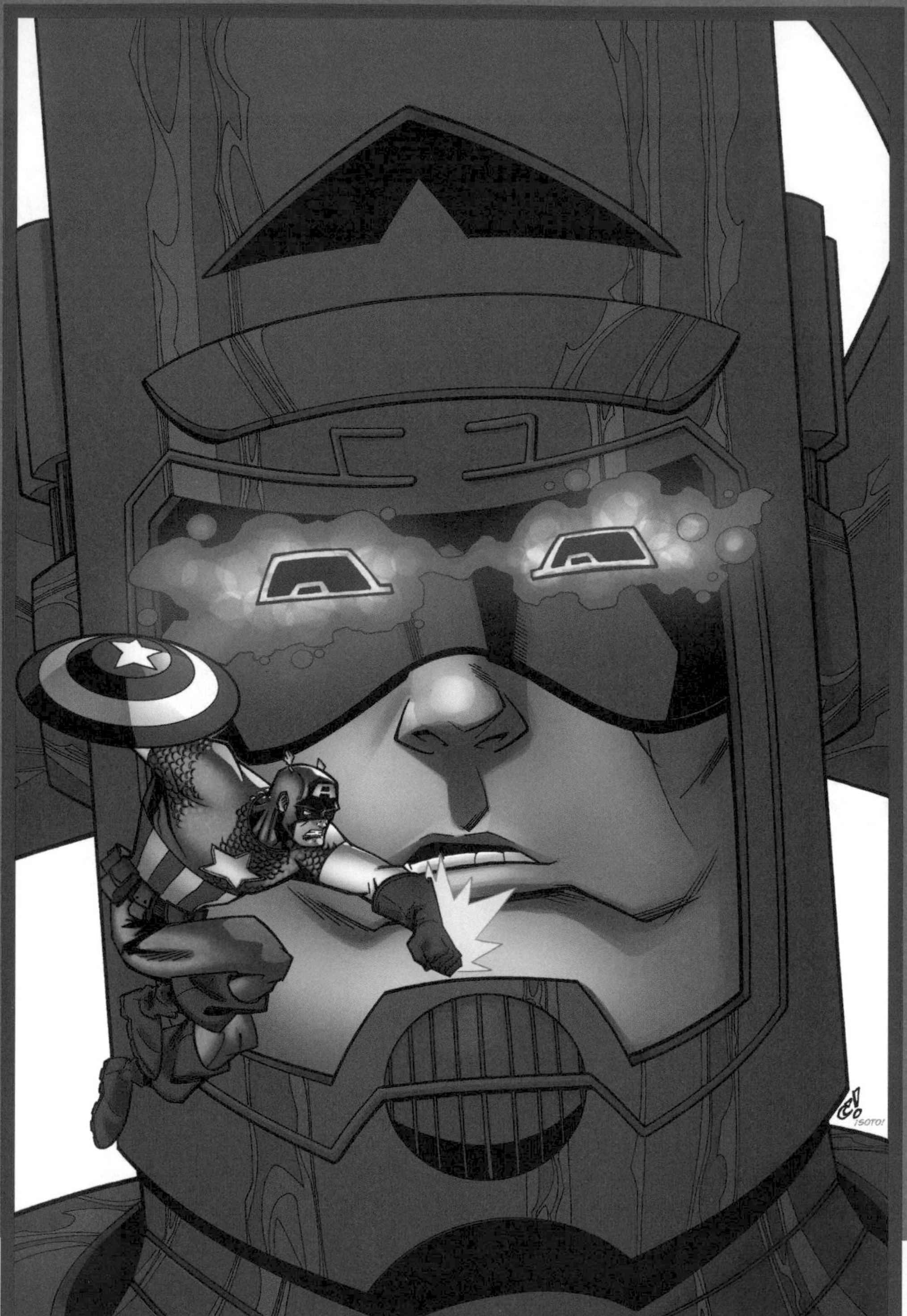
¡SOTO!

#4

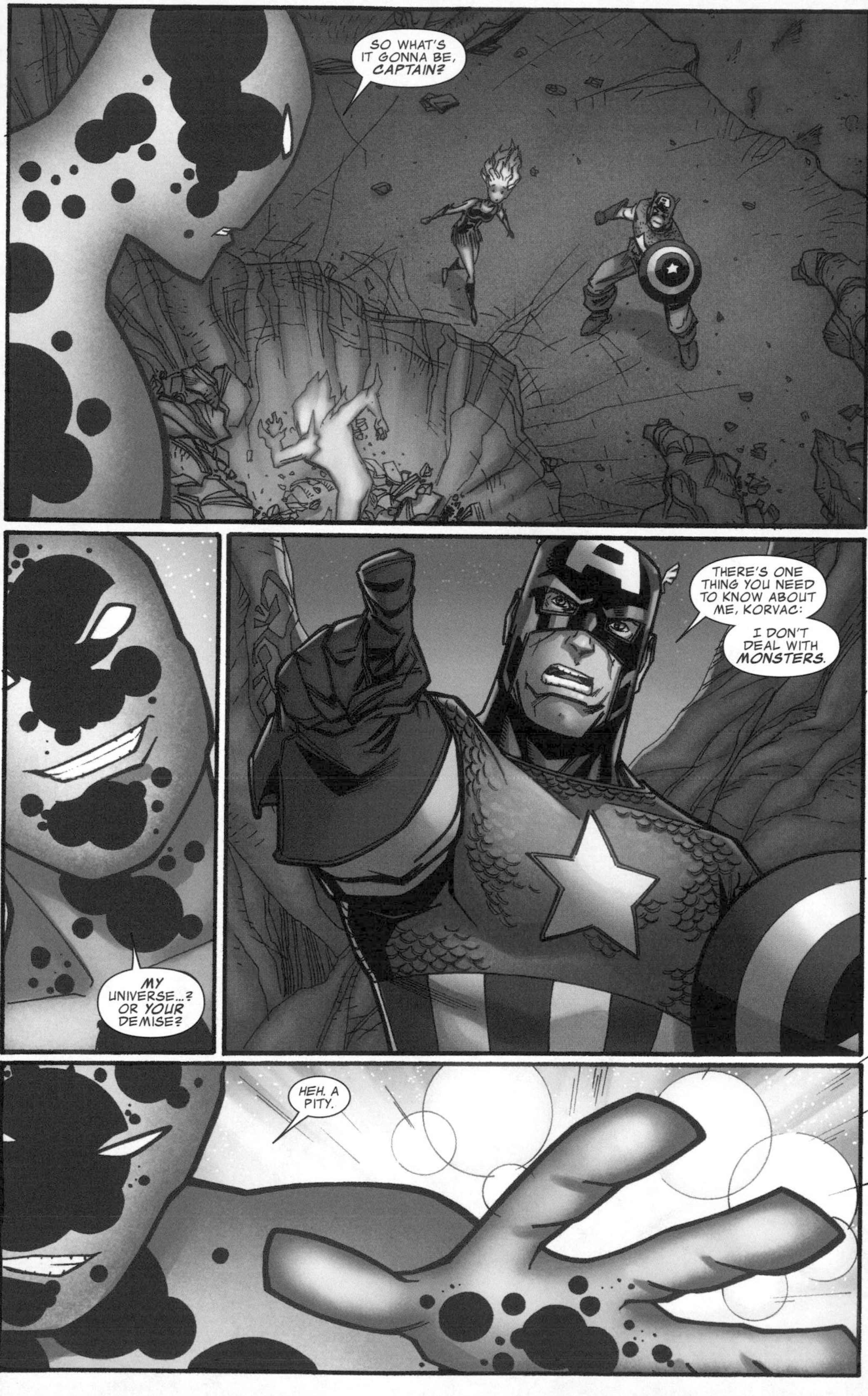
SO WHAT'S IT GONNA BE, CAPTAIN?
MY UNIVERSE...? OR YOUR DEMISE?
THERE'S ONE THING YOU NEED TO KNOW ABOUT ME, KORVAC:
I DON'T DEAL WITH MONSTERS.
HEH. A PITY.

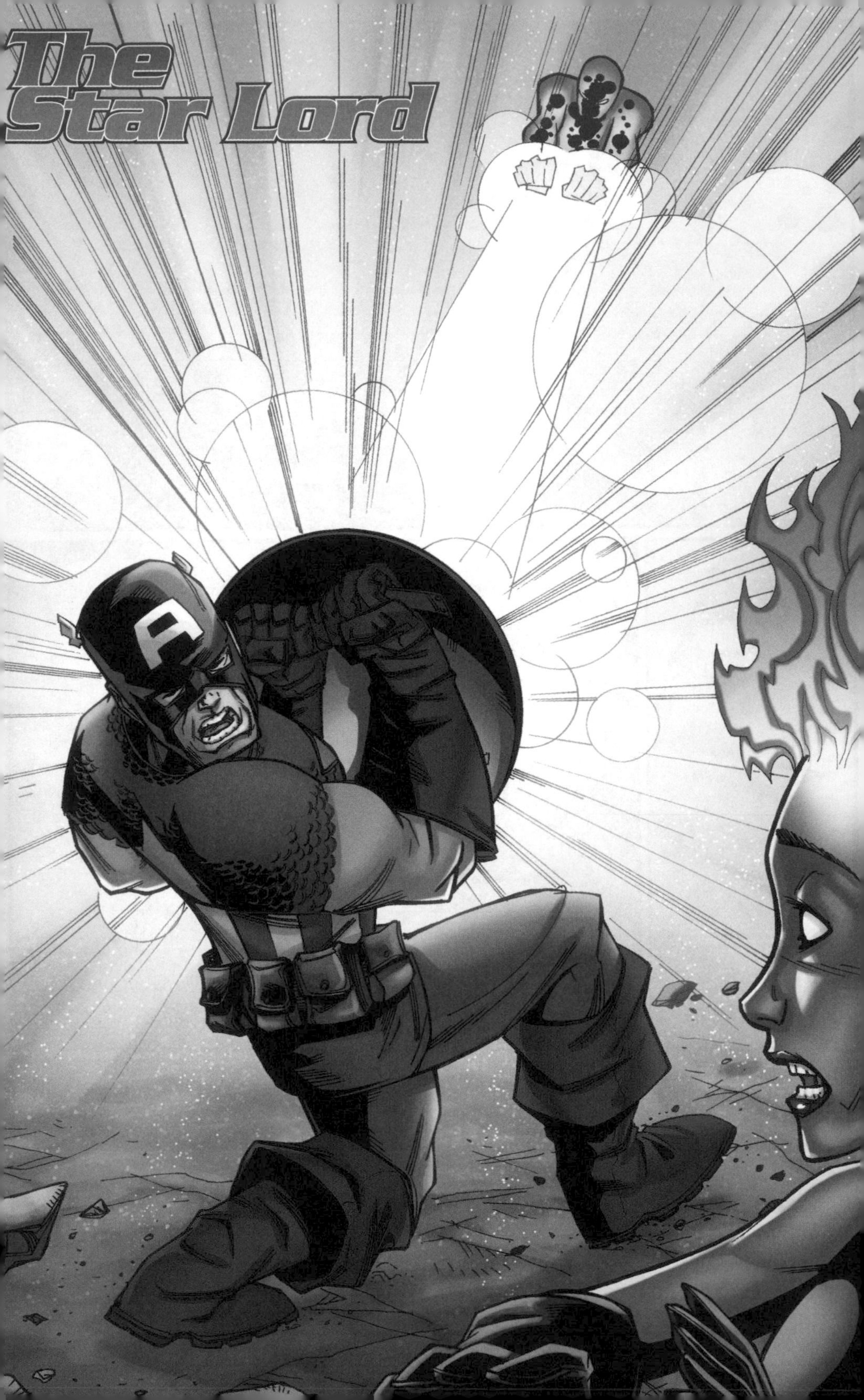
The Star Lord

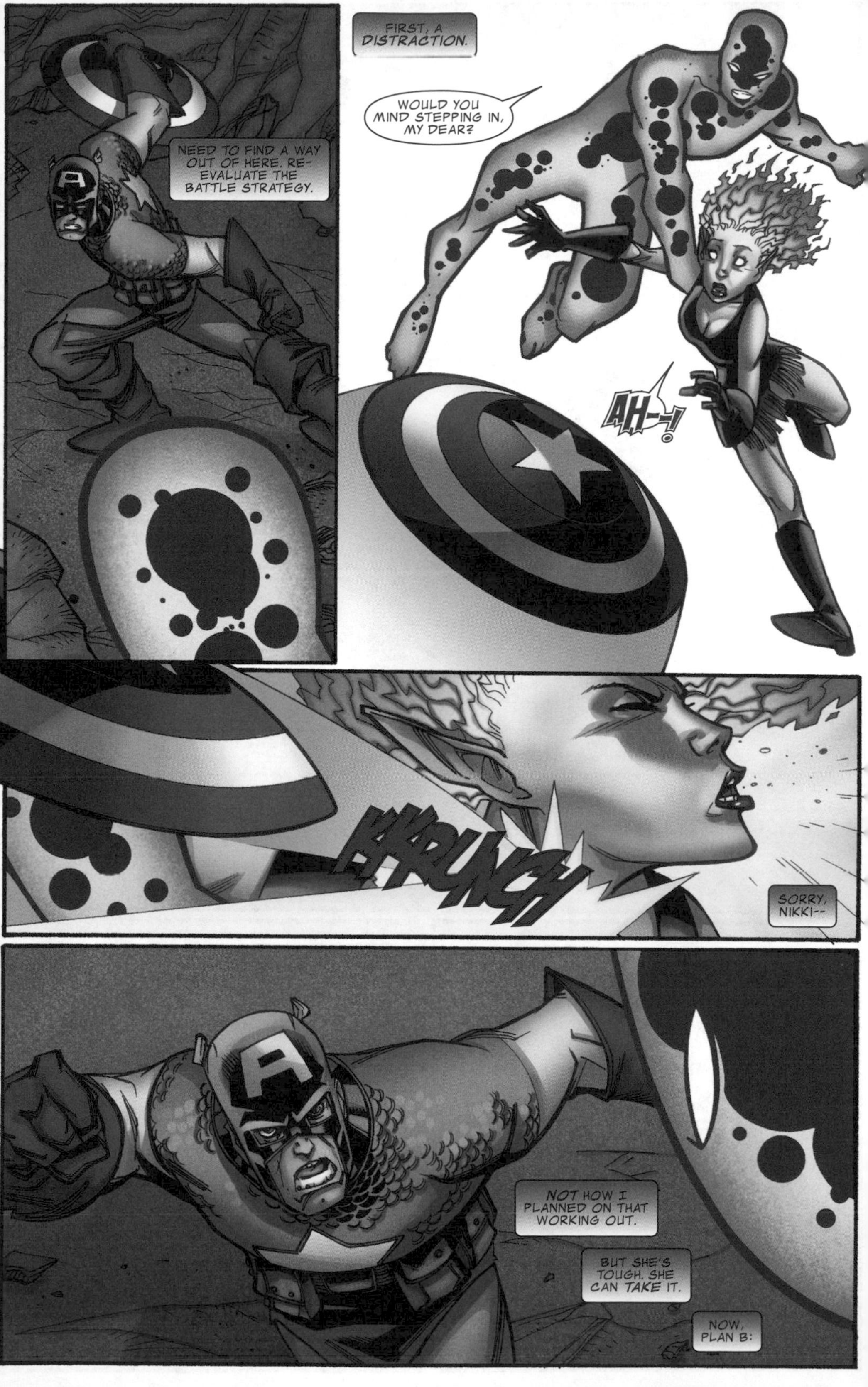
NEED TO FIND A WAY OUT OF HERE. RE-EVALUATE THE BATTLE STRATEGY.
FIRST, A DISTRACTION.
WOULD YOU MIND STEPPING IN, MY DEAR?
AH--!
KKRUNCH
SORRY, NIKKI--
NOT HOW I PLANNED ON THAT WORKING OUT.
BUT SHE'S TOUGH. SHE CAN TAKE IT.
NOW, PLAN B:

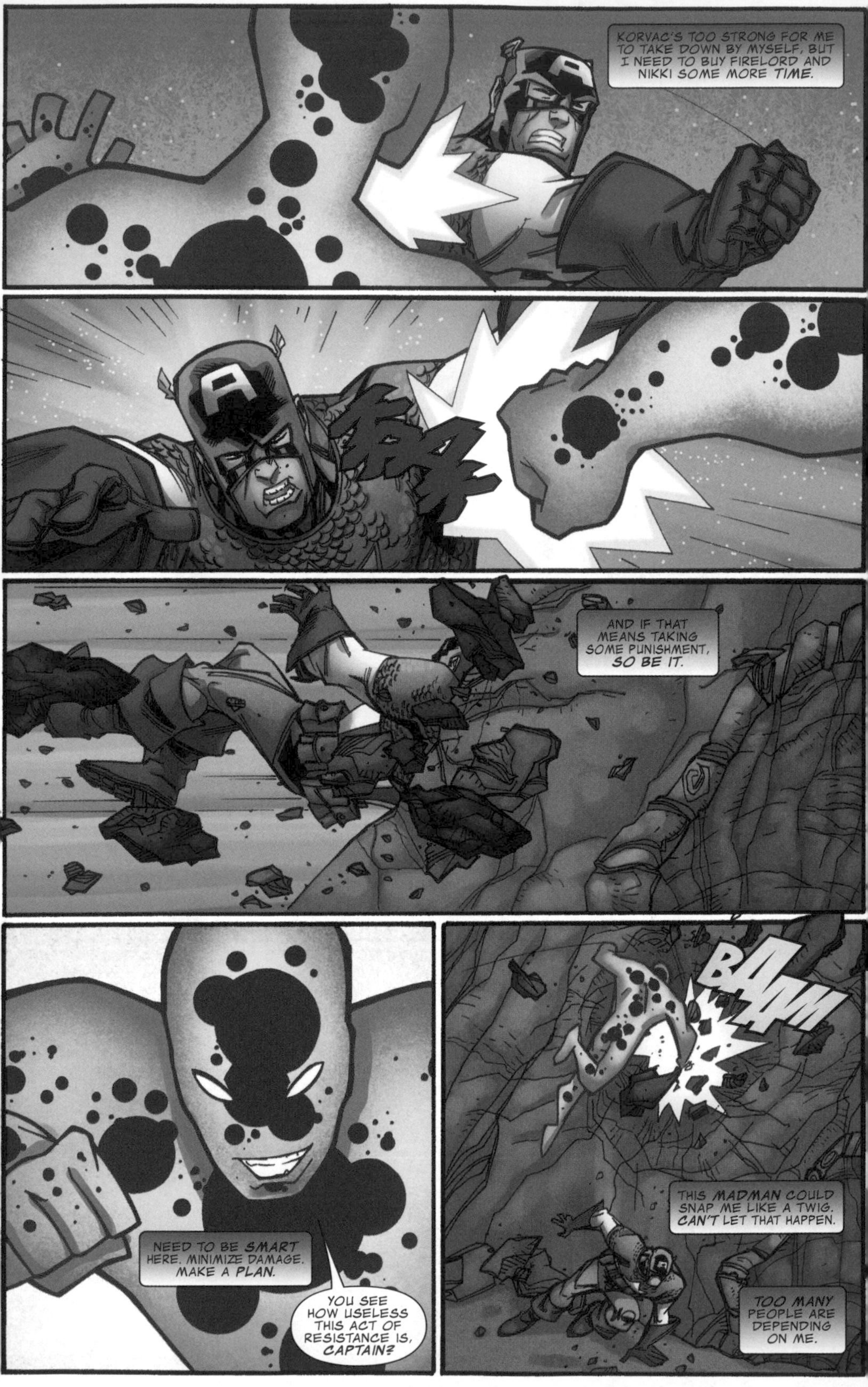

KORVAC'S TOO STRONG FOR ME TO TAKE DOWN BY MYSELF, BUT I NEED TO BUY FIRELORD AND NIKKI SOME MORE TIME.
AND IF THAT MEANS TAKING SOME PUNISHMENT, SO BE IT.
NEED TO BE SMART HERE. MINIMIZE DAMAGE. MAKE A PLAN.
YOU SEE HOW USELESS THIS ACT OF RESISTANCE IS, CAPTAIN?
BAAM
THIS MADMAN COULD SNAP ME LIKE A TWIG. CAN'T LET THAT HAPPEN.
TOO MANY PEOPLE ARE DEPENDING ON ME.

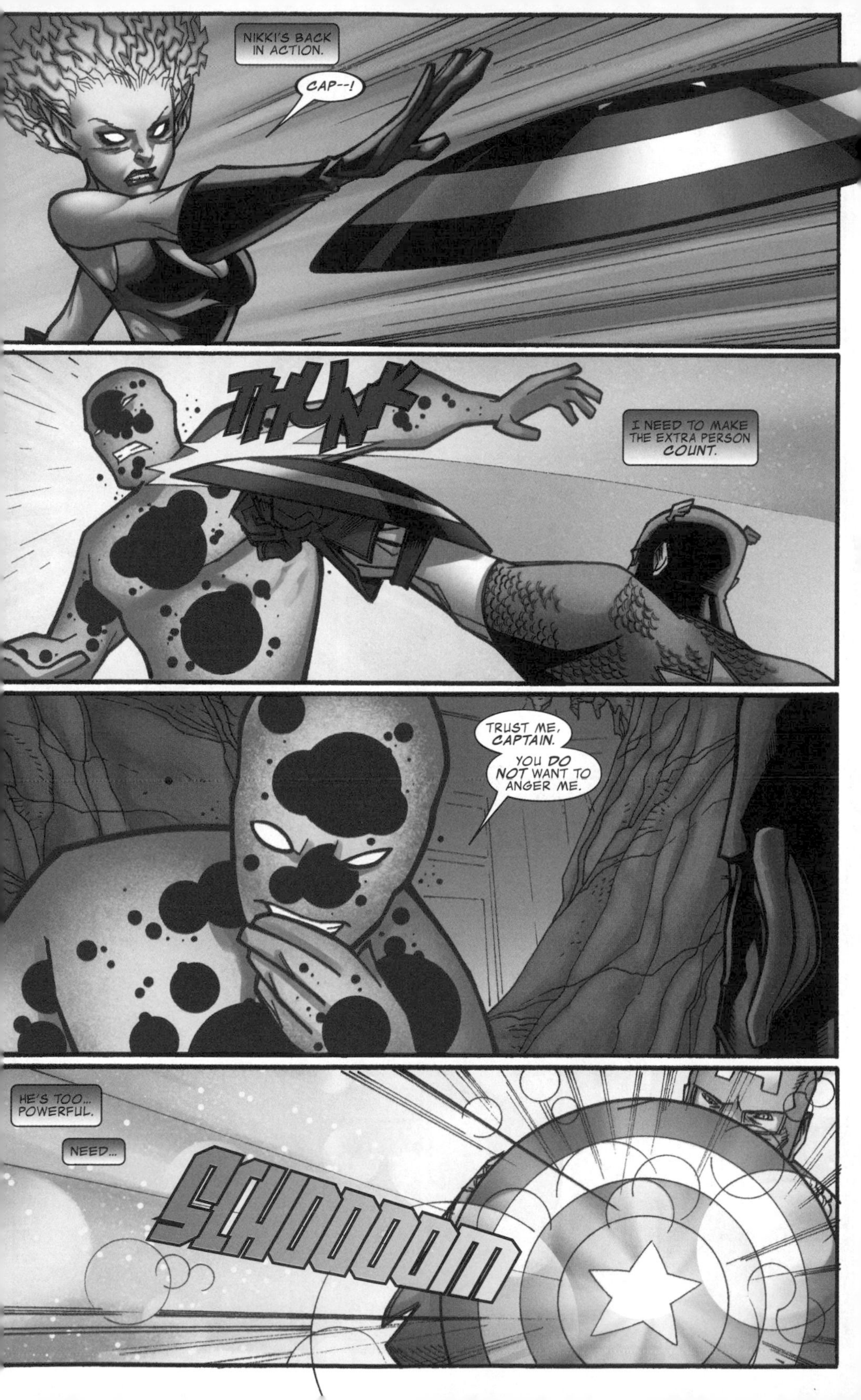
NIKKI'S BACK IN ACTION.
CAP--!
THUNK
I NEED TO MAKE THE EXTRA PERSON COUNT.
TRUST ME, CAPTAIN.
YOU DO NOT WANT TO ANGER ME.
HE'S TOO... POWERFUL.
NEED...
SCHOOOOOM

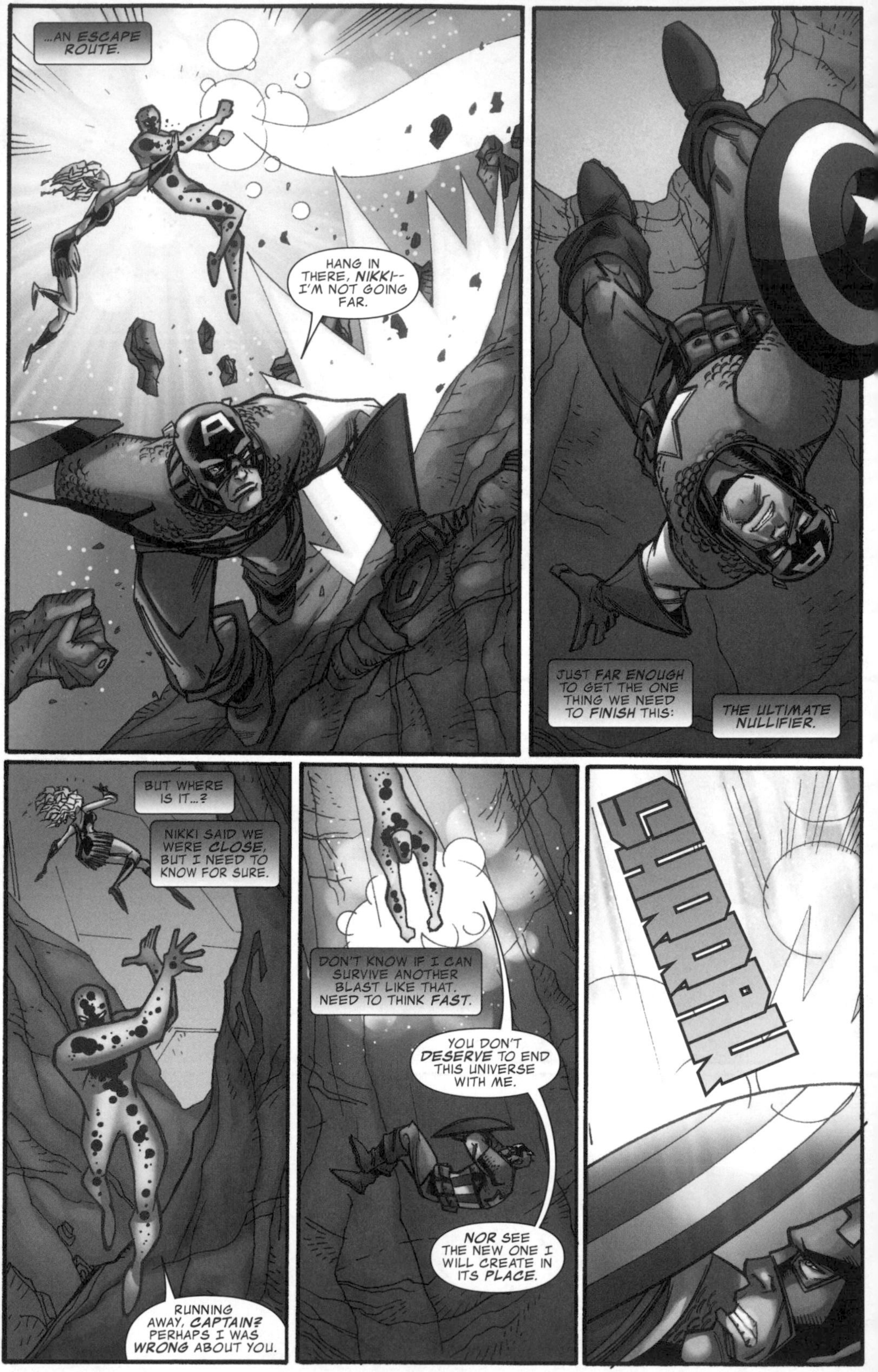
...AN ESCAPE ROUTE.
HANG IN THERE, NIKKI-- I'M NOT GOING FAR.
JUST FAR ENOUGH TO GET THE ONE THING WE NEED TO FINISH THIS:
THE ULTIMATE NULLIFIER.
BUT WHERE IS IT...?
NIKKI SAID WE WERE CLOSE, BUT I NEED TO KNOW FOR SURE.
RUNNING AWAY, CAPTAIN? PERHAPS I WAS WRONG ABOUT YOU.
DON'T KNOW IF I CAN SURVIVE ANOTHER BLAST LIKE THAT. NEED TO THINK FAST.
YOU DON'T DESERVE TO END THIS UNIVERSE WITH ME.
NOR SEE THE NEW ONE I WILL CREATE IN ITS PLACE.
CHRAK

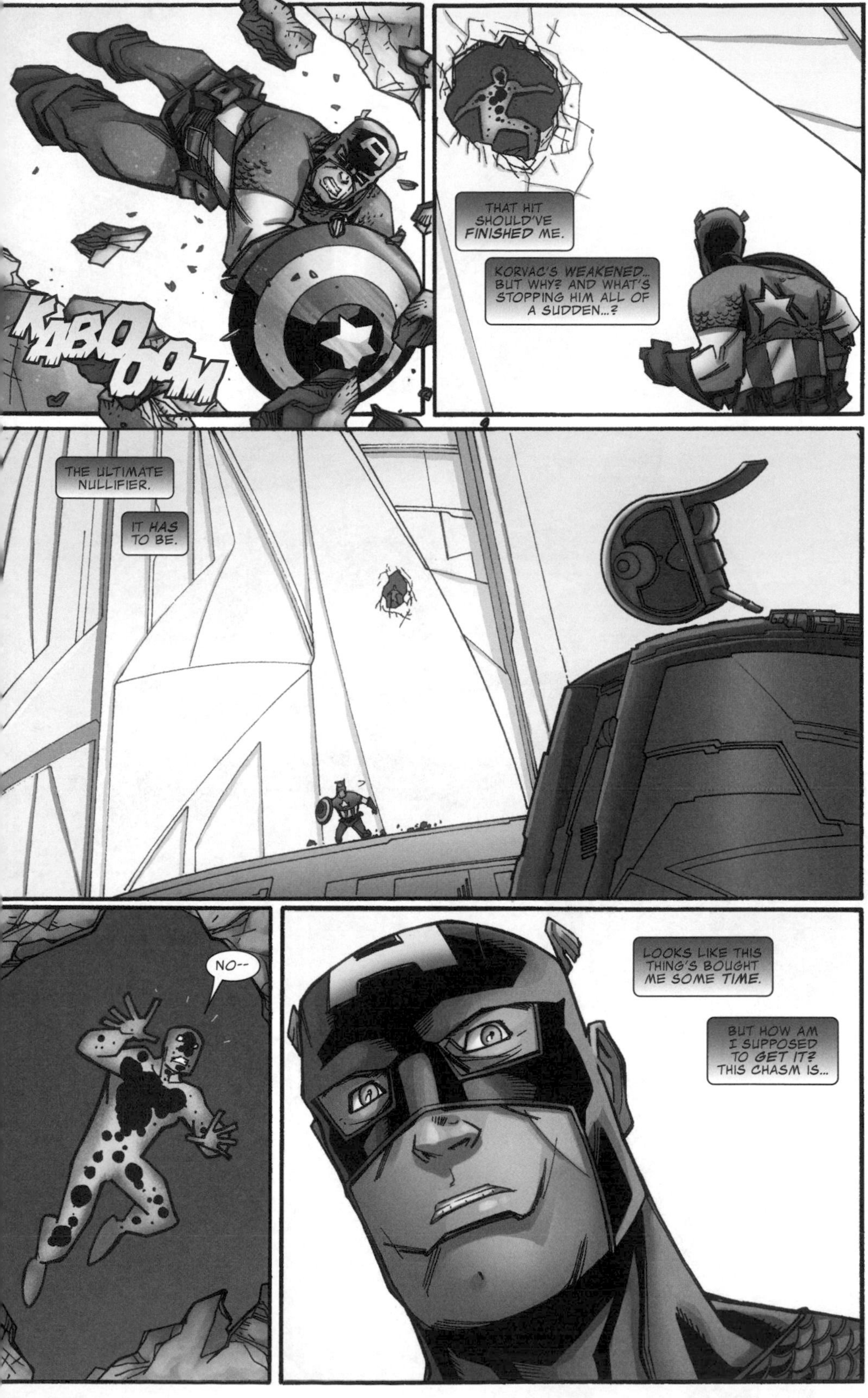
KABOOOM
THAT HIT SHOULD'VE FINISHED ME.
KORVAC'S WEAKENED... BUT WHY? AND WHAT'S STOPPING HIM ALL OF A SUDDEN...?
THE ULTIMATE NULLIFIER.
IT HAS TO BE.
NO--
LOOKS LIKE THIS THING'S BOUGHT ME SOME TIME.
BUT HOW AM I SUPPOSED TO GET IT? THIS CHASM IS...

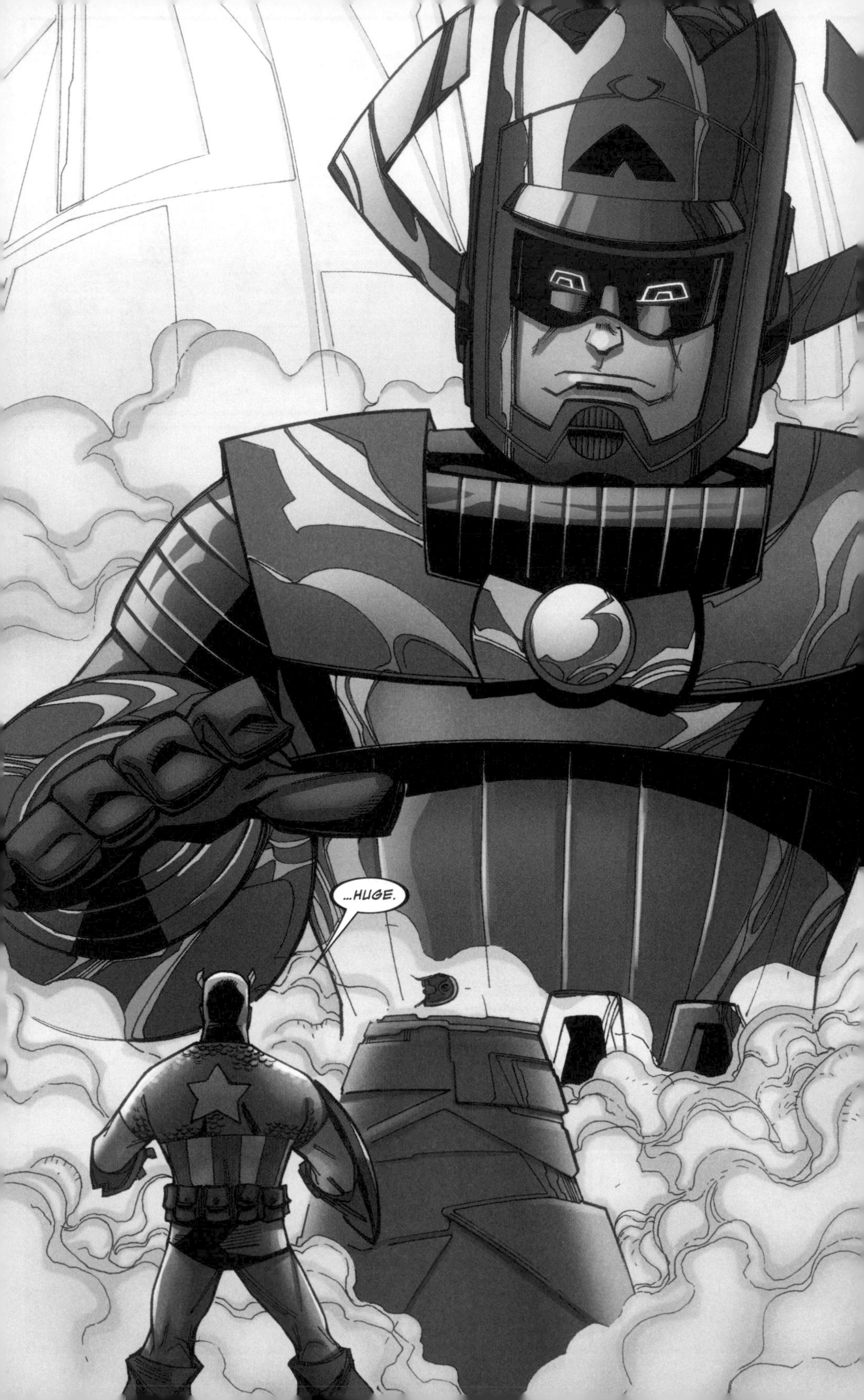
...HUGE.

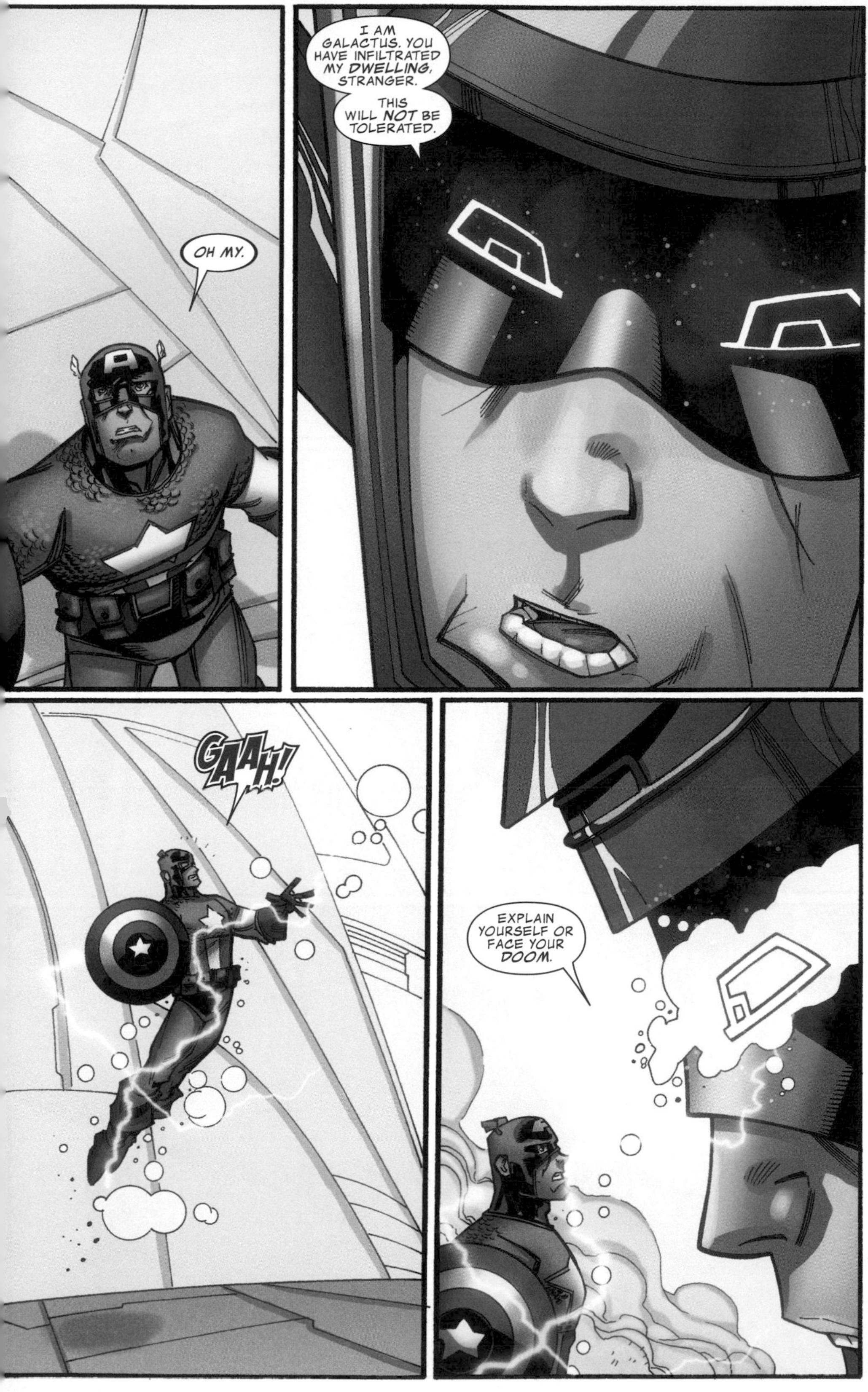
OH MY.
I AM GALACTUS. YOU HAVE INFILTRATED MY DWELLING, STRANGER.
THIS WILL NOT BE TOLERATED.
GAAH!
EXPLAIN YOURSELF OR FACE YOUR DOOM.

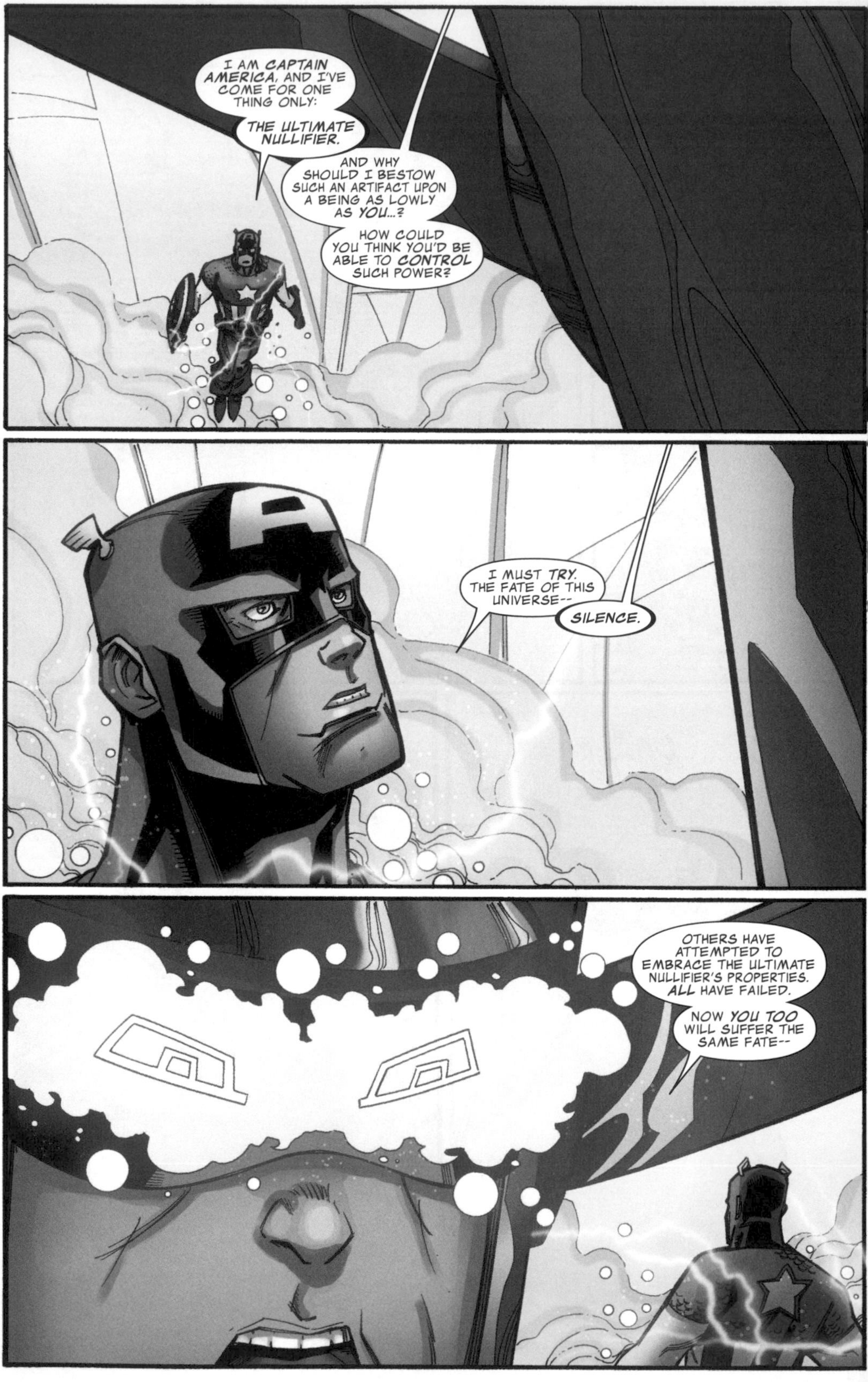
I AM CAPTAIN AMERICA, AND I'VE COME FOR ONE THING ONLY:
THE ULTIMATE NULLIFIER.
AND WHY SHOULD I BESTOW SUCH AN ARTIFACT UPON A BEING AS LOWLY AS YOU...?
HOW COULD YOU THINK YOU'D BE ABLE TO CONTROL SUCH POWER?
I MUST TRY. THE FATE OF THIS UNIVERSE--
SILENCE.
OTHERS HAVE ATTEMPTED TO EMBRACE THE ULTIMATE NULLIFIER'S PROPERTIES. ALL HAVE FAILED.
NOW YOU TOO WILL SUFFER THE SAME FATE--

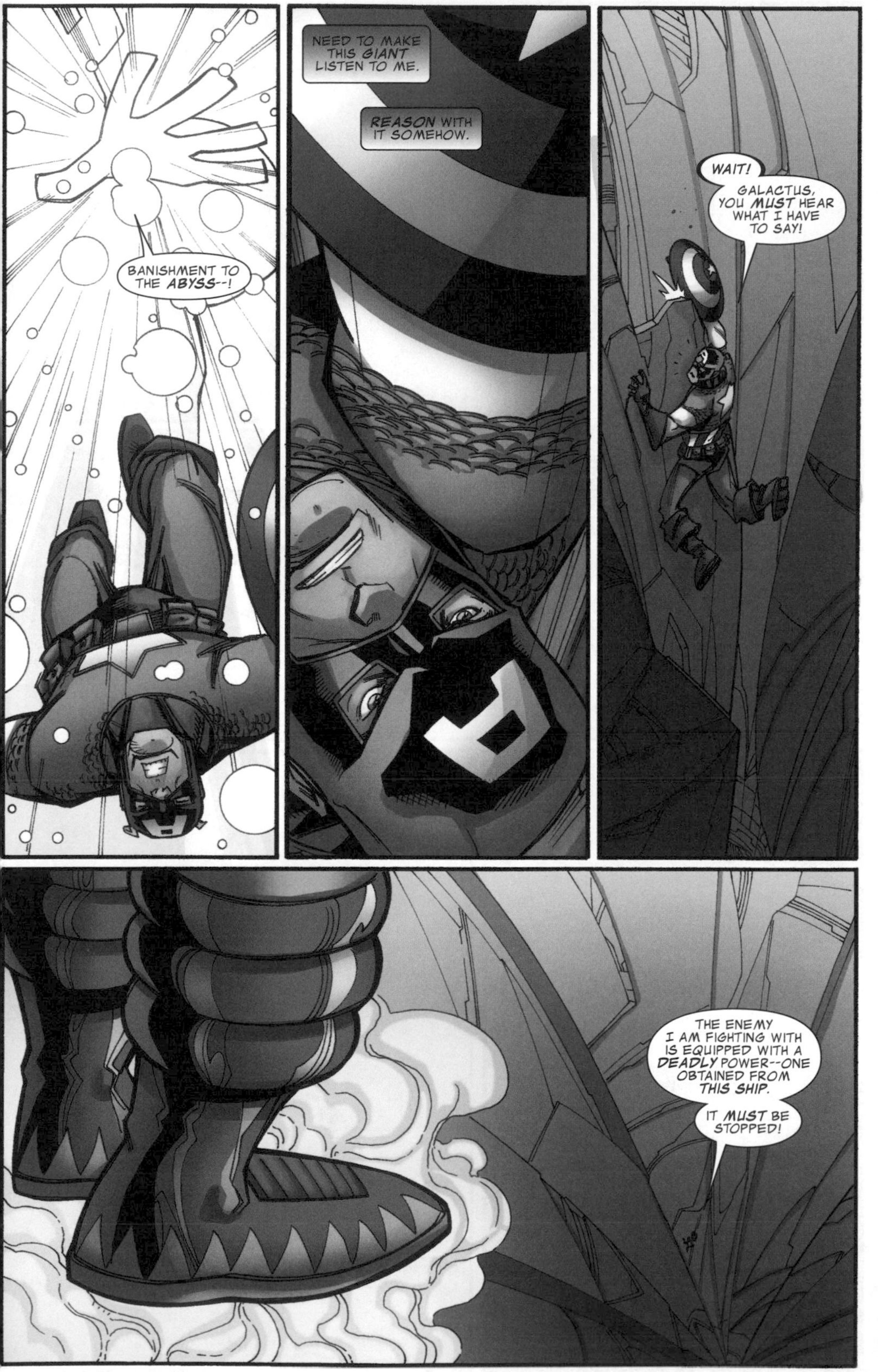
BANISHMENT TO THE ABYSS--!
NEED TO MAKE THIS GIANT LISTEN TO ME.
REASON WITH IT SOMEHOW.
WAIT!
GALACTUS, YOU MUST HEAR WHAT I HAVE TO SAY!
THE ENEMY I AM FIGHTING WITH IS EQUIPPED WITH A DEADLY POWER--ONE OBTAINED FROM THIS SHIP.
IT MUST BE STOPPED!

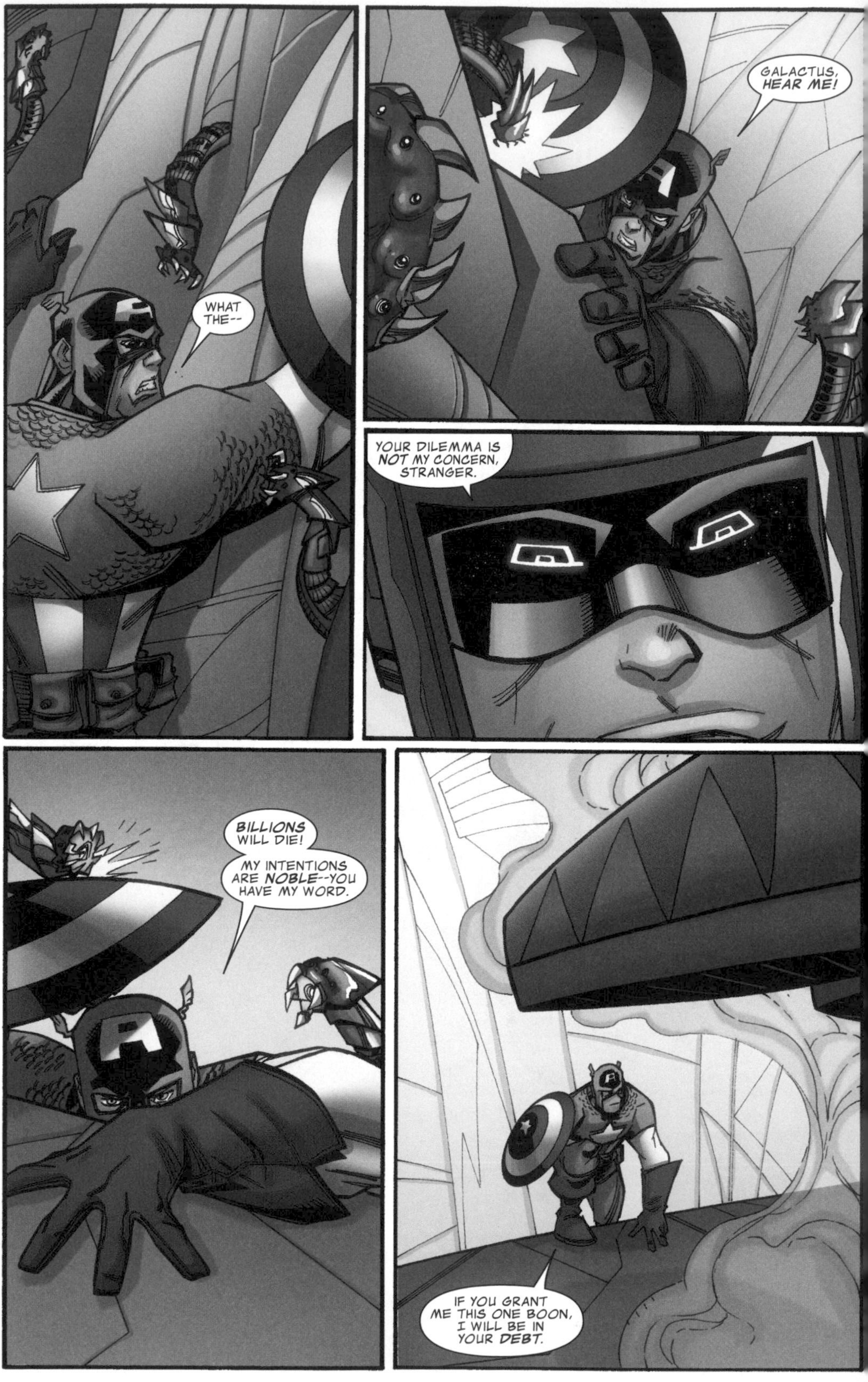
WHAT THE--
GALACTUS, HEAR ME!
YOUR DILEMMA IS NOT MY CONCERN, STRANGER.
BILLIONS WILL DIE!
MY INTENTIONS ARE NOBLE--YOU HAVE MY WORD.
IF YOU GRANT ME THIS ONE BOON, I WILL BE IN YOUR DEBT.

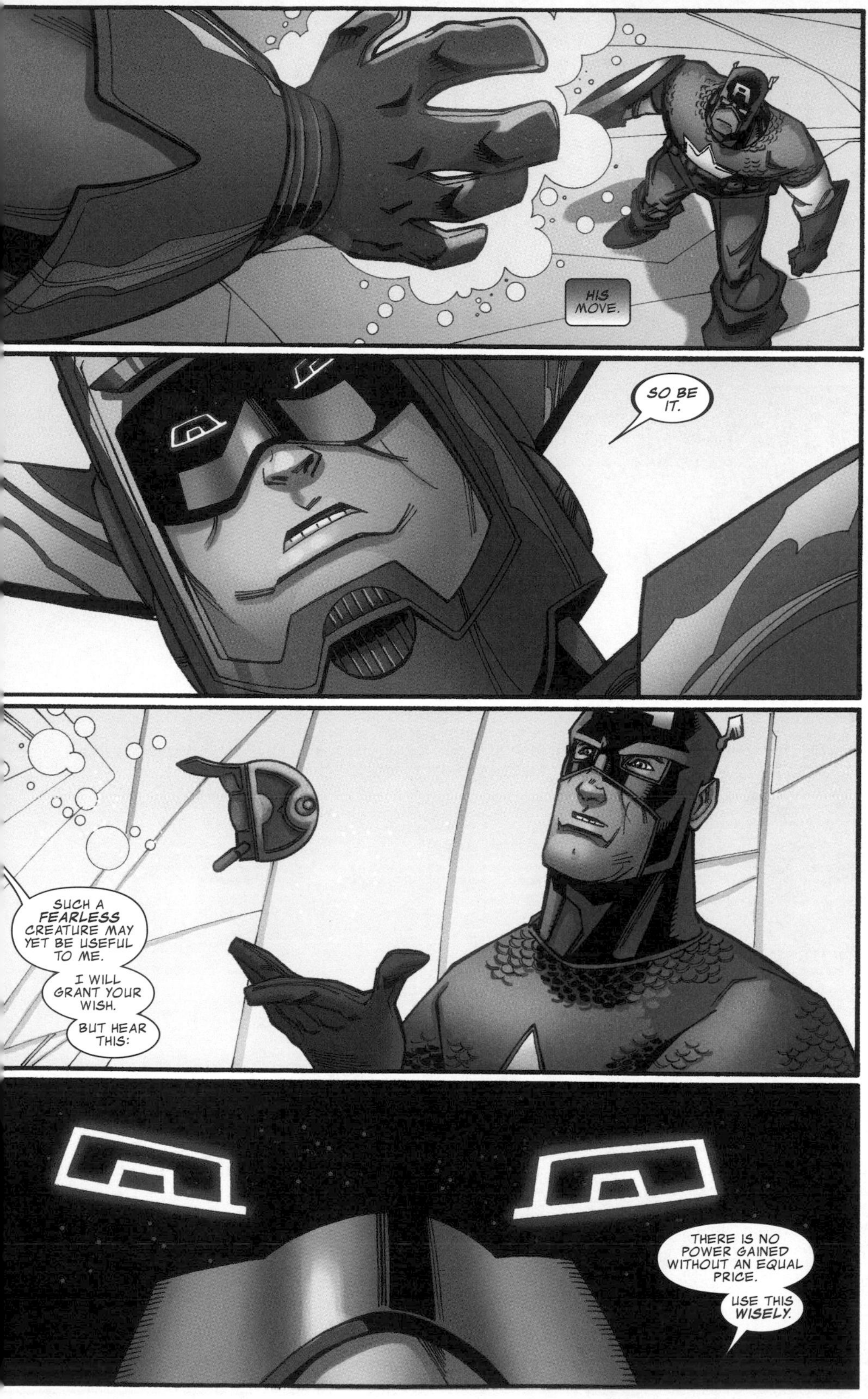
HIS MOVE.
SO BE IT.
SUCH A FEARLESS CREATURE MAY YET BE USEFUL TO ME.
I WILL GRANT YOUR WISH.
BUT HEAR THIS:
THERE IS NO POWER GAINED WITHOUT AN EQUAL PRICE.
USE THIS WISELY.

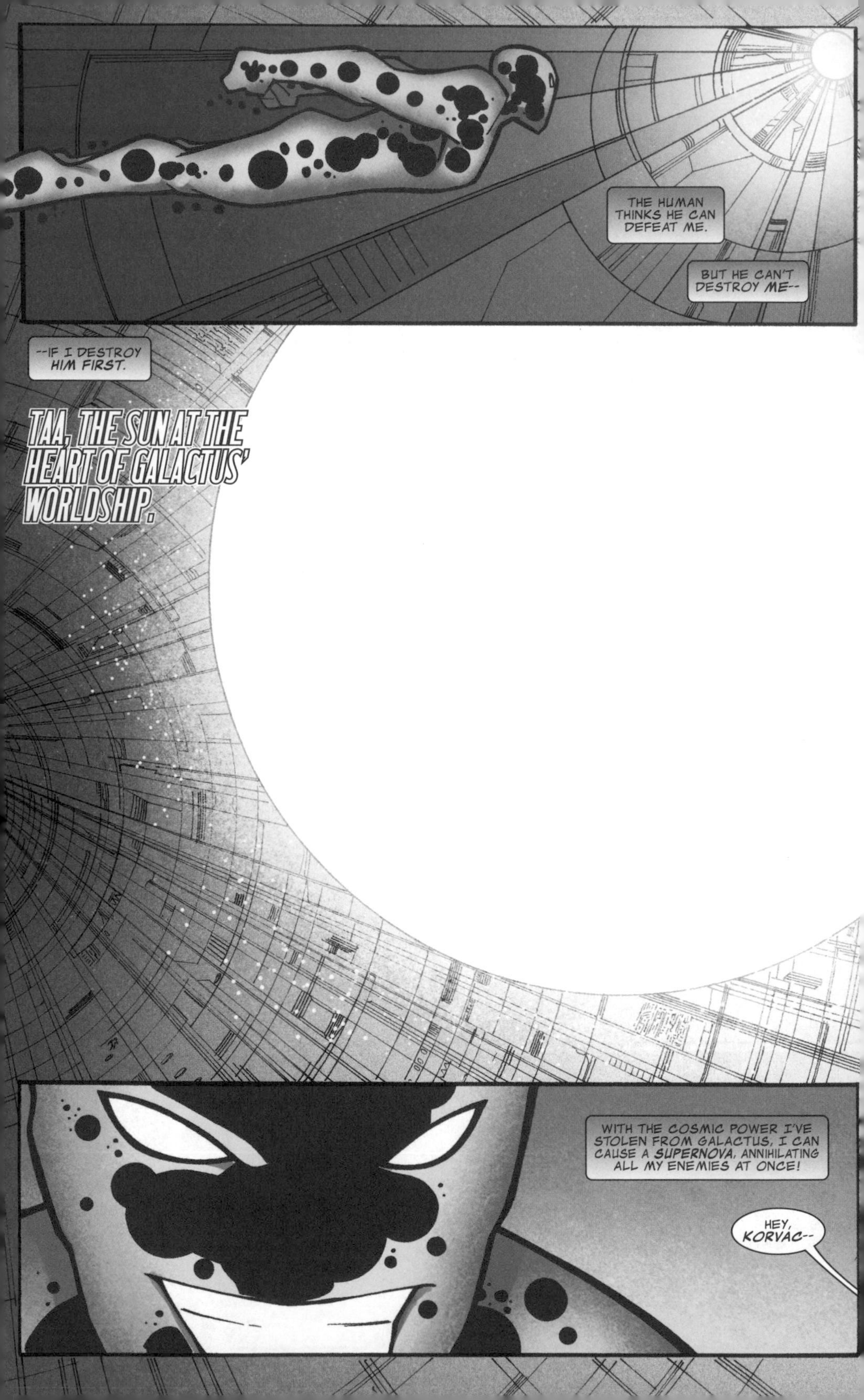
THE HUMAN THINKS HE CAN DEFEAT ME.
BUT HE CAN'T DESTROY ME--
--IF I DESTROY HIM FIRST.
TAA, THE SUN AT THE HEART OF GALACTUS' WORLDSHIP.
WITH THE COSMIC POWER I'VE STOLEN FROM GALACTUS, I CAN CAUSE A SUPERNOVA, ANNIHILATING ALL MY ENEMIES AT ONCE!
HEY, KORVAC--

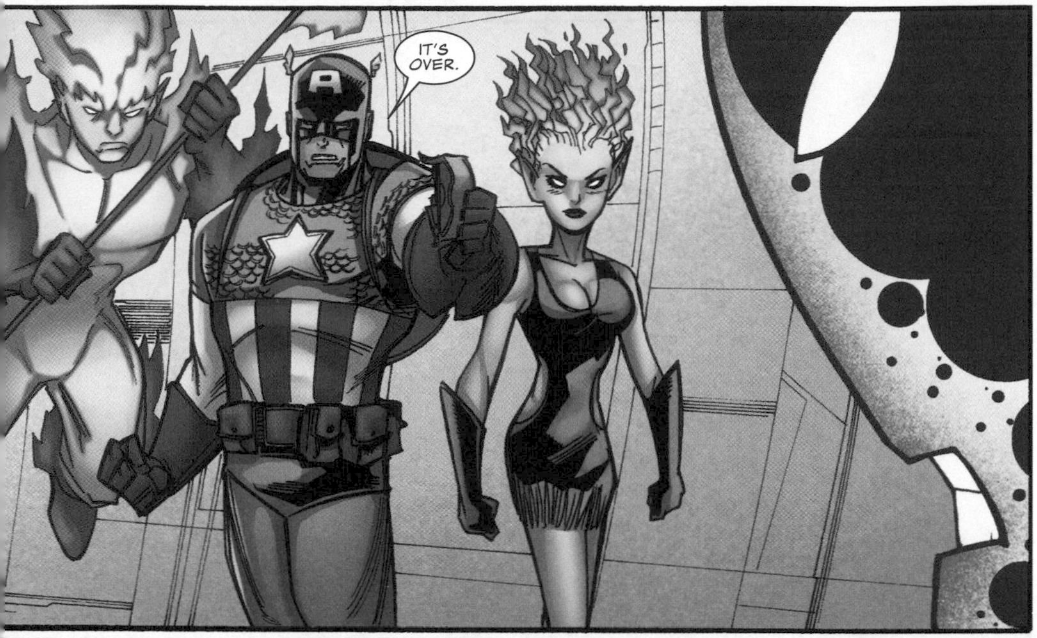
IT'S OVER.

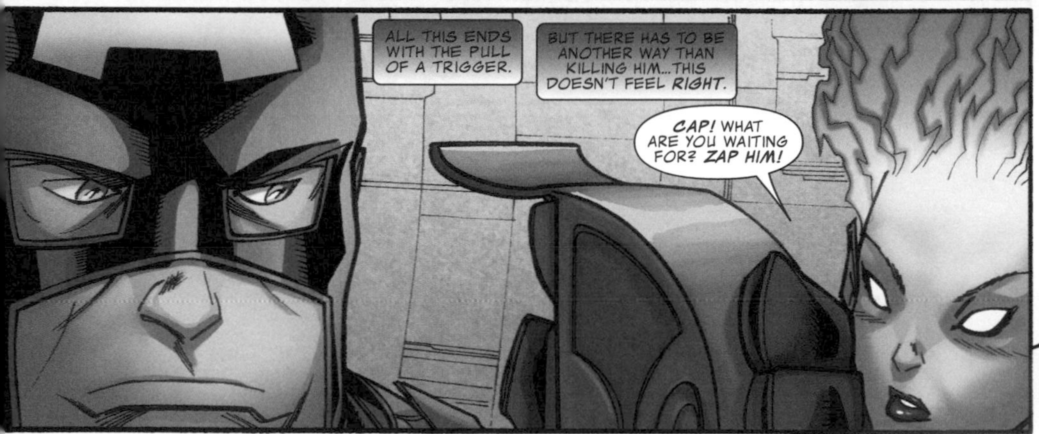
ALL THIS ENDS WITH THE PULL OF A TRIGGER.
BUT THERE HAS TO BE ANOTHER WAY THAN KILLING HIM...THIS DOESN'T FEEL RIGHT.
CAP! WHAT ARE YOU WAITING FOR? ZAP HIM!

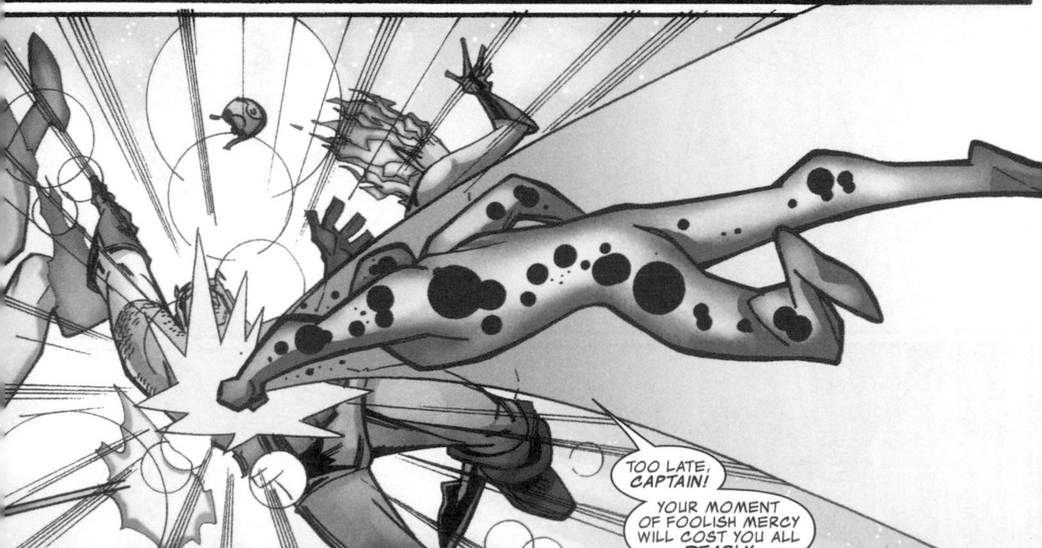
TOO LATE, CAPTAIN!
YOUR MOMENT OF FOOLISH MERCY WILL COST YOU ALL DEARLY.

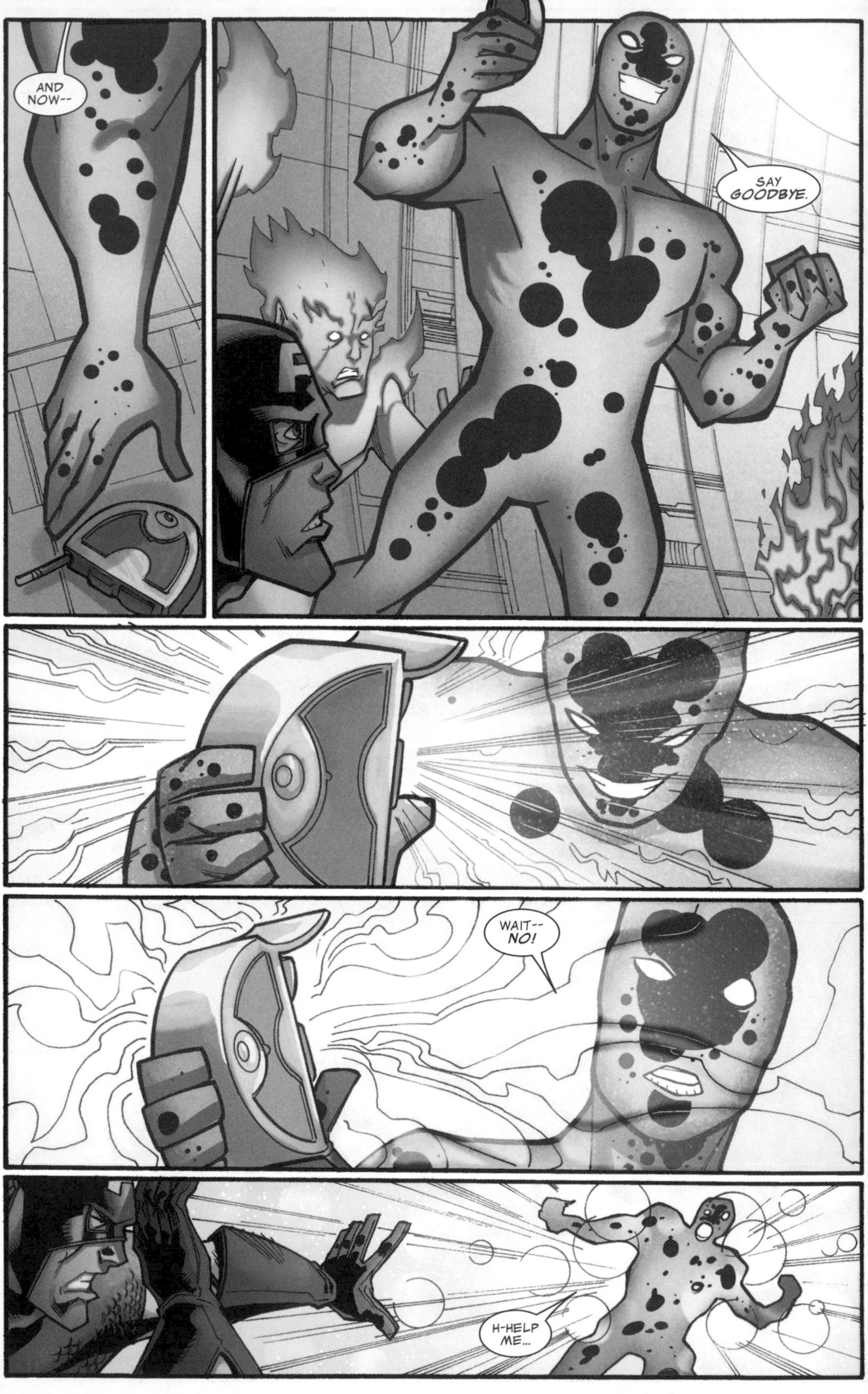
AND NOW--
SAY GOODBYE.
WAIT-- NO!
H-HELP ME...

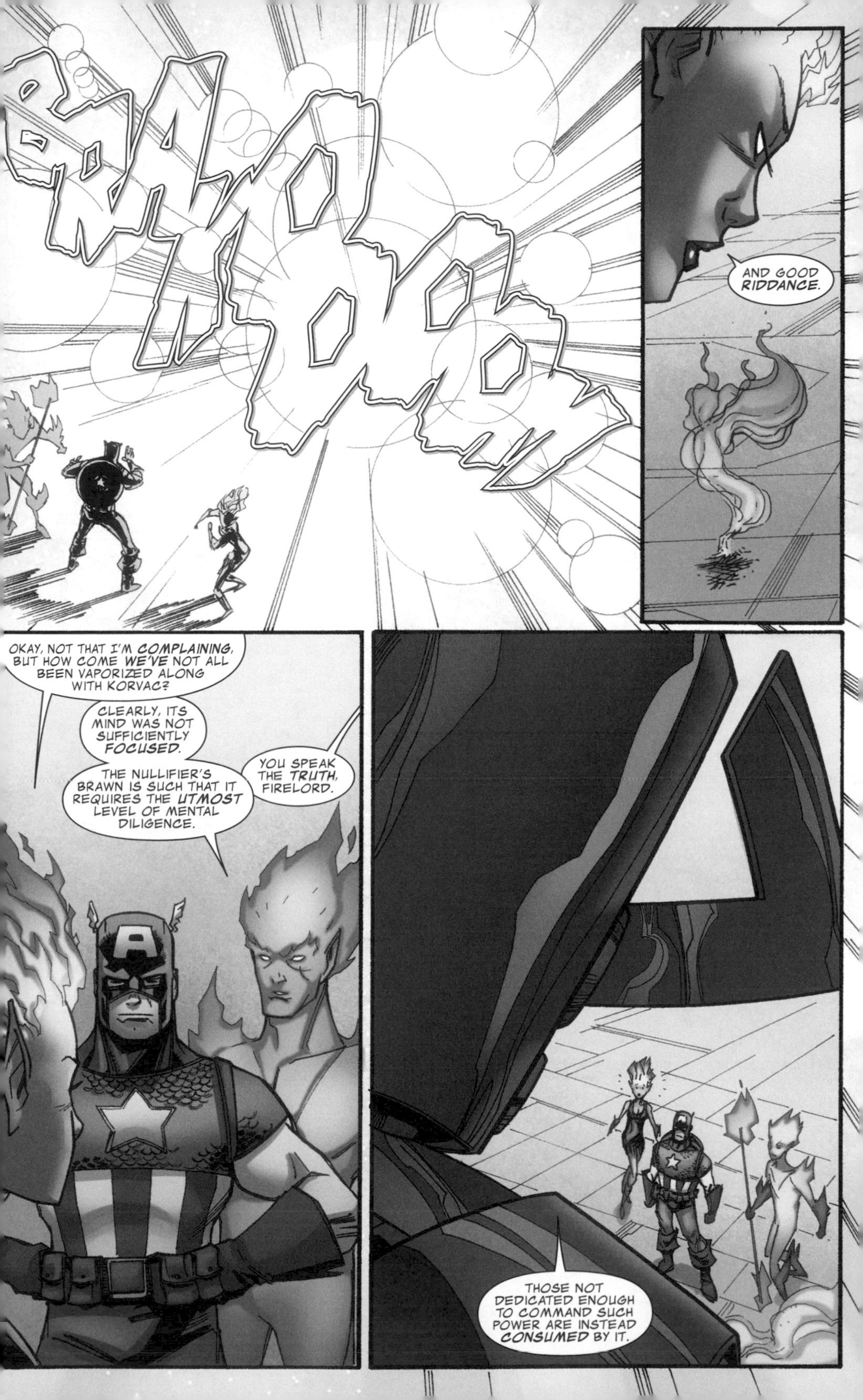
AND GOOD RIDDANCE.
OKAY, NOT THAT I'M COMPLAINING, BUT HOW COME WE'VE NOT ALL BEEN VAPORIZED ALONG WITH KORVAC?
CLEARLY, ITS MIND WAS NOT SUFFICIENTLY FOCUSED.
THE NULLIFIER'S BRAWN IS SUCH THAT IT REQUIRES THE UTMOST LEVEL OF MENTAL DILIGENCE.
YOU SPEAK THE TRUTH, FIRELORD.
THOSE NOT DEDICATED ENOUGH TO COMMAND SUCH POWER ARE INSTEAD CONSUMED BY IT.

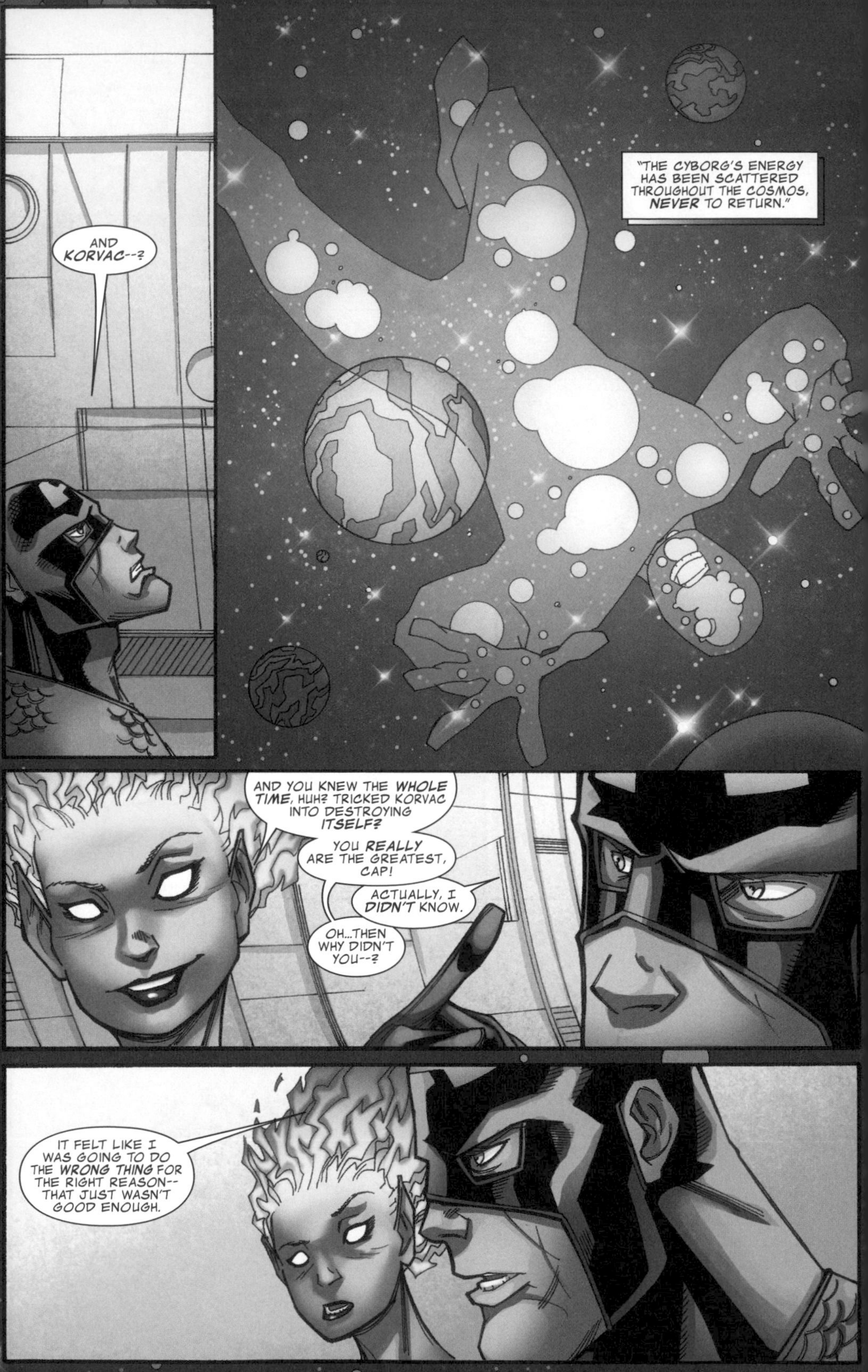
AND KORVAC--?
"THE CYBORG'S ENERGY HAS BEEN SCATTERED THROUGHOUT THE COSMOS, NEVER TO RETURN."
AND YOU KNEW THE WHOLE TIME, HUH? TRICKED KORVAC INTO DESTROYING ITSELF?
YOU REALLY ARE THE GREATEST, CAP!
ACTUALLY, I DIDN'T KNOW.
OH...THEN WHY DIDN'T YOU--?
IT FELT LIKE I WAS GOING TO DO THE WRONG THING FOR THE RIGHT REASON-- THAT JUST WASN'T GOOD ENOUGH.

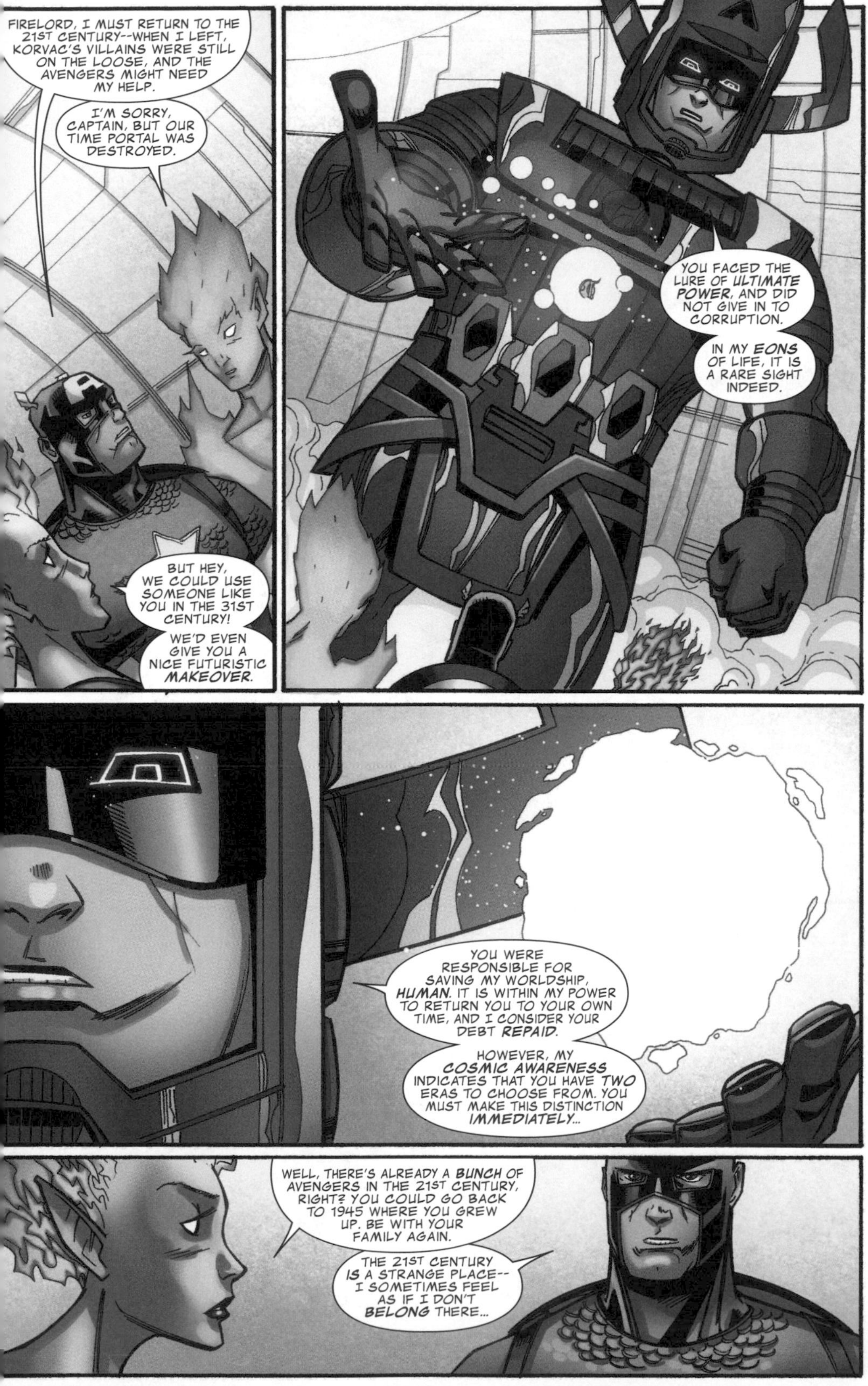
FIRELORD, I MUST RETURN TO THE 21ST CENTURY--WHEN I LEFT, KORVAC'S VILLAINS WERE STILL ON THE LOOSE, AND THE AVENGERS MIGHT NEED MY HELP.
I'M SORRY, CAPTAIN, BUT OUR TIME PORTAL WAS DESTROYED.
BUT HEY, WE COULD USE SOMEONE LIKE YOU IN THE 31ST CENTURY!
WE'D EVEN GIVE YOU A NICE FUTURISTIC MAKEOVER.
YOU FACED THE LURE OF ULTIMATE POWER, AND DID NOT GIVE IN TO CORRUPTION.
IN MY EONS OF LIFE, IT IS A RARE SIGHT INDEED.
YOU WERE RESPONSIBLE FOR SAVING MY WORLDSHIP, HUMAN. IT IS WITHIN MY POWER TO RETURN YOU TO YOUR OWN TIME, AND I CONSIDER YOUR DEBT REPAID.
HOWEVER, MY COSMIC AWARENESS INDICATES THAT YOU HAVE TWO ERAS TO CHOOSE FROM. YOU MUST MAKE THIS DISTINCTION IMMEDIATELY...
WELL, THERE'S ALREADY A BUNCH OF AVENGERS IN THE 21ST CENTURY, RIGHT? YOU COULD GO BACK TO 1945 WHERE YOU GREW UP. BE WITH YOUR FAMILY AGAIN.
THE 21ST CENTURY IS A STRANGE PLACE-- I SOMETIMES FEEL AS IF I DON'T BELONG THERE...

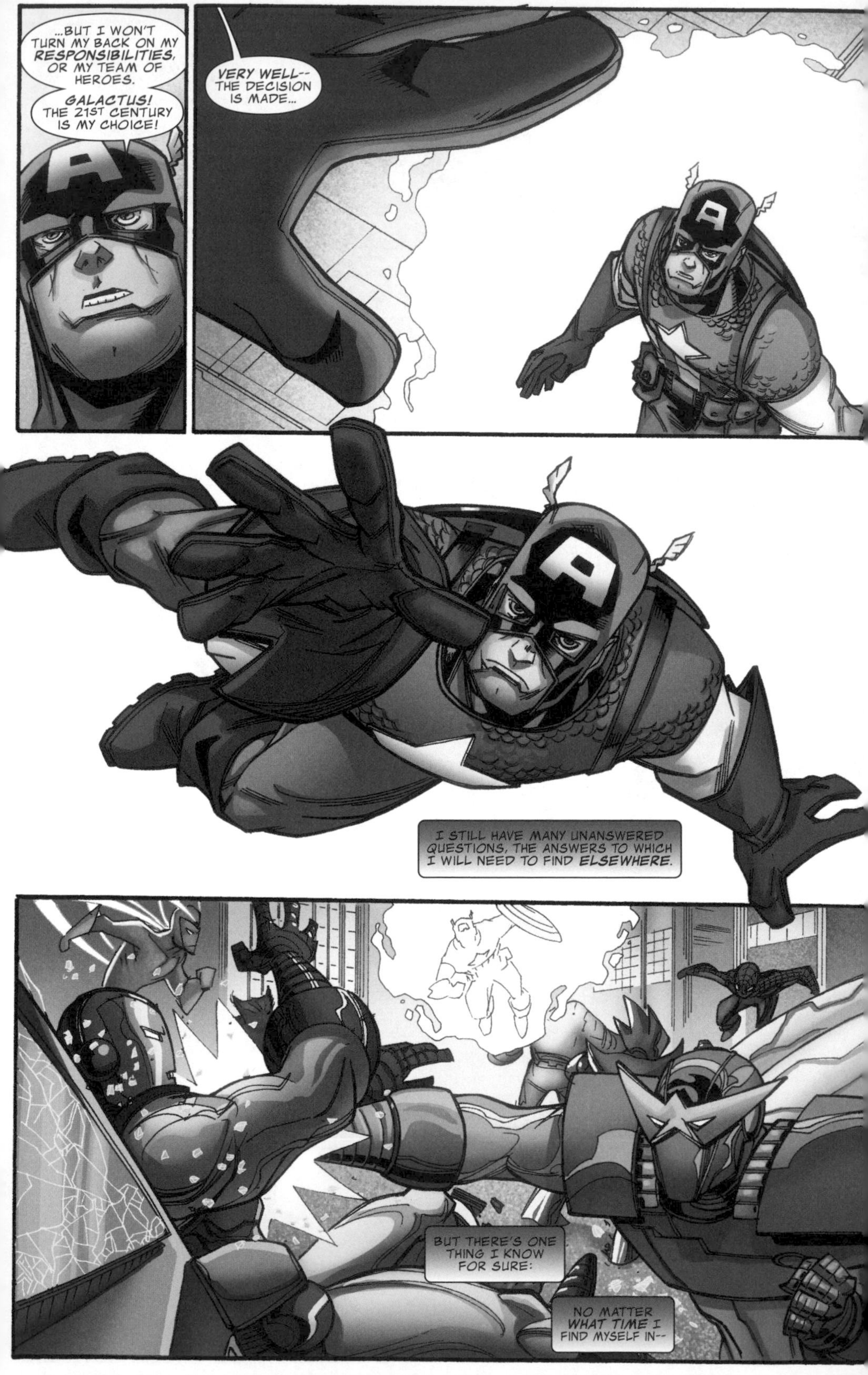
...BUT I WON'T TURN MY BACK ON MY RESPONSIBILITIES, OR MY TEAM OF HEROES.
GALACTUS! THE 21ST CENTURY IS MY CHOICE!
VERY WELL-- THE DECISION IS MADE...
I STILL HAVE MANY UNANSWERED QUESTIONS, THE ANSWERS TO WHICH I WILL NEED TO FIND ELSEWHERE.
BUT THERE'S ONE THING I KNOW FOR SURE:
NO MATTER WHAT TIME I FIND MYSELF IN--

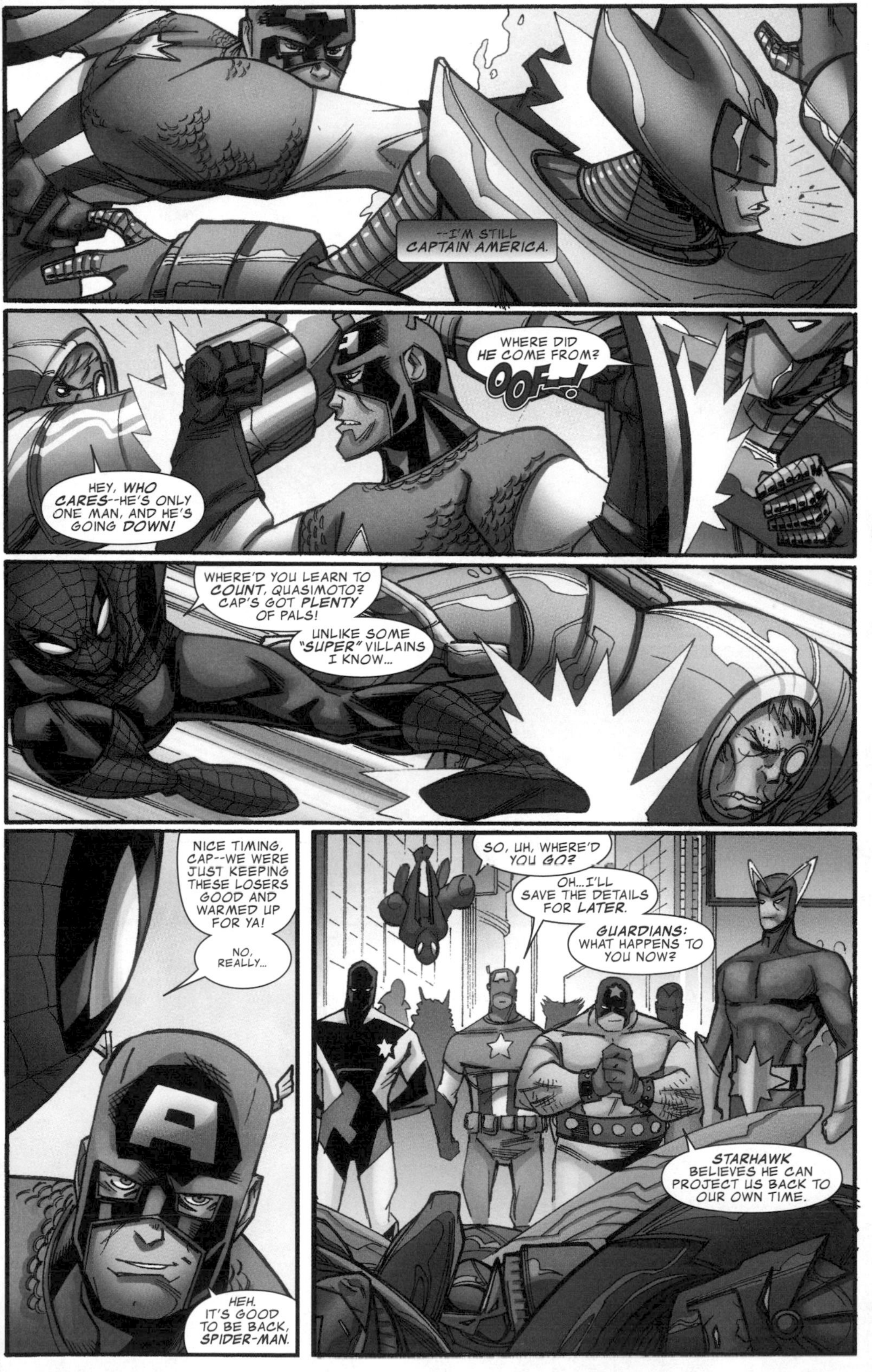
--I'M STILL CAPTAIN AMERICA.
WHERE DID HE COME FROM?
OOF--!
HEY, WHO CARES--HE'S ONLY ONE MAN, AND HE'S GOING DOWN!
WHERE'D YOU LEARN TO COUNT, QUASIMOTO? CAP'S GOT PLENTY OF PALS!
UNLIKE SOME "SUPER" VILLAINS I KNOW...
NICE TIMING, CAP--WE WERE JUST KEEPING THESE LOSERS GOOD AND WARMED UP FOR YA!
NO, REALLY...
HEH. IT'S GOOD TO BE BACK, SPIDER-MAN.
SO, UH, WHERE'D YOU GO?
OH...I'LL SAVE THE DETAILS FOR LATER.
GUARDIANS: WHAT HAPPENS TO YOU NOW?
STARHAWK BELIEVES HE CAN PROJECT US BACK TO OUR OWN TIME.

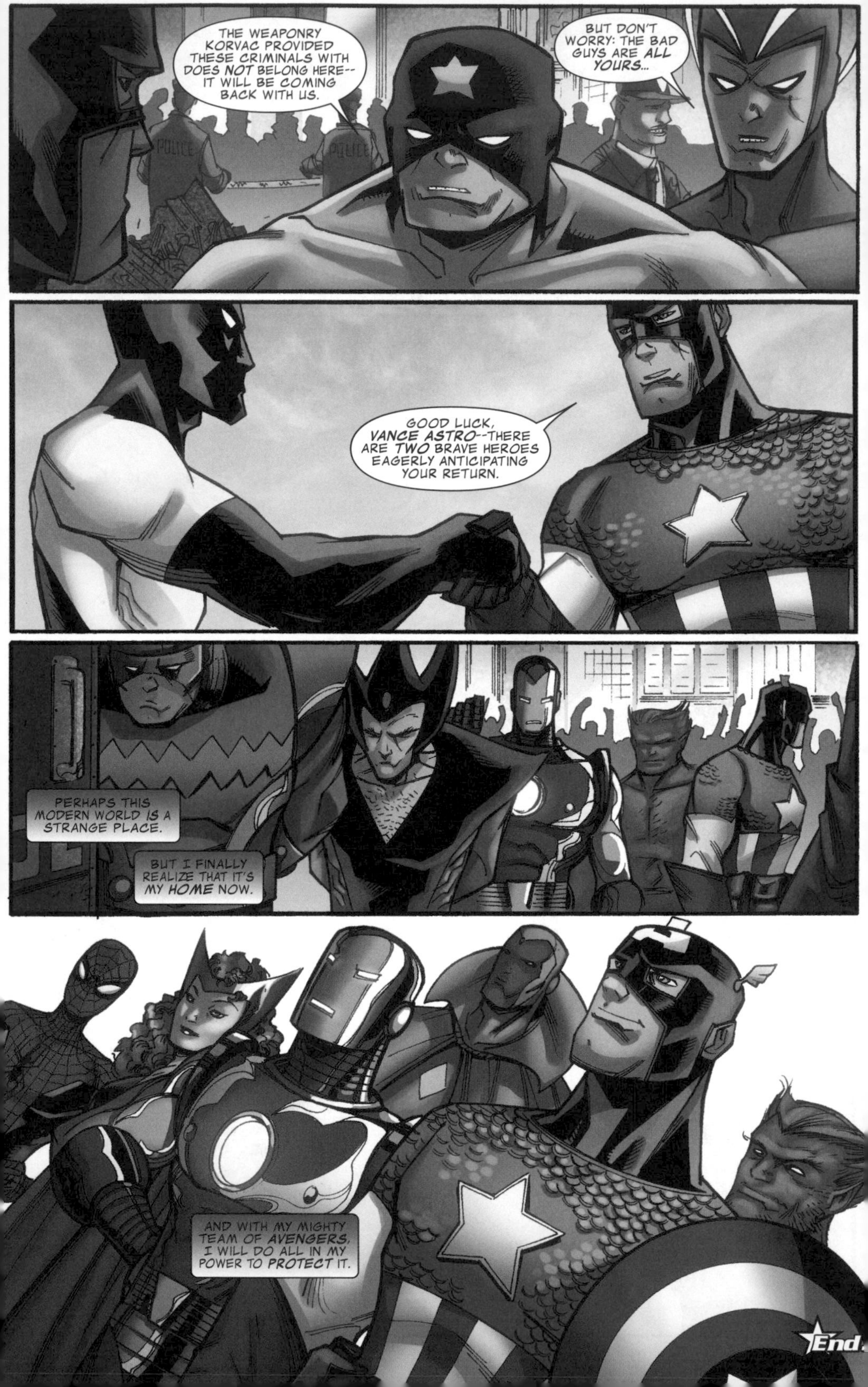
THE WEAPONRY KORVAC PROVIDED THESE CRIMINALS WITH DOES NOT BELONG HERE-- IT WILL BE COMING BACK WITH US.
BUT DON'T WORRY: THE BAD GUYS ARE ALL YOURS...
POLICE
POLICE
GOOD LUCK, VANCE ASTRO--THERE ARE TWO BRAVE HEROES EAGERLY ANTICIPATING YOUR RETURN.
PERHAPS THIS MODERN WORLD IS A STRANGE PLACE.
BUT I FINALLY REALIZE THAT IT'S MY HOME NOW.
AND WITH MY MIGHTY TEAM OF AVENGERS, I WILL DO ALL IN MY POWER TO PROTECT IT.
End.

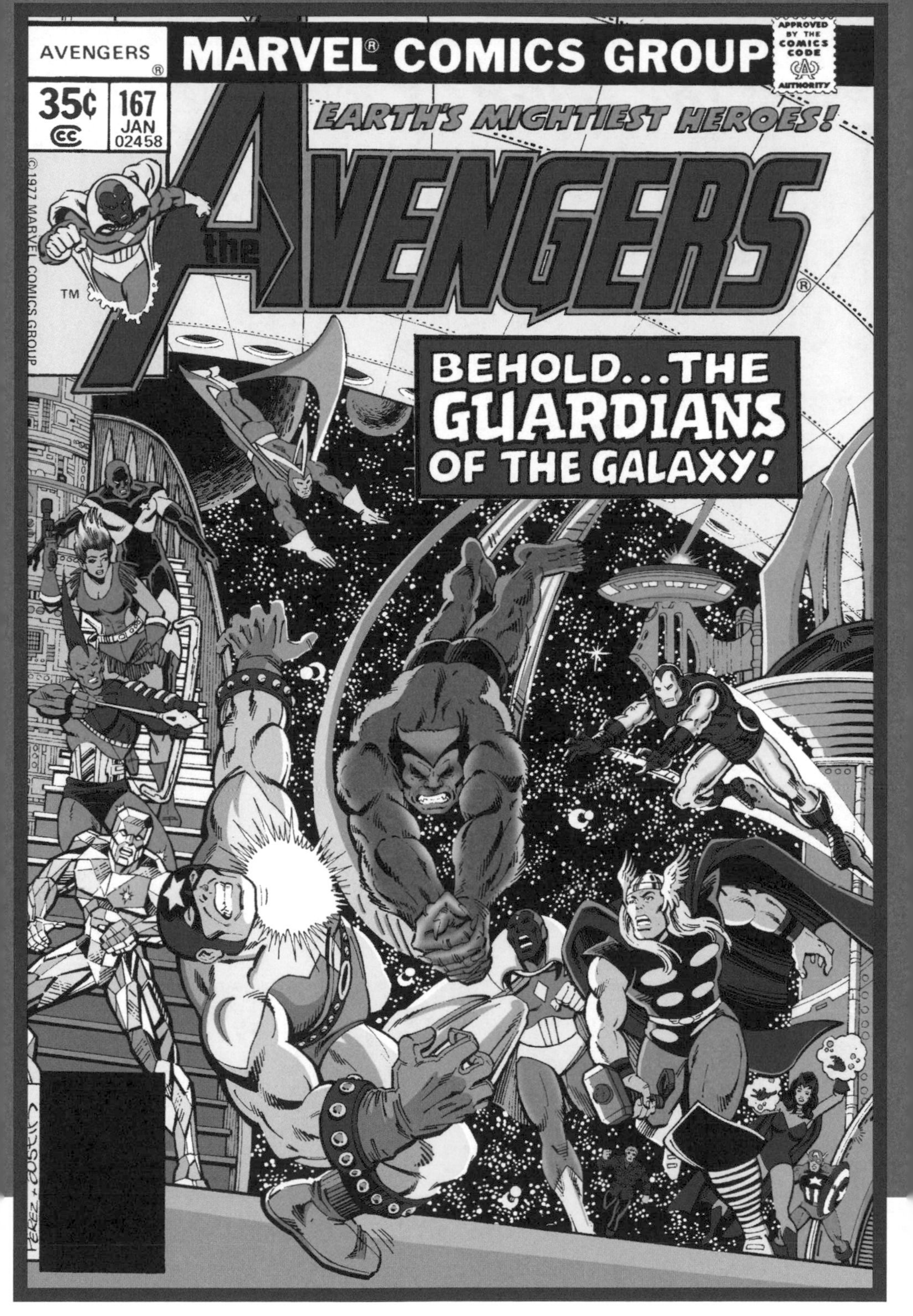
AVENGERS
MARVEL® COMICS GROUP
APPROVED BY THE COMICS CODE AUTHORITY
35¢
167
JAN
02458
© 1977 MARVEL COMICS GROUP
EARTH'S MIGHTIEST HEROES!
the AVENGERS®
TM
BEHOLD...THE
GUARDIANS
OF THE GALAXY!

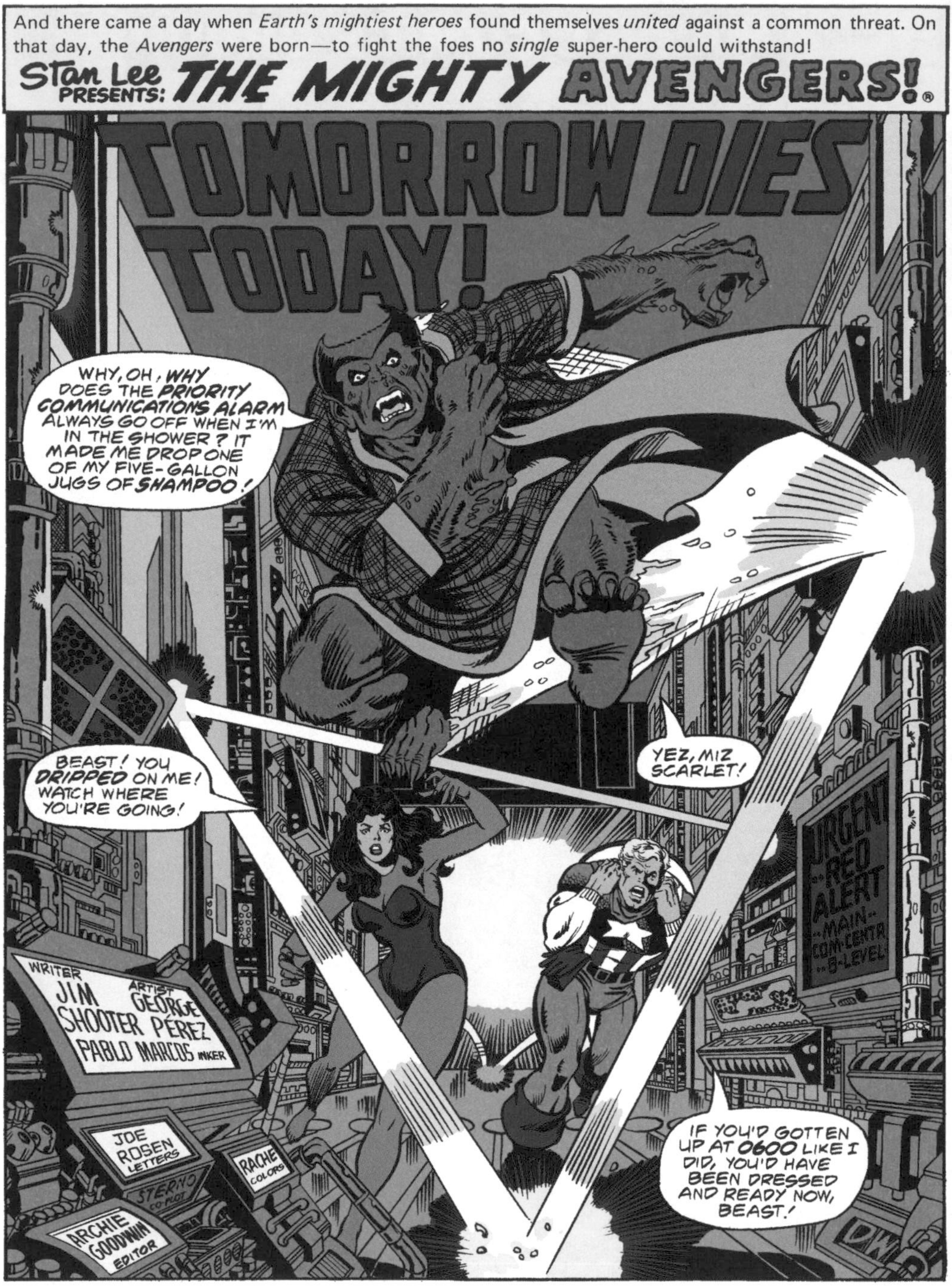
And there came a day when *Earth's mightiest heroes* found themselves *united* against a common threat. On that day, the *Avengers* were born—to fight the foes no *single* super-hero could withstand!
Stan Lee PRESENTS: THE MIGHTY AVENGERS!®
TOMORROW DIES TODAY!
WHY, OH, WHY DOES THE PRIORITY COMMUNICATIONS ALARM ALWAYS GO OFF WHEN I'M IN THE SHOWER? IT MADE ME DROP ONE OF MY FIVE-GALLON JUGS OF SHAMPOO!
BEAST! YOU DRIPPED ON ME! WATCH WHERE YOU'RE GOING!
YEZ, MIZ SCARLET!
IF YOU'D GOTTEN UP AT 0600 LIKE I DID, YOU'D HAVE BEEN DRESSED AND READY NOW, BEAST!
URGENT RED ALERT ..MAIN.. COM-CENTR ..B-LEVEL..
WRITER JIM SHOOTER
ARTIST GEORGE PÉREZ
PABLO MARCOS INKER
JOE ROSEN LETTERS
STERNO CO-PLOT
RACHE COLORS
ARCHIE GOODWIN EDITOR

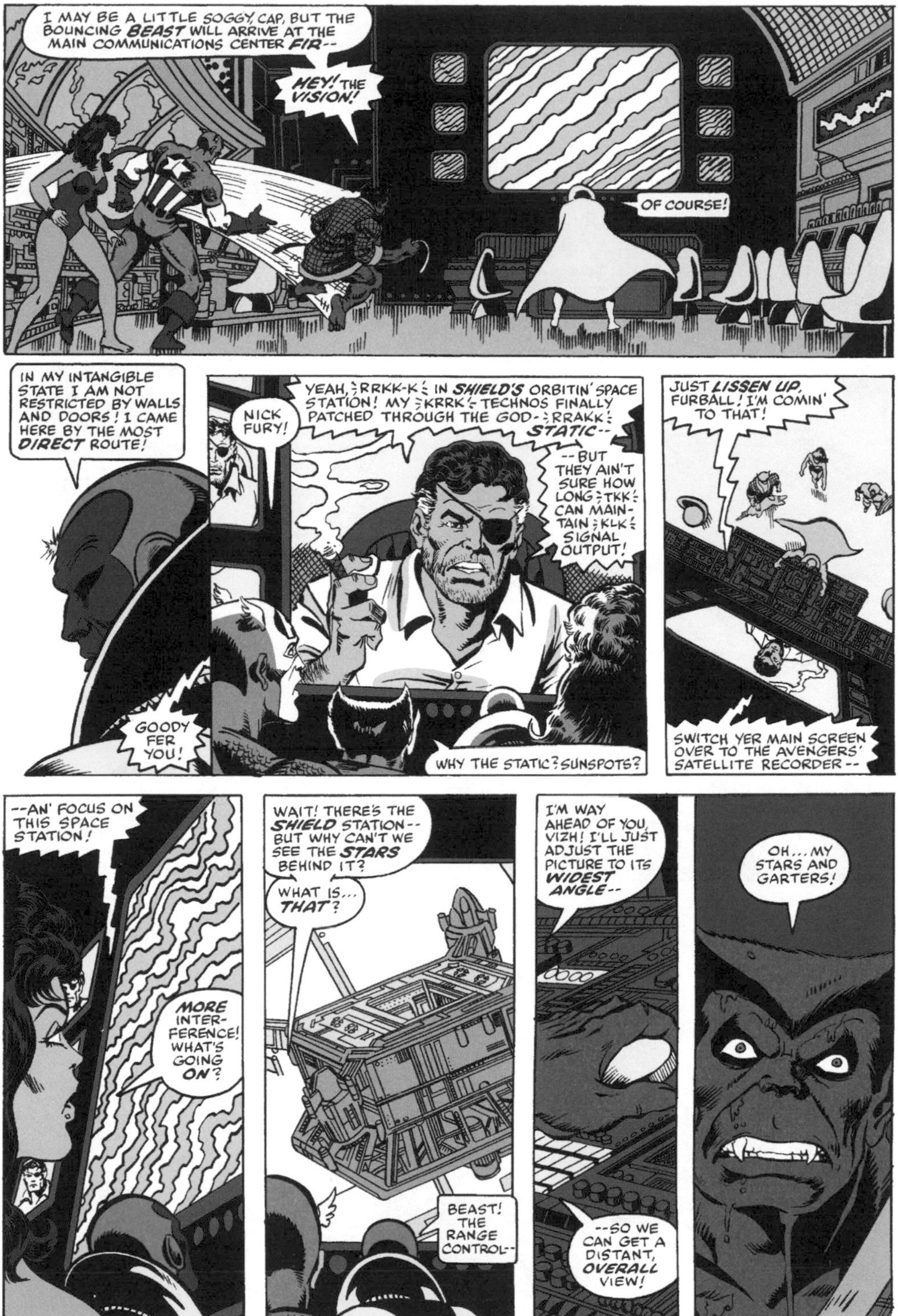
I MAY BE A LITTLE SOGGY, CAP, BUT THE BOUNCING BEAST WILL ARRIVE AT THE MAIN COMMUNICATIONS CENTER FIR--
HEY! THE VISION!
OF COURSE!
IN MY INTANGIBLE STATE I AM NOT RESTRICTED BY WALLS AND DOORS! I CAME HERE BY THE MOST DIRECT ROUTE!
GOODY FER YOU!
NICK FURY!
YEAH, RRKK-K IN SHIELD'S ORBITIN' SPACE STATION! MY KRRK TECHNOS FINALLY PATCHED THROUGH THE GOD- RRAKK STATIC--
--BUT THEY AIN'T SURE HOW LONG TKK CAN MAIN-TAIN KLK SIGNAL OUTPUT!
WHY THE STATIC? SUNSPOTS?
JUST LISSEN UP, FURBALL! I'M COMIN' TO THAT!
SWITCH YER MAIN SCREEN OVER TO THE AVENGERS' SATELLITE RECORDER--
--AN' FOCUS ON THIS SPACE STATION!
MORE INTER-FERENCE! WHAT'S GOING ON?
WAIT! THERE'S THE SHIELD STATION-- BUT WHY CAN'T WE SEE THE STARS BEHIND IT?
WHAT IS... THAT?
BEAST! THE RANGE CONTROL--
I'M WAY AHEAD OF YOU, VIZH! I'LL JUST ADJUST THE PICTURE TO ITS WIDEST ANGLE--
--SO WE CAN GET A DISTANT, OVERALL VIEW!
OH... MY STARS AND GARTERS!

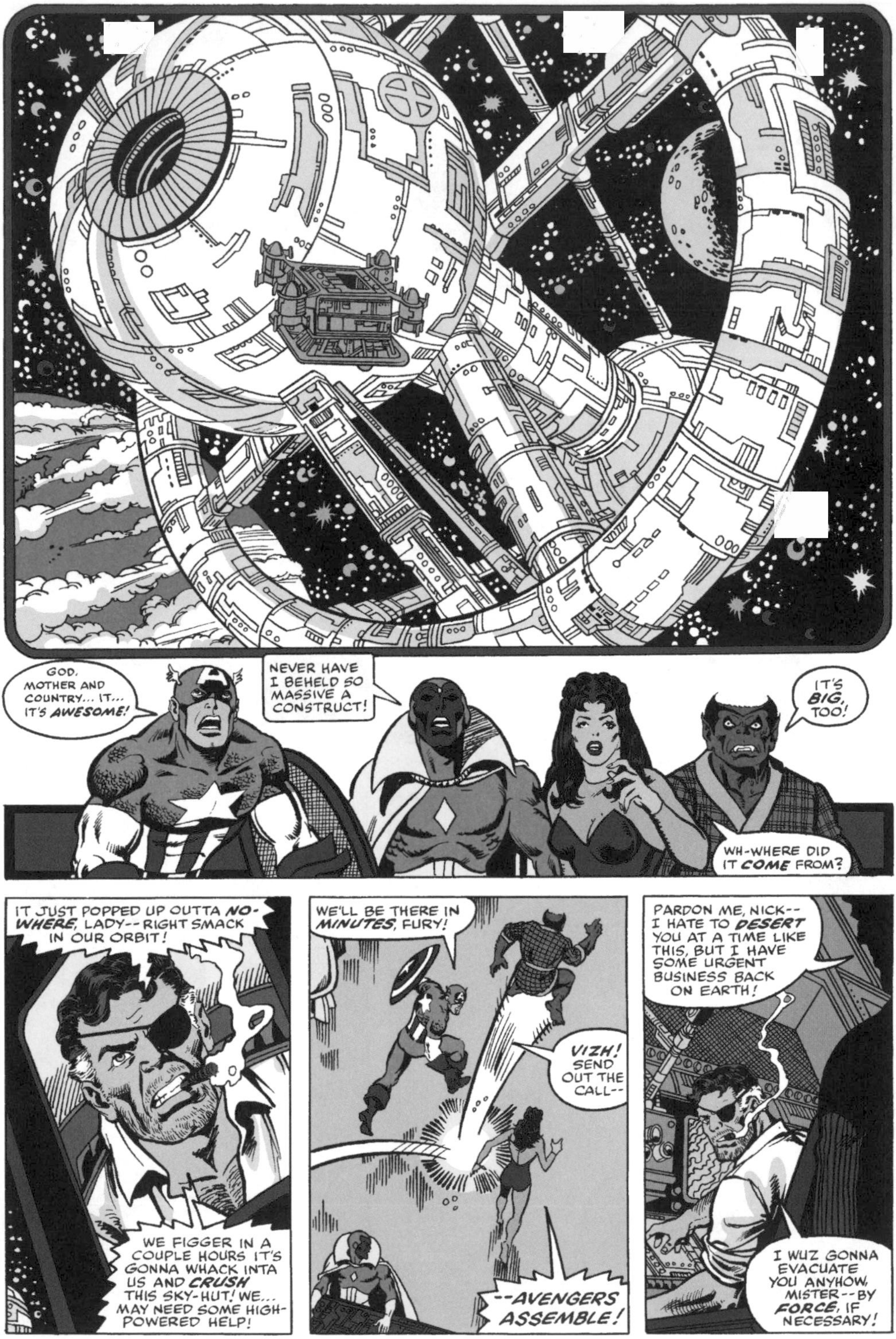
GOD, MOTHER AND COUNTRY... IT... IT'S AWESOME!
NEVER HAVE I BEHELD SO MASSIVE A CONSTRUCT!
IT'S BIG, TOO!
WH-WHERE DID IT COME FROM?
IT JUST POPPED UP OUTTA NO-WHERE, LADY-- RIGHT SMACK IN OUR ORBIT!
WE FIGGER IN A COUPLE HOURS IT'S GONNA WHACK INTA US AND CRUSH THIS SKY-HUT! WE... MAY NEED SOME HIGH-POWERED HELP!
WE'LL BE THERE IN MINUTES, FURY!
VIZH! SEND OUT THE CALL--
--AVENGERS ASSEMBLE!
PARDON ME, NICK-- I HATE TO DESERT YOU AT A TIME LIKE THIS, BUT I HAVE SOME URGENT BUSINESS BACK ON EARTH!
I WUZ GONNA EVACUATE YOU ANYHOW, MISTER--BY FORCE, IF NECESSARY!

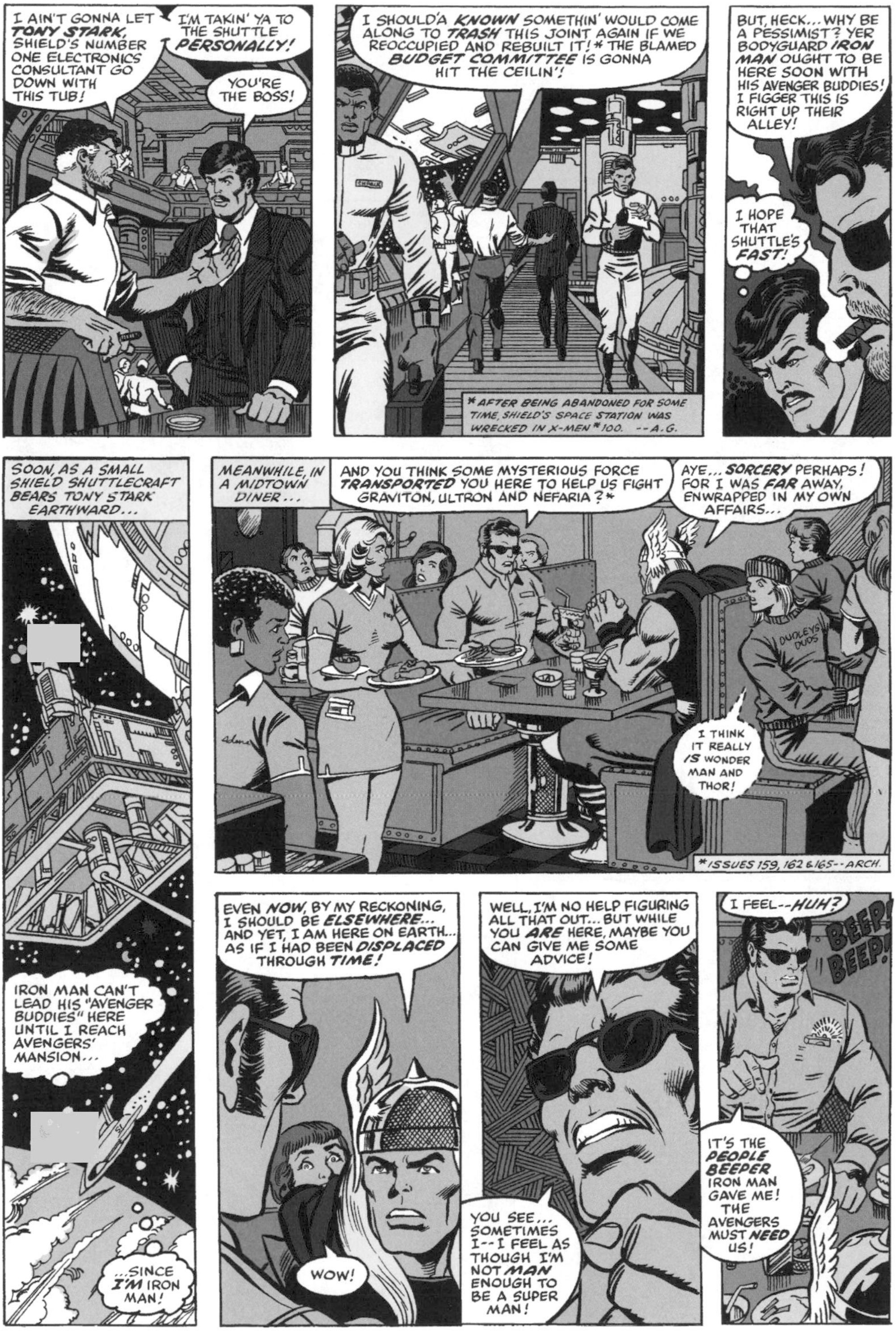
I AIN'T GONNA LET TONY STARK, SHIELD'S NUMBER ONE ELECTRONICS CONSULTANT GO DOWN WITH THIS TUB!
I'M TAKIN' YA TO THE SHUTTLE PERSONALLY!
YOU'RE THE BOSS!
I SHOULD'A KNOWN SOMETHIN' WOULD COME ALONG TO TRASH THIS JOINT AGAIN IF WE REOCCUPIED AND REBUILT IT!* THE BLAMED BUDGET COMMITTEE IS GONNA HIT THE CEILIN'!
*AFTER BEING ABANDONED FOR SOME TIME, SHIELD'S SPACE STATION WAS WRECKED IN X-MEN*100. --A.G.
BUT, HECK...WHY BE A PESSIMIST? YER BODYGUARD IRON MAN OUGHT TO BE HERE SOON WITH HIS AVENGER BUDDIES! I FIGGER THIS IS RIGHT UP THEIR ALLEY!
I HOPE THAT SHUTTLE'S FAST!
SOON, AS A SMALL SHIELD SHUTTLECRAFT BEARS TONY STARK EARTHWARD...
IRON MAN CAN'T LEAD HIS "AVENGER BUDDIES" HERE UNTIL I REACH AVENGERS' MANSION...
...SINCE I'M IRON MAN!
MEANWHILE, IN A MIDTOWN DINER...
AND YOU THINK SOME MYSTERIOUS FORCE TRANSPORTED YOU HERE TO HELP US FIGHT GRAVITON, ULTRON AND NEFARIA?*
AYE... SORCERY PERHAPS! FOR I WAS FAR AWAY, ENWRAPPED IN MY OWN AFFAIRS...
DUDLEY'S DUDS
I THINK IT REALLY IS WONDER MAN AND THOR!
*ISSUES 159, 162 & 165--ARCH.
EVEN NOW, BY MY RECKONING, I SHOULD BE ELSEWHERE... AND YET, I AM HERE ON EARTH... AS IF I HAD BEEN DISPLACED THROUGH TIME!
WOW!
WELL, I'M NO HELP FIGURING ALL THAT OUT... BUT WHILE YOU ARE HERE, MAYBE YOU CAN GIVE ME SOME ADVICE!
YOU SEE... SOMETIMES I--I FEEL AS THOUGH I'M NOT MAN ENOUGH TO BE A SUPER MAN!
I FEEL--HUH?
BEEP! BEEP!
IT'S THE PEOPLE BEEPER IRON MAN GAVE ME! THE AVENGERS MUST NEED US!

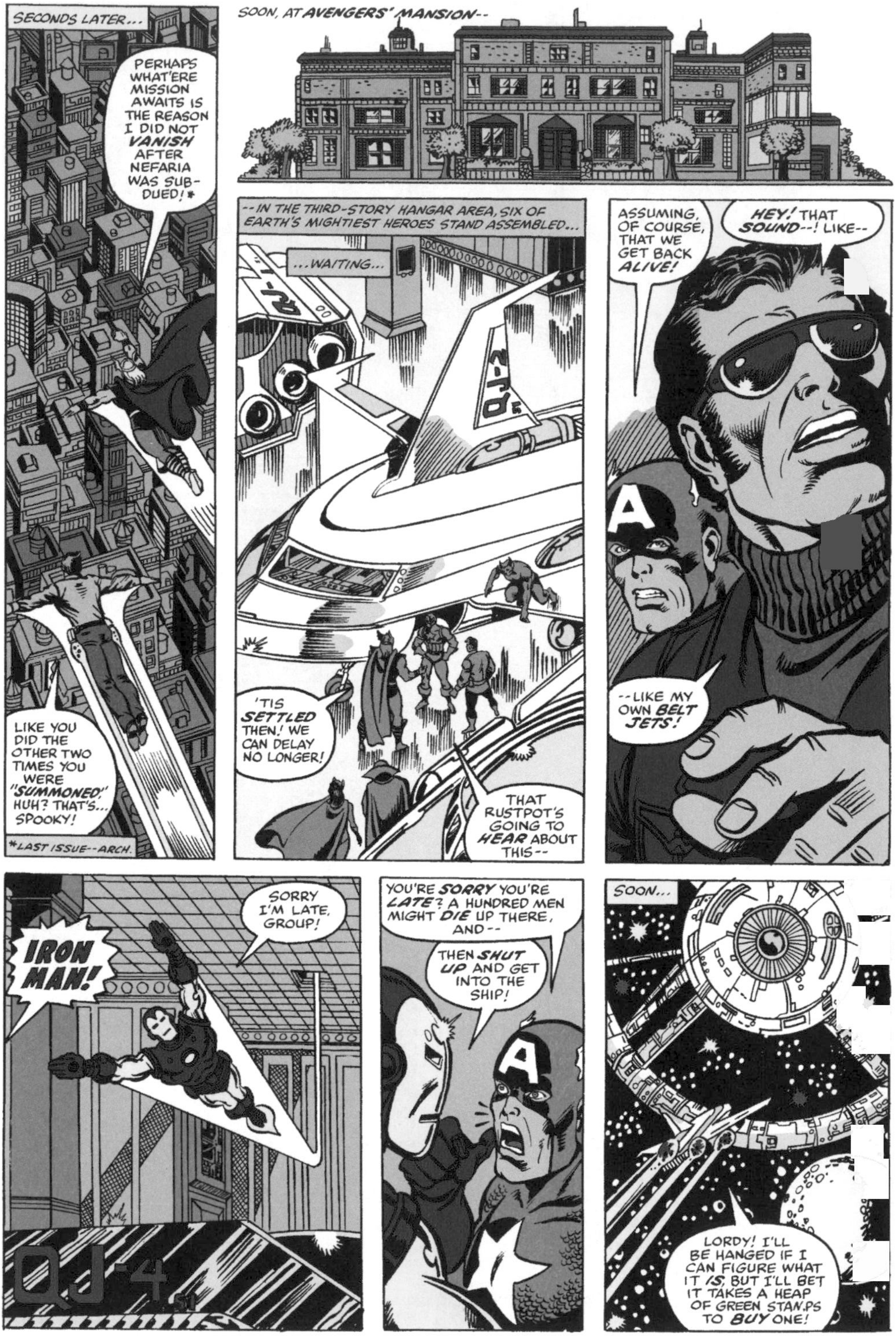
SECONDS LATER...
PERHAPS WHAT'ERE MISSION AWAITS IS THE REASON I DID NOT VANISH AFTER NEFARIA WAS SUBDUED! *
LIKE YOU DID THE OTHER TWO TIMES YOU WERE "SUMMONED," HUH? THAT'S... SPOOKY!
*LAST ISSUE--ARCH.
SOON, AT AVENGERS' MANSION--
--IN THE THIRD-STORY HANGAR AREA, SIX OF EARTH'S MIGHTIEST HEROES STAND ASSEMBLED...
...WAITING...
'TIS SETTLED THEN! WE CAN DELAY NO LONGER!
THAT RUSTPOT'S GOING TO HEAR ABOUT THIS--
ASSUMING, OF COURSE, THAT WE GET BACK ALIVE!
HEY! THAT SOUND--! LIKE--
--LIKE MY OWN BELT JETS!
IRON MAN!
SORRY I'M LATE, GROUP!
QJ-4
YOU'RE SORRY YOU'RE LATE? A HUNDRED MEN MIGHT DIE UP THERE, AND--
THEN SHUT UP AND GET INTO THE SHIP!
SOON...
LORDY! I'LL BE HANGED IF I CAN FIGURE WHAT IT IS, BUT I'LL BET IT TAKES A HEAP OF GREEN STAN.PS TO BUY ONE!

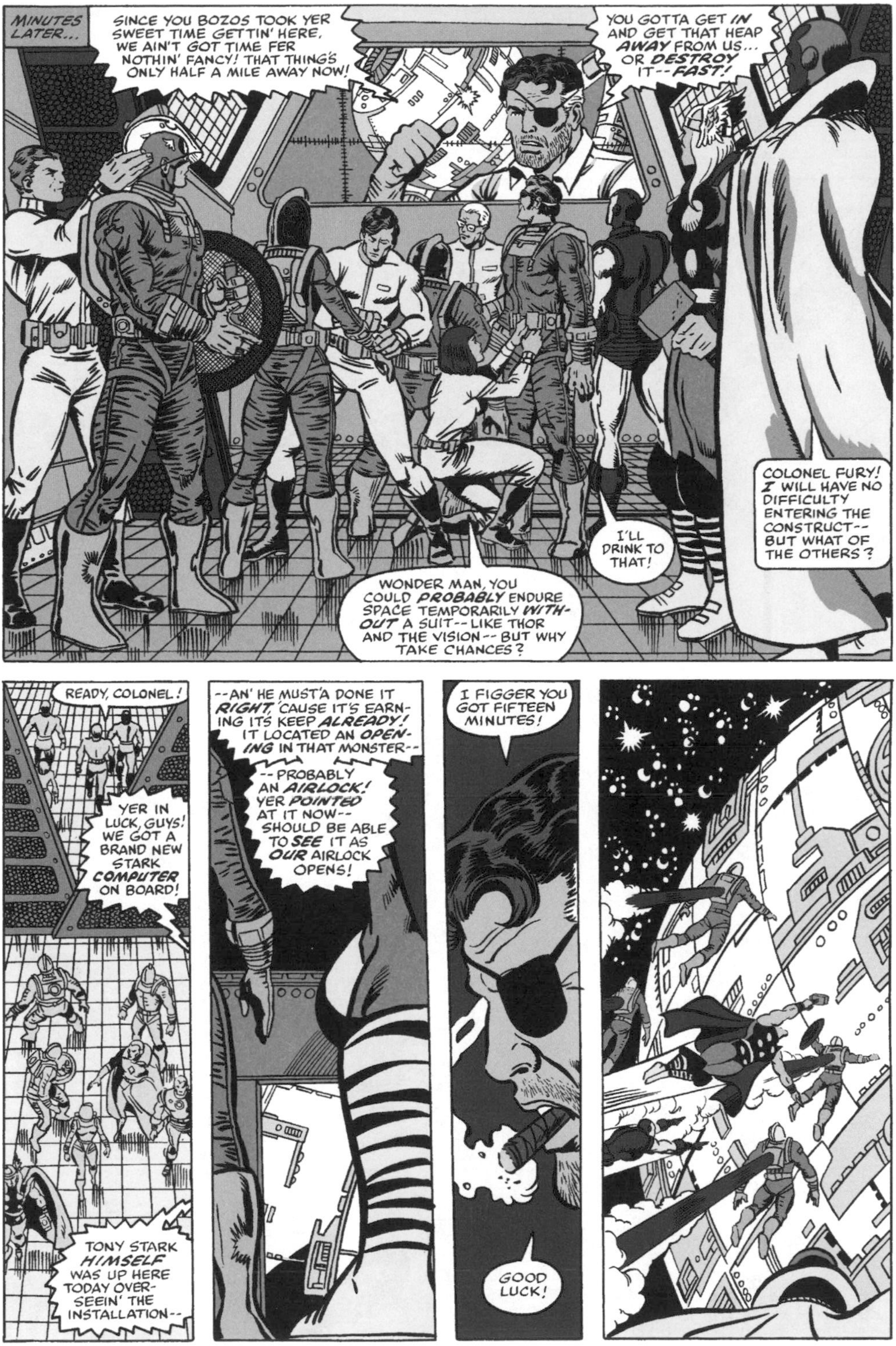
MINUTES LATER...
SINCE YOU BOZOS TOOK YER SWEET TIME GETTIN' HERE, WE AIN'T GOT TIME FER NOTHIN' FANCY! THAT THING'S ONLY HALF A MILE AWAY NOW!
YOU GOTTA GET IN AND GET THAT HEAP AWAY FROM US... OR DESTROY IT--FAST!
COLONEL FURY! I WILL HAVE NO DIFFICULTY ENTERING THE CONSTRUCT--BUT WHAT OF THE OTHERS?
I'LL DRINK TO THAT!
WONDER MAN, YOU COULD PROBABLY ENDURE SPACE TEMPORARILY WITHOUT A SUIT--LIKE THOR AND THE VISION--BUT WHY TAKE CHANCES?
READY, COLONEL!
YER IN LUCK, GUYS! WE GOT A BRAND NEW STARK COMPUTER ON BOARD!
TONY STARK HIMSELF WAS UP HERE TODAY OVER-SEEIN' THE INSTALLATION--
--AN' HE MUST'A DONE IT RIGHT, 'CAUSE IT'S EARNING ITS KEEP ALREADY! IT LOCATED AN OPENING IN THAT MONSTER--
--PROBABLY AN AIRLOCK! YER POINTED AT IT NOW--SHOULD BE ABLE TO SEE IT AS OUR AIRLOCK OPENS!
I FIGGER YOU GOT FIFTEEN MINUTES!
GOOD LUCK!

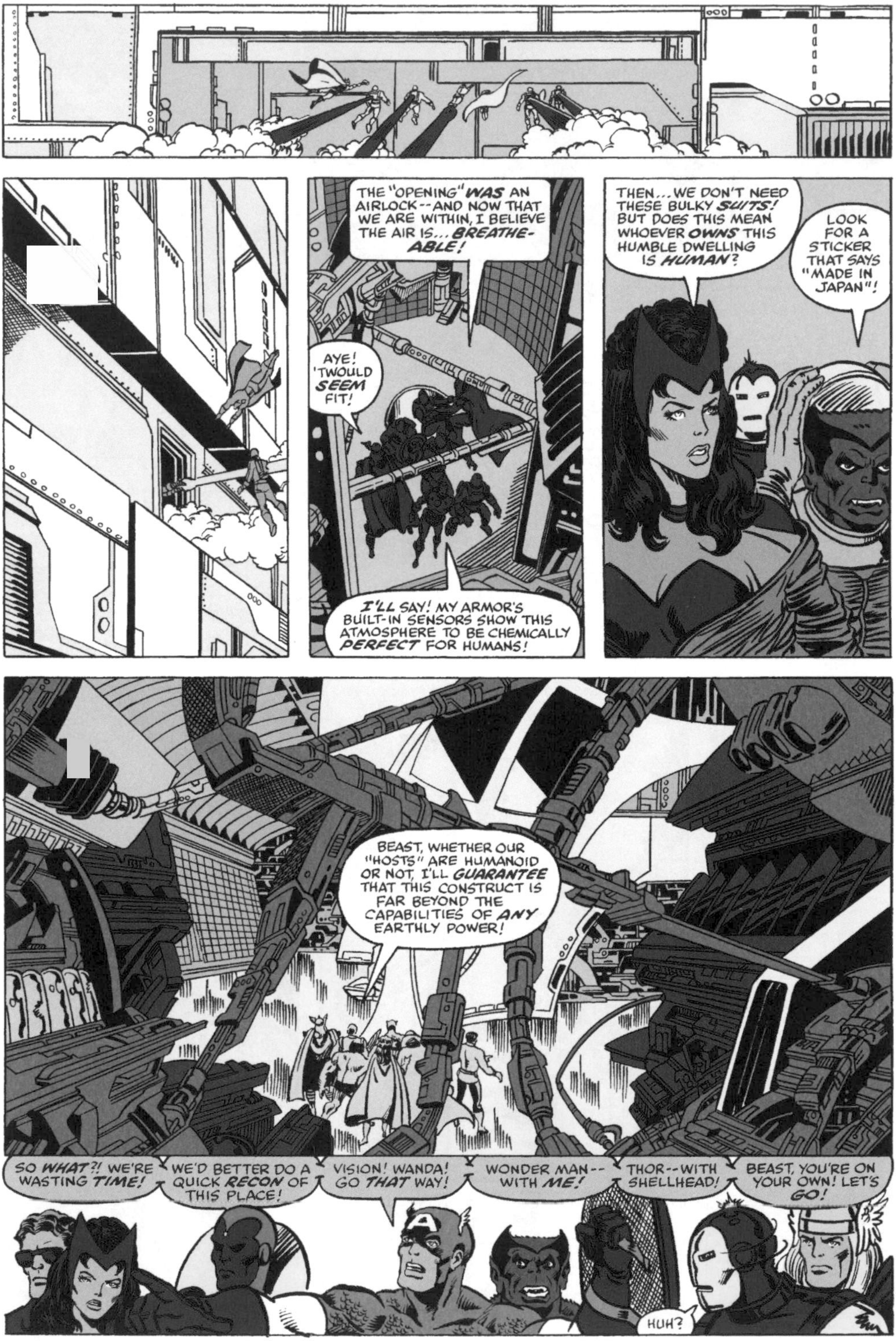

THE "OPENING" WAS AN AIRLOCK--AND NOW THAT WE ARE WITHIN, I BELIEVE THE AIR IS... BREATHE-ABLE!
AYE! 'TWOULD SEEM FIT!
I'LL SAY! MY ARMOR'S BUILT-IN SENSORS SHOW THIS ATMOSPHERE TO BE CHEMICALLY PERFECT FOR HUMANS!
THEN... WE DON'T NEED THESE BULKY SUITS! BUT DOES THIS MEAN WHOEVER OWNS THIS HUMBLE DWELLING IS HUMAN?
LOOK FOR A STICKER THAT SAYS "MADE IN JAPAN"!
BEAST, WHETHER OUR "HOSTS" ARE HUMANOID OR NOT, I'LL GUARANTEE THAT THIS CONSTRUCT IS FAR BEYOND THE CAPABILITIES OF ANY EARTHLY POWER!
SO WHAT?! WE'RE WASTING TIME!
WE'D BETTER DO A QUICK RECON OF THIS PLACE!
VISION! WANDA! GO THAT WAY!
WONDER MAN--WITH ME!
THOR--WITH SHELLHEAD!
BEAST, YOU'RE ON YOUR OWN! LET'S GO!
HUH?

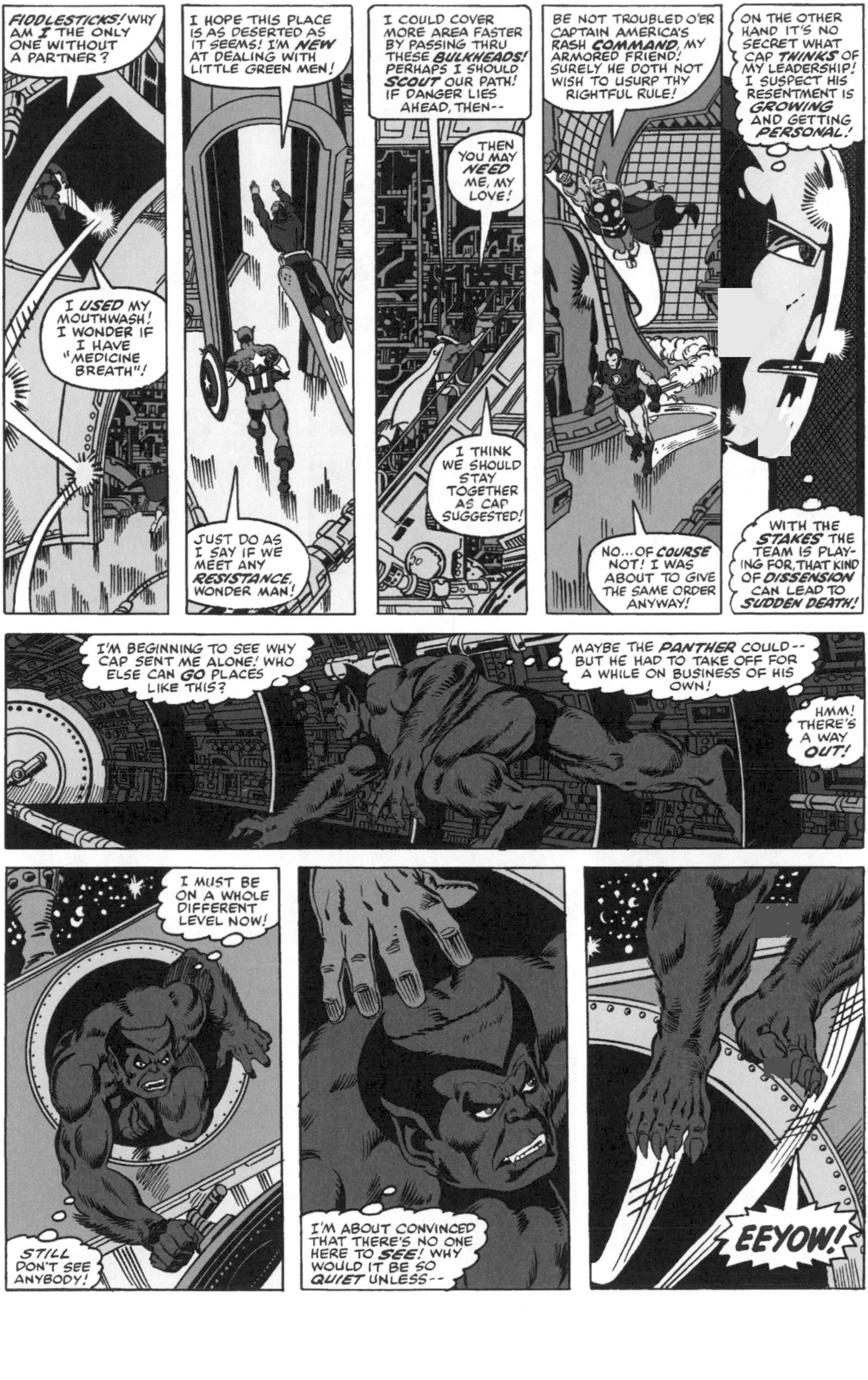

FIDDLESTICKS! WHY AM I THE ONLY ONE WITHOUT A PARTNER?
I USED MY MOUTHWASH! I WONDER IF I HAVE "MEDICINE BREATH"!
I HOPE THIS PLACE IS AS DESERTED AS IT SEEMS! I'M NEW AT DEALING WITH LITTLE GREEN MEN!
JUST DO AS I SAY IF WE MEET ANY RESISTANCE, WONDER MAN!
I COULD COVER MORE AREA FASTER BY PASSING THRU THESE BULKHEADS! PERHAPS I SHOULD SCOUT OUR PATH! IF DANGER LIES AHEAD, THEN--
THEN YOU MAY NEED ME, MY LOVE!
I THINK WE SHOULD STAY TOGETHER AS CAP SUGGESTED!
BE NOT TROUBLED O'ER CAPTAIN AMERICA'S RASH COMMAND, MY ARMORED FRIEND! SURELY HE DOTH NOT WISH TO USURP THY RIGHTFUL RULE!
NO... OF COURSE NOT! I WAS ABOUT TO GIVE THE SAME ORDER ANYWAY!
ON THE OTHER HAND IT'S NO SECRET WHAT CAP THINKS OF MY LEADERSHIP! I SUSPECT HIS RESENTMENT IS GROWING AND GETTING PERSONAL!
WITH THE STAKES THE TEAM IS PLAYING FOR, THAT KIND OF DISSENSION CAN LEAD TO SUDDEN DEATH!
I'M BEGINNING TO SEE WHY CAP SENT ME ALONE! WHO ELSE CAN GO PLACES LIKE THIS?
MAYBE THE PANTHER COULD-- BUT HE HAD TO TAKE OFF FOR A WHILE ON BUSINESS OF HIS OWN!
HMM! THERE'S A WAY OUT!
I MUST BE ON A WHOLE DIFFERENT LEVEL NOW!
STILL DON'T SEE ANYBODY!
I'M ABOUT CONVINCED THAT THERE'S NO ONE HERE TO SEE! WHY WOULD IT BE SO QUIET UNLESS--
EEYOW!

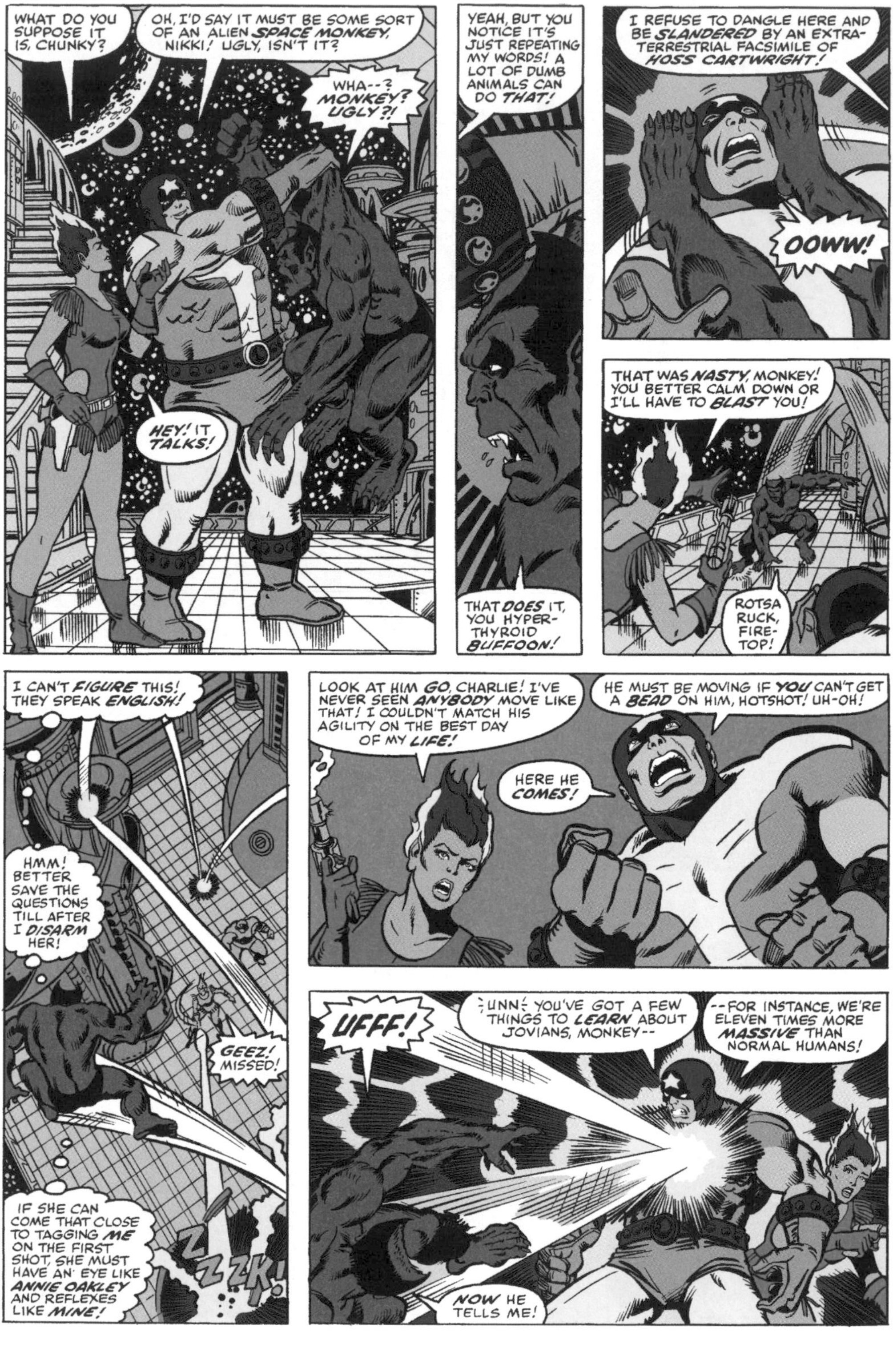
WHAT DO YOU SUPPOSE IT IS, CHUNKY?
OH, I'D SAY IT MUST BE SOME SORT OF AN ALIEN SPACE MONKEY, NIKKI! UGLY, ISN'T IT?
WHA--? MONKEY? UGLY?!
HEY! IT TALKS!
YEAH, BUT YOU NOTICE IT'S JUST REPEATING MY WORDS! A LOT OF DUMB ANIMALS CAN DO THAT!
THAT DOES IT, YOU HYPER-THYROID BUFFOON!
I REFUSE TO DANGLE HERE AND BE SLANDERED BY AN EXTRA-TERRESTRIAL FACSIMILE OF HOSS CARTWRIGHT!
OOWW!
THAT WAS NASTY, MONKEY! YOU BETTER CALM DOWN OR I'LL HAVE TO BLAST YOU!
ROTSA RUCK, FIRE-TOP!
I CAN'T FIGURE THIS! THEY SPEAK ENGLISH!
HMM! BETTER SAVE THE QUESTIONS TILL AFTER I DISARM HER!
GEEZ! MISSED!
IF SHE CAN COME THAT CLOSE TO TAGGING ME ON THE FIRST SHOT, SHE MUST HAVE AN' EYE LIKE ANNIE OAKLEY AND REFLEXES LIKE MINE!
ZZZK!
LOOK AT HIM GO, CHARLIE! I'VE NEVER SEEN ANYBODY MOVE LIKE THAT! I COULDN'T MATCH HIS AGILITY ON THE BEST DAY OF MY LIFE!
HE MUST BE MOVING IF YOU CAN'T GET A BEAD ON HIM, HOTSHOT! UH-OH!
HERE HE COMES!
UFFF!
UNN! YOU'VE GOT A FEW THINGS TO LEARN ABOUT JOVIANS, MONKEY--
--FOR INSTANCE, WE'RE ELEVEN TIMES MORE MASSIVE THAN NORMAL HUMANS!
NOW HE TELLS ME!

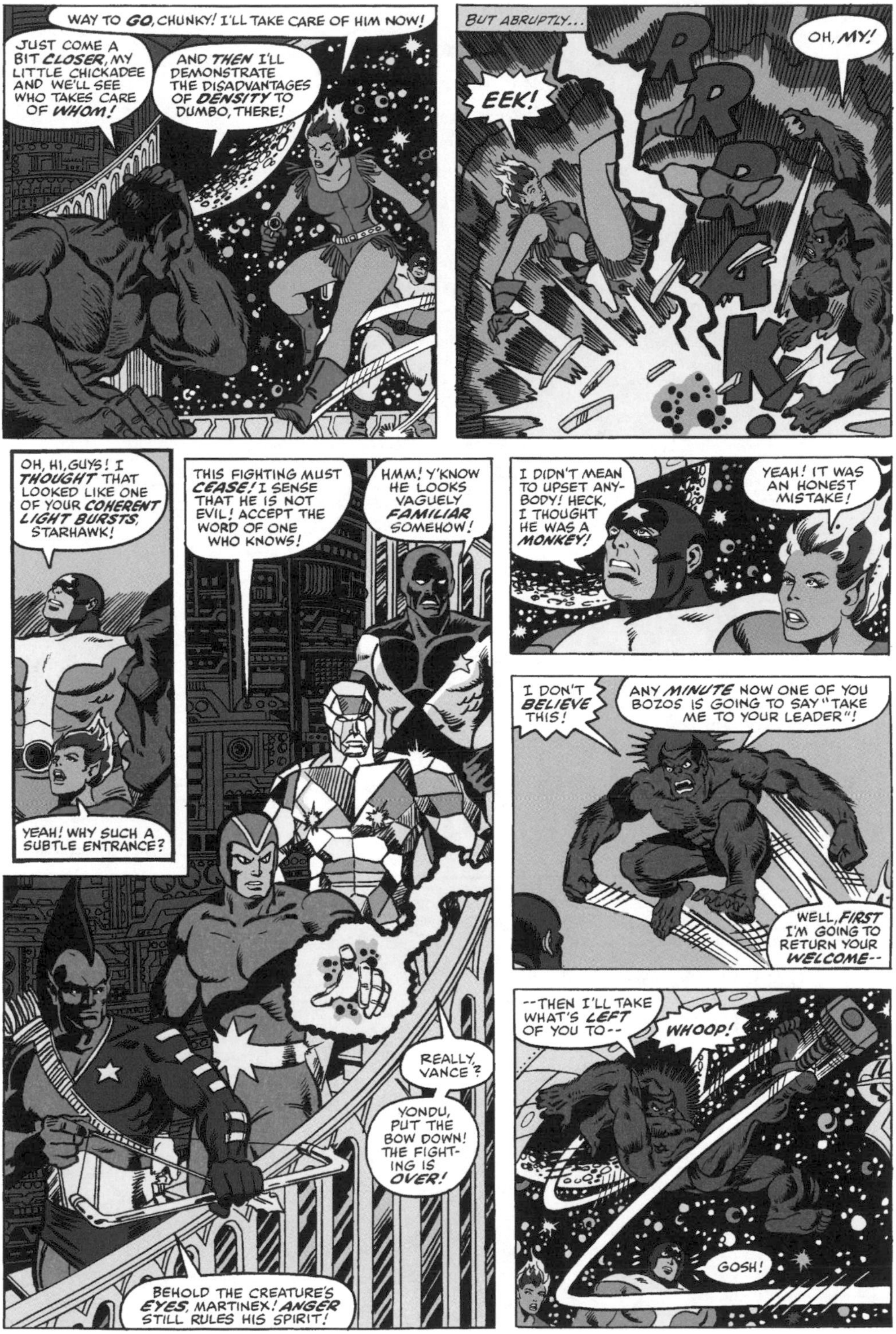
WAY TO GO, CHUNKY! I'LL TAKE CARE OF HIM NOW!
JUST COME A BIT CLOSER, MY LITTLE CHICKADEE AND WE'LL SEE WHO TAKES CARE OF WHOM!
AND THEN I'LL DEMONSTRATE THE DISADVANTAGES OF DENSITY TO DUMBO, THERE!
BUT ABRUPTLY...
RRRAK
EEK!
OH, MY!
OH, HI, GUYS! I THOUGHT THAT LOOKED LIKE ONE OF YOUR COHERENT LIGHT BURSTS, STARHAWK!
YEAH! WHY SUCH A SUBTLE ENTRANCE?
THIS FIGHTING MUST CEASE! I SENSE THAT HE IS NOT EVIL! ACCEPT THE WORD OF ONE WHO KNOWS!
HMM! Y'KNOW HE LOOKS VAGUELY FAMILIAR SOMEHOW!
REALLY, VANCE?
YONDU, PUT THE BOW DOWN! THE FIGHTING IS OVER!
BEHOLD THE CREATURE'S EYES, MARTINEX! ANGER STILL RULES HIS SPIRIT!
I DIDN'T MEAN TO UPSET ANYBODY! HECK, I THOUGHT HE WAS A MONKEY!
YEAH! IT WAS AN HONEST MISTAKE!
I DON'T BELIEVE THIS!
ANY MINUTE NOW ONE OF YOU BOZOS IS GOING TO SAY "TAKE ME TO YOUR LEADER"!
WELL, FIRST I'M GOING TO RETURN YOUR WELCOME--
--THEN I'LL TAKE WHAT'S LEFT OF YOU TO--
WHOOP!
GOSH!

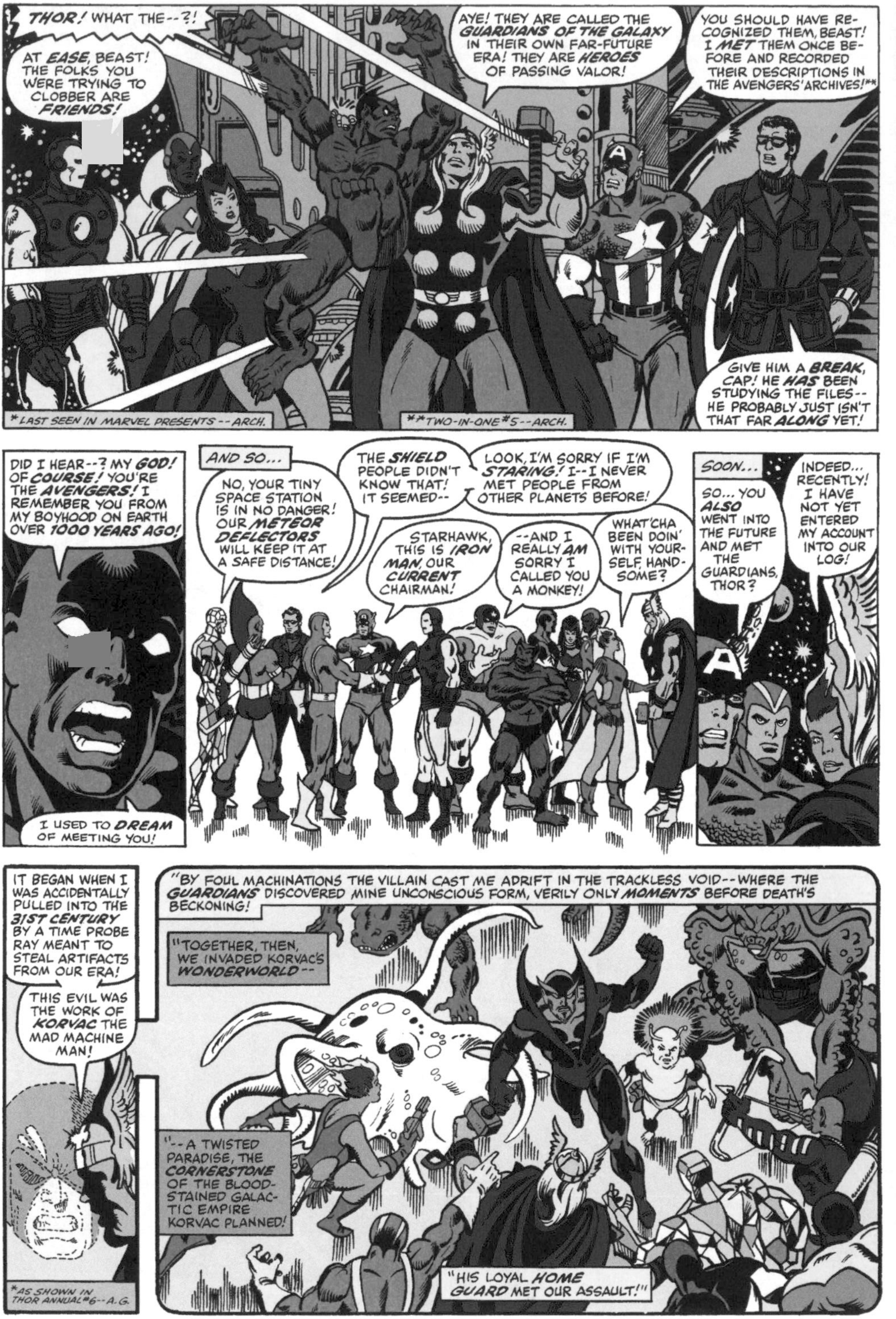

THOR! WHAT THE--?!
AT EASE, BEAST! THE FOLKS YOU WERE TRYING TO CLOBBER ARE FRIENDS!
AYE! THEY ARE CALLED THE GUARDIANS OF THE GALAXY IN THEIR OWN FAR-FUTURE ERA! THEY ARE HEROES OF PASSING VALOR!
YOU SHOULD HAVE RECOGNIZED THEM, BEAST! I MET THEM ONCE BEFORE AND RECORDED THEIR DESCRIPTIONS IN THE AVENGERS' ARCHIVES!**
GIVE HIM A BREAK, CAP! HE HAS BEEN STUDYING THE FILES-- HE PROBABLY JUST ISN'T THAT FAR ALONG YET!
*LAST SEEN IN MARVEL PRESENTS--ARCH.
**TWO-IN-ONE #5--ARCH.
DID I HEAR--? MY GOD! OF COURSE! YOU'RE THE AVENGERS! I REMEMBER YOU FROM MY BOYHOOD ON EARTH OVER 1000 YEARS AGO!
I USED TO DREAM OF MEETING YOU!
AND SO...
NO, YOUR TINY SPACE STATION IS IN NO DANGER! OUR METEOR DEFLECTORS WILL KEEP IT AT A SAFE DISTANCE!
THE SHIELD PEOPLE DIDN'T KNOW THAT! IT SEEMED--
LOOK, I'M SORRY IF I'M STARING! I--I NEVER MET PEOPLE FROM OTHER PLANETS BEFORE!
STARHAWK, THIS IS IRON MAN, OUR CURRENT CHAIRMAN!
--AND I REALLY AM SORRY I CALLED YOU A MONKEY!
WHAT'CHA BEEN DOIN' WITH YOURSELF, HANDSOME?
SOON...
SO... YOU ALSO WENT INTO THE FUTURE AND MET THE GUARDIANS, THOR?
INDEED... RECENTLY! I HAVE NOT YET ENTERED MY ACCOUNT INTO OUR LOG!
IT BEGAN WHEN I WAS ACCIDENTALLY PULLED INTO THE 31ST CENTURY BY A TIME PROBE RAY MEANT TO STEAL ARTIFACTS FROM OUR ERA!
THIS EVIL WAS THE WORK OF KORVAC THE MAD MACHINE MAN!
*AS SHOWN IN THOR ANNUAL #6--A.G.
"BY FOUL MACHINATIONS THE VILLAIN CAST ME ADRIFT IN THE TRACKLESS VOID--WHERE THE GUARDIANS DISCOVERED MINE UNCONSCIOUS FORM, VERILY ONLY MOMENTS BEFORE DEATH'S BECKONING!
"TOGETHER, THEN, WE INVADED KORVAC'S WONDERWORLD--
"--A TWISTED PARADISE, THE CORNERSTONE OF THE BLOOD-STAINED GALACTIC EMPIRE KORVAC PLANNED!
"HIS LOYAL HOME GUARD MET OUR ASSAULT!"

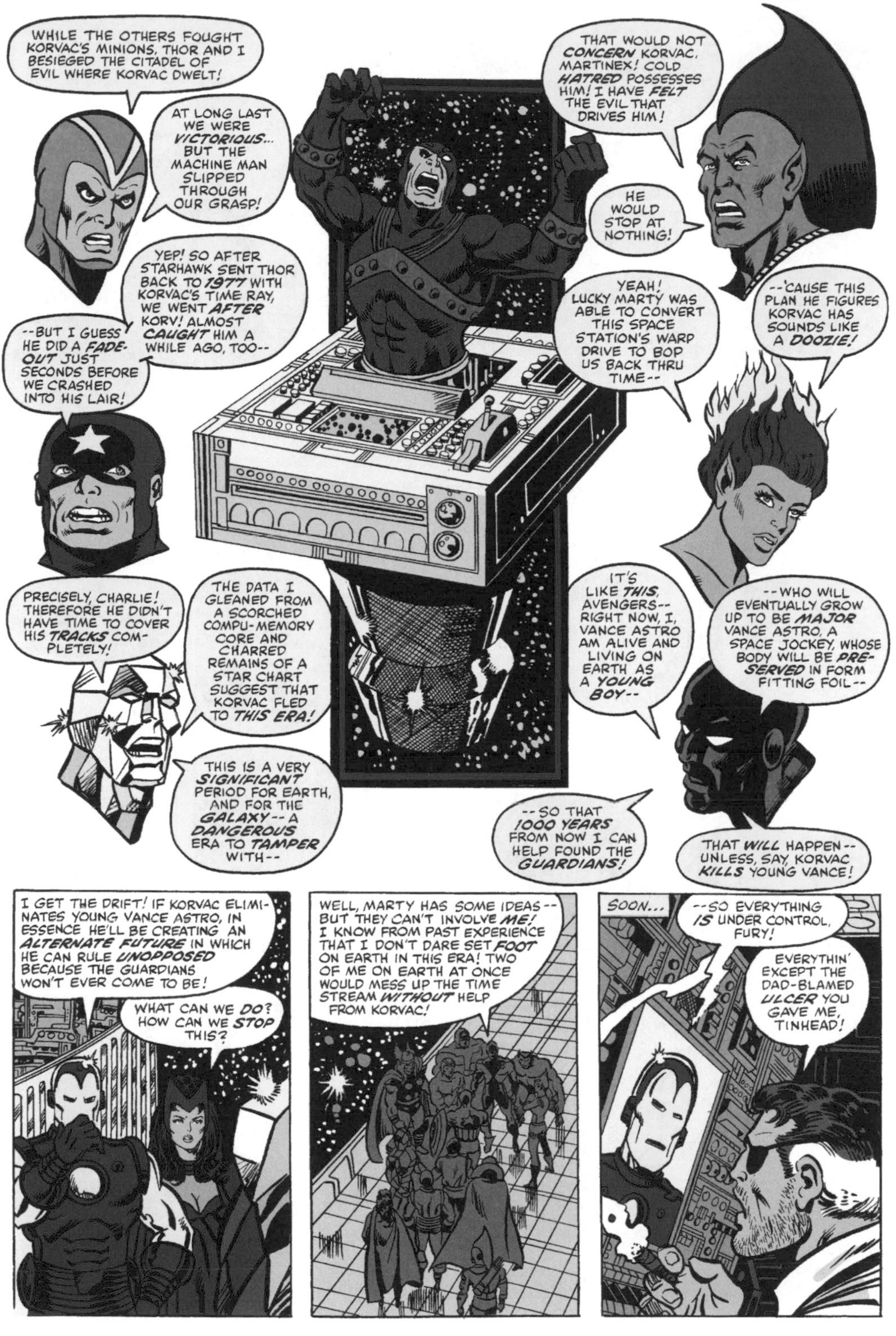
WHILE THE OTHERS FOUGHT KORVAC'S MINIONS, THOR AND I BESIEGED THE CITADEL OF EVIL WHERE KORVAC DWELT!
AT LONG LAST WE WERE VICTORIOUS... BUT THE MACHINE MAN SLIPPED THROUGH OUR GRASP!
THAT WOULD NOT CONCERN KORVAC, MARTINEX! COLD HATRED POSSESSES HIM! I HAVE FELT THE EVIL THAT DRIVES HIM!
HE WOULD STOP AT NOTHING!
YEP! SO AFTER STARHAWK SENT THOR BACK TO 1977 WITH KORVAC'S TIME RAY, WE WENT AFTER KORV! ALMOST CAUGHT HIM A WHILE AGO, TOO--
--BUT I GUESS HE DID A FADE-OUT JUST SECONDS BEFORE WE CRASHED INTO HIS LAIR!
YEAH! LUCKY MARTY WAS ABLE TO CONVERT THIS SPACE STATION'S WARP DRIVE TO BOP US BACK THRU TIME--
--'CAUSE THIS PLAN HE FIGURES KORVAC HAS SOUNDS LIKE A DOOZIE!
PRECISELY, CHARLIE! THEREFORE HE DIDN'T HAVE TIME TO COVER HIS TRACKS COMPLETELY!
THE DATA I GLEANED FROM A SCORCHED COMPU-MEMORY CORE AND CHARRED REMAINS OF A STAR CHART SUGGEST THAT KORVAC FLED TO THIS ERA!
THIS IS A VERY SIGNIFICANT PERIOD FOR EARTH, AND FOR THE GALAXY -- A DANGEROUS ERA TO TAMPER WITH--
IT'S LIKE THIS, AVENGERS-- RIGHT NOW, I, VANCE ASTRO AM ALIVE AND LIVING ON EARTH AS A YOUNG BOY--
--WHO WILL EVENTUALLY GROW UP TO BE MAJOR VANCE ASTRO, A SPACE JOCKEY, WHOSE BODY WILL BE PRESERVED IN FORM FITTING FOIL--
--SO THAT 1000 YEARS FROM NOW I CAN HELP FOUND THE GUARDIANS!
THAT WILL HAPPEN-- UNLESS, SAY, KORVAC KILLS YOUNG VANCE!
I GET THE DRIFT! IF KORVAC ELIMINATES YOUNG VANCE ASTRO, IN ESSENCE HE'LL BE CREATING AN ALTERNATE FUTURE IN WHICH HE CAN RULE UNOPPOSED BECAUSE THE GUARDIANS WON'T EVER COME TO BE!
WHAT CAN WE DO? HOW CAN WE STOP THIS?
WELL, MARTY HAS SOME IDEAS-- BUT THEY CAN'T INVOLVE ME! I KNOW FROM PAST EXPERIENCE THAT I DON'T DARE SET FOOT ON EARTH IN THIS ERA! TWO OF ME ON EARTH AT ONCE WOULD MESS UP THE TIME STREAM WITHOUT HELP FROM KORVAC!
SOON...
--SO EVERYTHING IS UNDER CONTROL, FURY!
EVERYTHIN' EXCEPT THE DAD-BLAMED ULCER YOU GAVE ME, TINHEAD!

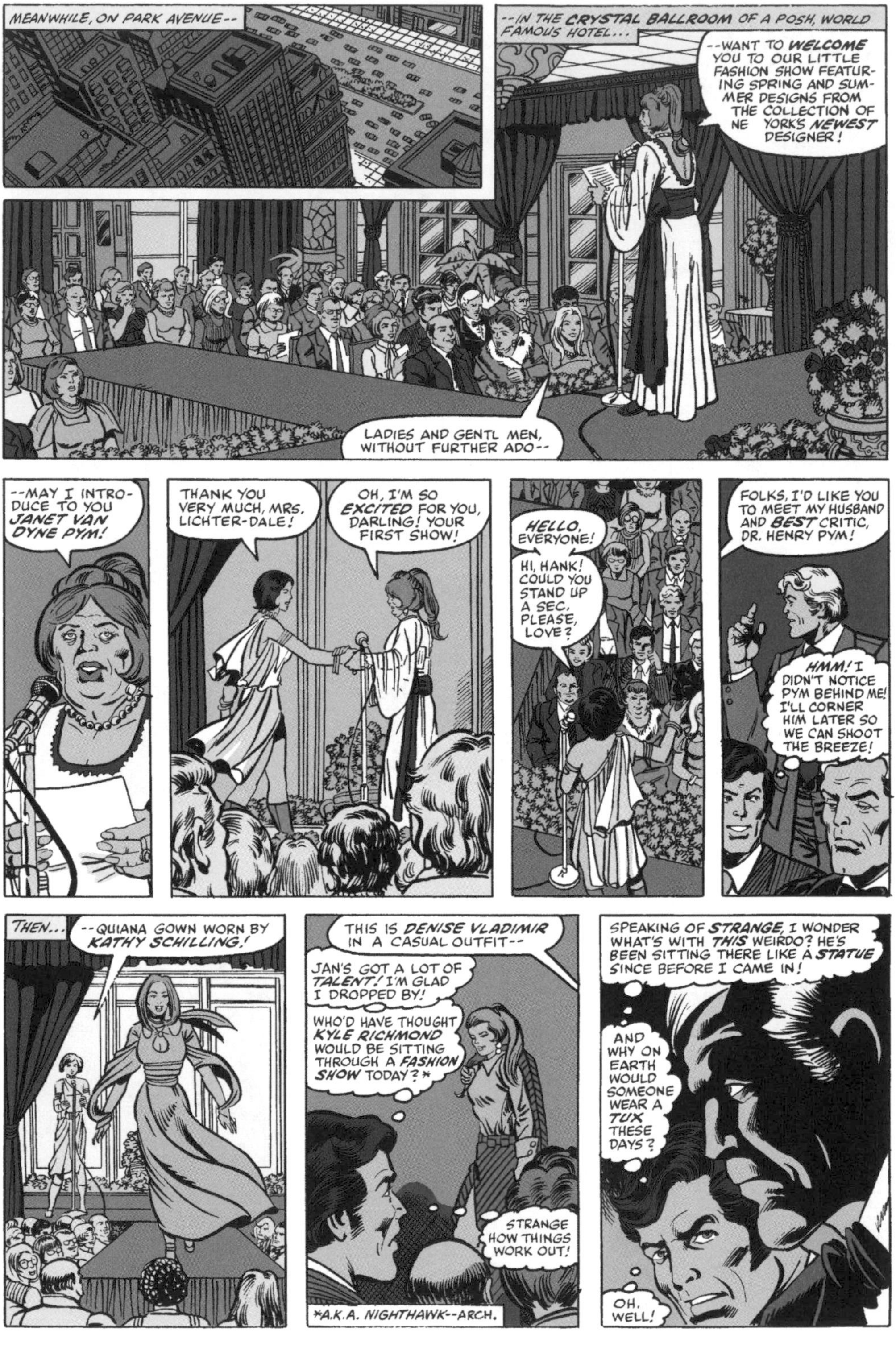
MEANWHILE, ON PARK AVENUE--
--IN THE CRYSTAL BALLROOM OF A POSH, WORLD FAMOUS HOTEL...
--WANT TO WELCOME YOU TO OUR LITTLE FASHION SHOW FEATURING SPRING AND SUMMER DESIGNS FROM THE COLLECTION OF NE YORK'S NEWEST DESIGNER!
LADIES AND GENTL MEN, WITHOUT FURTHER ADO--
--MAY I INTRODUCE TO YOU JANET VAN DYNE PYM!
THANK YOU VERY MUCH, MRS. LICHTER-DALE!
OH, I'M SO EXCITED FOR YOU, DARLING! YOUR FIRST SHOW!
HELLO, EVERYONE!
HI, HANK! COULD YOU STAND UP A SEC, PLEASE, LOVE?
FOLKS, I'D LIKE YOU TO MEET MY HUSBAND AND BEST CRITIC, DR. HENRY PYM!
HMM! I DIDN'T NOTICE PYM BEHIND ME! I'LL CORNER HIM LATER SO WE CAN SHOOT THE BREEZE!
THEN...
--QUIANA GOWN WORN BY KATHY SCHILLING!
THIS IS DENISE VLADIMIR IN A CASUAL OUTFIT--
JAN'S GOT A LOT OF TALENT! I'M GLAD I DROPPED BY!
WHO'D HAVE THOUGHT KYLE RICHMOND WOULD BE SITTING THROUGH A FASHION SHOW TODAY?*
STRANGE HOW THINGS WORK OUT!
*A.K.A. NIGHTHAWK--ARCH.
SPEAKING OF STRANGE, I WONDER WHAT'S WITH THIS WEIRDO? HE'S BEEN SITTING THERE LIKE A STATUE SINCE BEFORE I CAME IN!
AND WHY ON EARTH WOULD SOMEONE WEAR A TUX THESE DAYS?
OH, WELL!

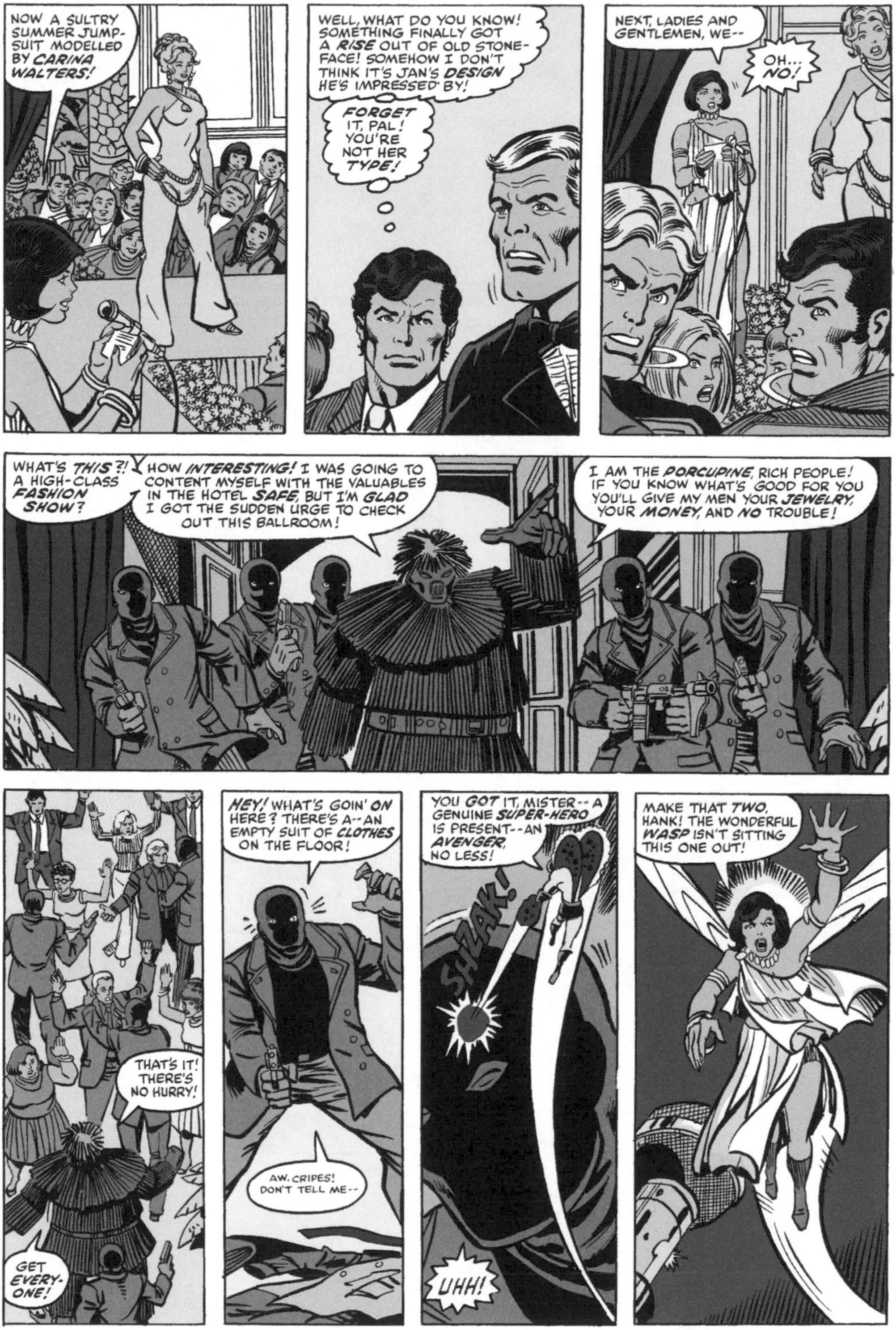
NOW A SULTRY SUMMER JUMP-SUIT MODELLED BY CARINA WALTERS!
WELL, WHAT DO YOU KNOW! SOMETHING FINALLY GOT A RISE OUT OF OLD STONE-FACE! SOMEHOW I DON'T THINK IT'S JAN'S DESIGN HE'S IMPRESSED BY!
FORGET IT, PAL! YOU'RE NOT HER TYPE!
NEXT, LADIES AND GENTLEMEN, WE--
OH... NO!
WHAT'S THIS?! A HIGH-CLASS FASHION SHOW?
HOW INTERESTING! I WAS GOING TO CONTENT MYSELF WITH THE VALUABLES IN THE HOTEL SAFE, BUT I'M GLAD I GOT THE SUDDEN URGE TO CHECK OUT THIS BALLROOM!
I AM THE PORCUPINE, RICH PEOPLE! IF YOU KNOW WHAT'S GOOD FOR YOU YOU'LL GIVE MY MEN YOUR JEWELRY, YOUR MONEY, AND NO TROUBLE!
THAT'S IT! THERE'S NO HURRY!
GET EVERY-ONE!
HEY! WHAT'S GOIN' ON HERE? THERE'S A--AN EMPTY SUIT OF CLOTHES ON THE FLOOR!
AW, CRIPES! DON'T TELL ME--
YOU GOT IT, MISTER-- A GENUINE SUPER-HERO IS PRESENT--AN AVENGER, NO LESS!
SHZAK!
UHH!
MAKE THAT TWO, HANK! THE WONDERFUL WASP ISN'T SITTING THIS ONE OUT!

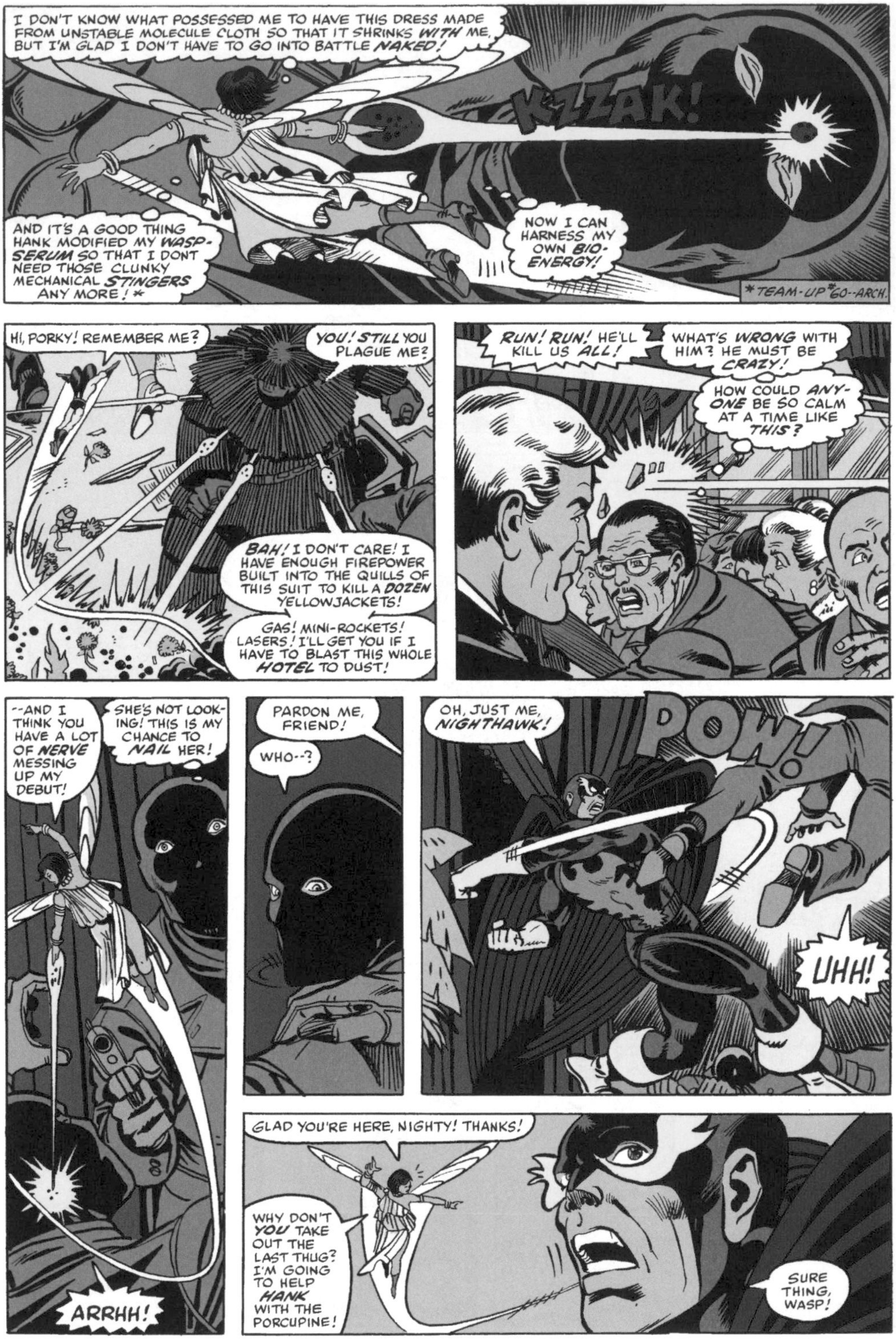
I DON'T KNOW WHAT POSSESSED ME TO HAVE THIS DRESS MADE FROM UNSTABLE MOLECULE CLOTH SO THAT IT SHRINKS WITH ME, BUT I'M GLAD I DON'T HAVE TO GO INTO BATTLE NAKED!
KZZAK!
AND IT'S A GOOD THING HANK MODIFIED MY WASP-SERUM SO THAT I DONT NEED THOSE CLUNKY MECHANICAL STINGERS ANY MORE! *
NOW I CAN HARNESS MY OWN BIO-ENERGY!
*TEAM-UP #60--ARCH.
HI, PORKY! REMEMBER ME?
YOU! STILL YOU PLAGUE ME?
BAH! I DON'T CARE! I HAVE ENOUGH FIREPOWER BUILT INTO THE QUILLS OF THIS SUIT TO KILL A DOZEN YELLOWJACKETS!
GAS! MINI-ROCKETS! LASERS! I'LL GET YOU IF I HAVE TO BLAST THIS WHOLE HOTEL TO DUST!
RUN! RUN! HE'LL KILL US ALL!
WHAT'S WRONG WITH HIM? HE MUST BE CRAZY!
HOW COULD ANYONE BE SO CALM AT A TIME LIKE THIS?
--AND I THINK YOU HAVE A LOT OF NERVE MESSING UP MY DEBUT!
SHE'S NOT LOOKING! THIS IS MY CHANCE TO NAIL HER!
ARRHH!
PARDON ME, FRIEND!
WHO--?
OH, JUST ME, NIGHTHAWK!
POW!
UHH!
GLAD YOU'RE HERE, NIGHTY! THANKS!
WHY DON'T YOU TAKE OUT THE LAST THUG? I'M GOING TO HELP HANK WITH THE PORCUPINE!
SURE THING, WASP!

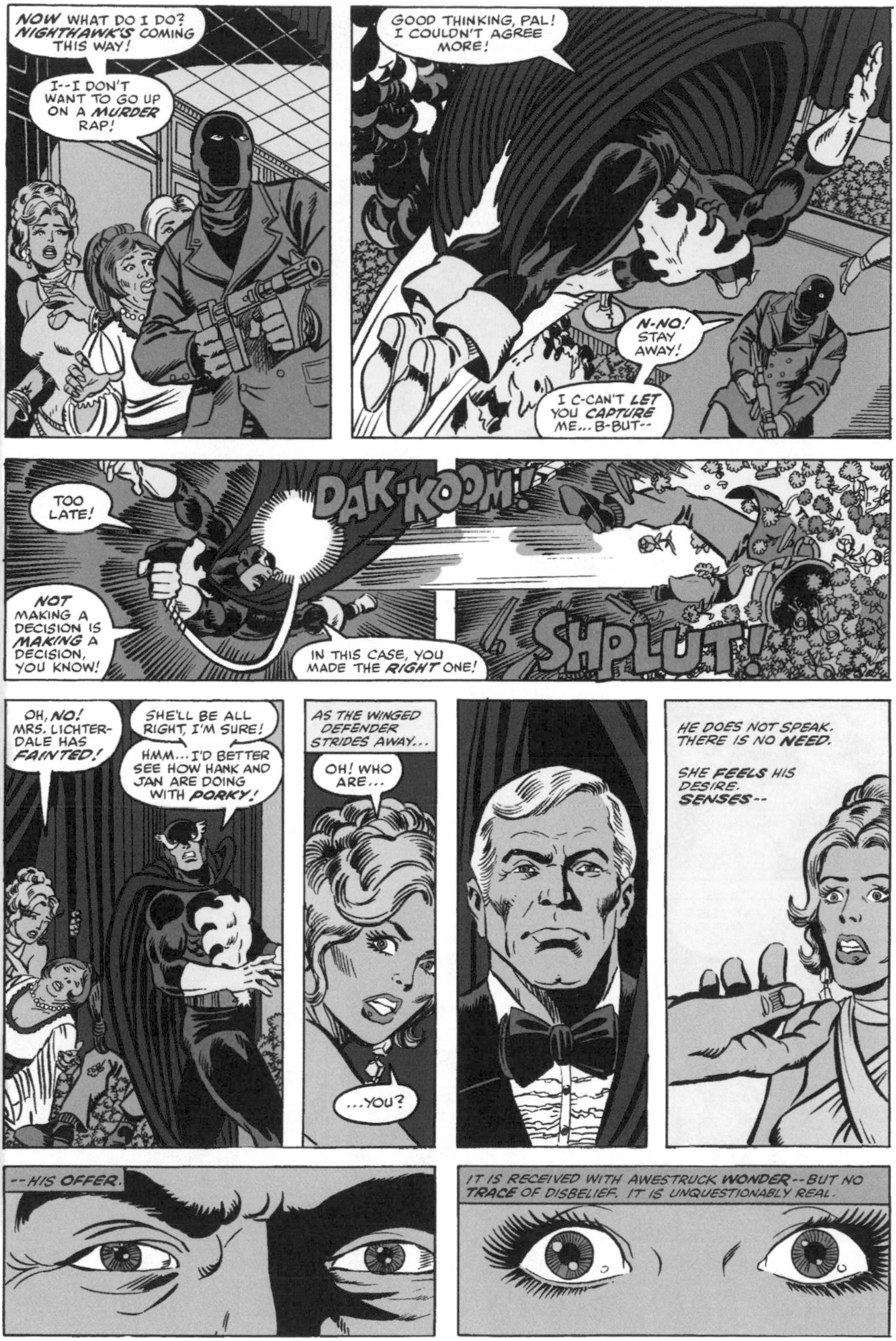

NOW WHAT DO I DO? NIGHTHAWK'S COMING THIS WAY!
I--I DON'T WANT TO GO UP ON A MURDER RAP!
GOOD THINKING, PAL! I COULDN'T AGREE MORE!
N-NO! STAY AWAY!
I C-CAN'T LET YOU CAPTURE ME... B-BUT--
TOO LATE!
DAK-KOOM!
NOT MAKING A DECISION IS MAKING A DECISION, YOU KNOW!
IN THIS CASE, YOU MADE THE RIGHT ONE!
SHPLUT!
OH, NO! MRS. LICHTER-DALE HAS FAINTED!
SHE'LL BE ALL RIGHT, I'M SURE!
HMM... I'D BETTER SEE HOW HANK AND JAN ARE DOING WITH PORKY!
AS THE WINGED DEFENDER STRIDES AWAY...
OH! WHO ARE...
...YOU?
HE DOES NOT SPEAK. THERE IS NO NEED.
SHE FEELS HIS DESIRE. SENSES--
--HIS OFFER.
IT IS RECEIVED WITH AWESTRUCK WONDER--BUT NO TRACE OF DISBELIEF. IT IS UNQUESTIONABLY REAL.

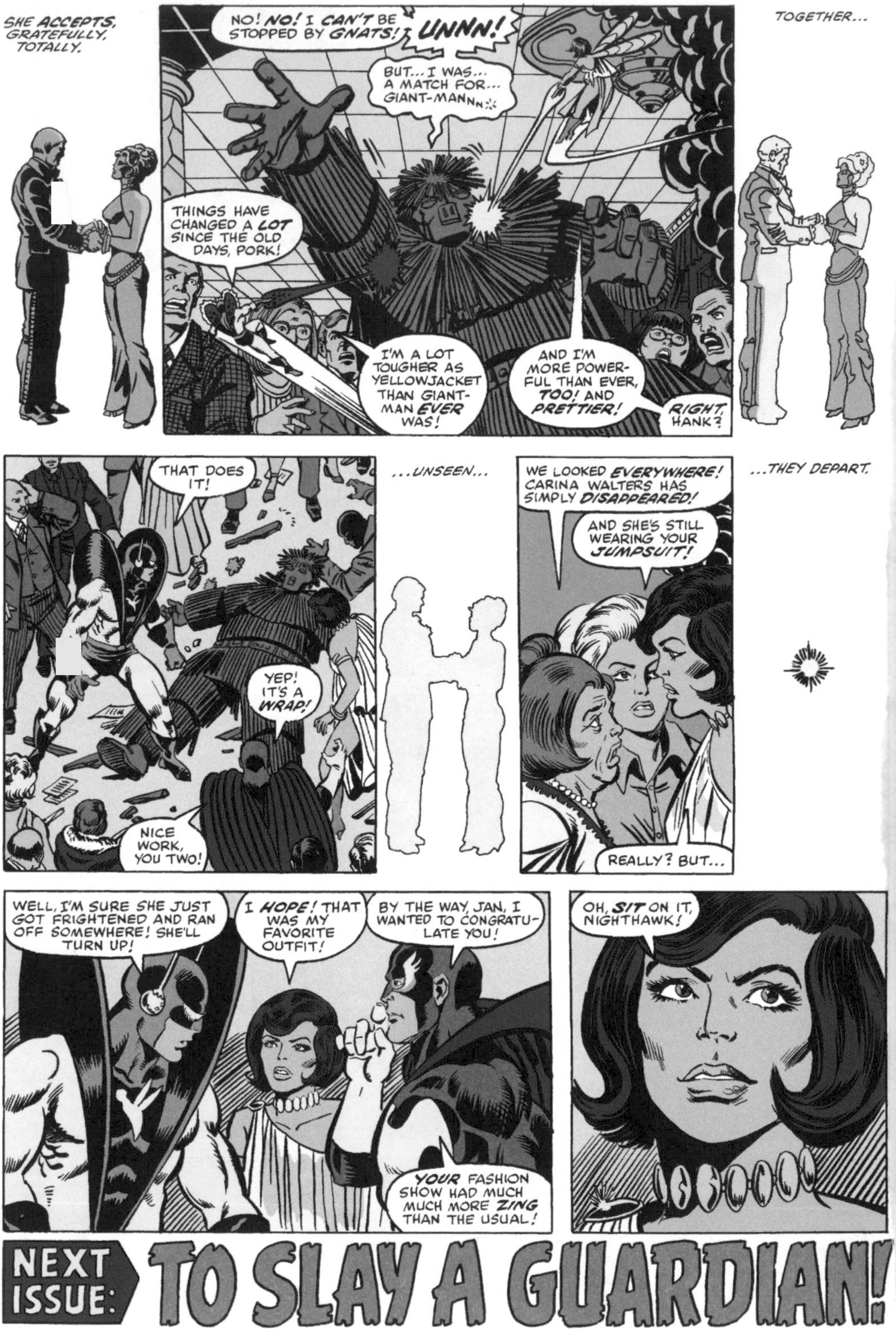

SHE ACCEPTS, GRATEFULLY, TOTALLY.
NO! NO! I CAN'T BE STOPPED BY GNATS!
UNNN!
BUT... I WAS... A MATCH FOR... GIANT-MANNN
THINGS HAVE CHANGED A LOT SINCE THE OLD DAYS, PORK!
I'M A LOT TOUGHER AS YELLOWJACKET THAN GIANT-MAN EVER WAS!
AND I'M MORE POWERFUL THAN EVER, TOO! AND PRETTIER!
RIGHT, HANK?
TOGETHER...
THAT DOES IT!
YEP! IT'S A WRAP!
NICE WORK, YOU TWO!
...UNSEEN...
WE LOOKED EVERYWHERE! CARINA WALTERS HAS SIMPLY DISAPPEARED!
AND SHE'S STILL WEARING YOUR JUMPSUIT!
REALLY? BUT...
...THEY DEPART.
WELL, I'M SURE SHE JUST GOT FRIGHTENED AND RAN OFF SOMEWHERE! SHE'LL TURN UP!
I HOPE! THAT WAS MY FAVORITE OUTFIT!
BY THE WAY, JAN, I WANTED TO CONGRATULATE YOU!
YOUR FASHION SHOW HAD MUCH MUCH MORE ZING THAN THE USUAL!
OH, SIT ON IT, NIGHTHAWK!
NEXT ISSUE: TO SLAY A GUARDIAN!